Lois A. Hill

FOR THE INWARD JOURNEY

FOR THE INWARD JOURNEY

The Writings of Howard Thurman

SELECTED BY

ANNE SPENCER THURMAN

INTRODUCTION BY

VINCENT HARDING

HARCOURT BRACE JOVANOVICH, PUBLISHERS

San Diego   New York   London

Grateful acknowledgment to reprint the selection from Howard Thurman's
Mysticism and the Experience of Love is hereby made to Pendle Hill Publications,
Wallingford, Pa. 19086 (Pamphlet 115, 1961).

Library of Congress Cataloging in Publication Data
Thurman, Howard, 1900–1981.
For the inward journey.
Bibliography: p.
1. Spiritual life—Addresses, essays, lectures.
I. Thurman, Anne.   II. Title.
BV4501.2. T524   1984   230'.044   83-26366
ISBN 0-15-132656-8

Designed by Christine Aulicino
Printed in the United States of America
First edition
A   B   C   D   E

CONTENTS

CONTENTS

CONTENTS

THE CENTERING MOMENT

INTRODUCTION

How shall we approach Howard Thurman? He seems to present a marvelous difficulty. When a life is opened at so many deep levels, filled with such spontaneous richness, and joined with so great a variety of intricate parts, introductions do not come easily. Any brief overview can only be suggestive, tentative, unfinished.

Thurman himself may have unintentionally provided us with the best summary we have of the man and his work. Writing in his autobiography, *With Head and Heart,* about the transformative experiences of a visit to India in the mid-1930s, Thurman explained why he and his wife, Sue Bailey Thurman, felt such an overwhelming desire to meet with Rabindranath Tagore, the mystic and Nobel Prize laureate who was often called "the poet of Asia." Thurman said of Tagore:

> He was the poet of India who soared above the political and social patterns of exclusiveness dividing mankind. His tremendous spiritual insight created a mood unique among the voices of the world. He moved deep into the heart of his own spiritual idiom and came up inside all peoples, all cultures, and all faiths.

Perhaps no single description better captures the essence of the life, work, and magnificent vision of Howard Thurman than that last sentence. For this was precisely the direction of Thurman's own "God-intoxicated" pilgrimage—constantly moving toward the source of all human life and truth by way of the concrete beauty and terror of the Black experience in the United States. In the course of that harrowing and redemptive journey, he became poet, teacher, mystic, preacher, counselor, friend, and guide to thousands of men and women in this nation and overseas. It is good that we now have this anthology of selections from ten of Thurman's more than twenty books to offer us some taste of the man in his many, fully integrated parts, some sense of his pilgrimage, his movement toward the "inside."

For Howard Thurman the personal journey began in Daytona Beach, Florida, in 1900. From the very outset his life was profoundly affected by the nurturing dynamics of the church and the larger Black community, the wisdom and disciplined spirituality of his maternal grandmother, Nancy Ambrose, and the powerful, ever-present rhythms of nature. Apparently, in the midst of that rich gathering of forces, Thurman the American mystic began to be formed. Later he remembered:

> As a boy in Florida, I walked along the beach of the Atlantic in the quiet stillness. . . . I held my breath against the night and watched the stars etch their brightness on the face of the darkened canopy of the heavens. I had the sense that all things, the sand, the sea, the night, and I, were one lung through which all of life breathed.

The night became an even more constant companion after tragedy struck the family. Thurman's father died when the boy was seven years old, and from that point on his deep thirst for knowledge and for schooling—along with solitude—had to compete with the family's poverty. Nevertheless, a combination of friends, relatives, unexpected patrons, and much hard and imaginative work and prayer on his part kept him moving. From Daytona he went on to attend high school in Jacksonville, Florida. (There were only three high schools for Black young people in Florida before World War I, all privately operated.) After Jacksonville, the goal was Atlanta, Georgia, where he attended Morehouse College with Martin Luther King, Sr.

Inspired by some of the powerful and committed teachers and preachers in Atlanta and elsewhere, Thurman went on from

Morehouse to Rochester Theological Seminary in 1923. Three years later, shortly after his graduation from seminary, he married Kate Kelly, a Spelman graduate from La Grange, Georgia, who had been doing social work in New Jersey. Together they went to Oberlin, Ohio, where Howard served his first full-time pastorate at Mount Zion, a Black Baptist church. It was there that the Thurmans' daughter, Olive, was born. It was also in Oberlin that Kate was diagnosed as having contracted tuberculosis.

Partly as a result of his wife's illness, the next period was a very difficult one for Thurman. At the same time, it was also a period of much growth—he always found difficulty and growth to be in creative tension within his life. In January 1929, Thurman left the church at Oberlin and went to Haverford College in Pennsylvania to study with the Quaker mystic Rufus Jones in a special one-to-one relationship. Meanwhile, Kate and the baby returned to Georgia. The family was gathered again in Atlanta that fall when Thurman accepted an invitation to teach at Morehouse and Spelman. But the reunion was relatively brief. Kate died near the end of December 1930.

Thurman began a new marriage and a new teaching career in 1932. He married Sue Bailey, a friend from college days and a highly considered staff member with the national board of the Y.W.C.A. Together they moved to Washington, D.C., where Thurman joined the School of Religion at Howard University and later became dean of the university's Rankin Chapel. The Thurmans developed together as a magnificent team in their ministry to students and others, and they became the parents of a second daughter, Anne Spencer Thurman.

It was during the Howard University period that Thurman's reputation as a creative teacher, preacher, and worship leader was first established. Partly as a result, he was invited to lead a small delegation of Afro-Americans on "a pilgrimage of friendship" as guests of the Student Christian Movement of India, Burma, and Ceylon (now Sri Lanka). The Thurmans and another couple, Edward and Phenola Carroll, made up the delegation that traveled from the fall of 1935 to the summer of 1936.

As Thurman often said later, that journey, coming at a formative point in his career, was "a watershed experience in my life." The encounters with Tagore, Gandhi, and others, the constant demand from Hindus, Buddhists, and Moslems that he explain his connections to the Christianity of the slaveholders, lynch mobs, and other white supremacists in the U.S.A. set him on pathways that he never abandoned. The journey strengthened him in his instinctive movement toward making "a careful distinction between Christianity and the religion of Jesus"—and identifying himself primarily with the latter. From these powerful and often shaking encounters he began to formulate the ideas and convictions that eventually formed the substance of his best-known work, *Jesus and the Disinherited.* On this journey, at the Khyber Pass, Thurman first caught a vision of creating a religious fellowship that would open its life to all seekers, of all colors and creeds.

Howard and Sue returned to Howard University and continued to expand and deepen their creative ministry there, paying even more attention than before to the needs of international students (a special concern of Sue's) and to the development of worship experiences that drew people together across all lines. Then in 1943 they received an invitation that seemed to make it possible for them to focus their energies on the fulfillment of the vision Thurman had had at the Khyber Pass. In the fall of 1944, with the war still raging, the Thurmans left behind a secure academic position and moved to San Francisco. There Howard became copastor of the newly formed Church for the Fellowship of All Peoples, the nation's first really interracial church congregation. It was an act of faith, a movement of vision, for very little was assured financially; but Howard and Sue were sure that this was where they should be.

The time at Fellowship Church provided the first opportunities for Howard Thurman's poetic meditations to be published. This style became his hallmark, and many of these brief but powerful openings to the spirit are included in the present volume. (Many of the tapes that contain his sermons and meditations over a span of some twenty-five years are available through the Howard Thurman Educational Trust in San Francisco. They are important, for Thurman never hesitated to say, "Though I have published [many] books, my craft remains the spoken word.")

After nine years of creative and pathbreaking ministry at Fellowship, the Thurmans accepted an invitation to return to the East Coast, this time with Howard as dean of the chapel at Boston University. In 1953 that was an unheard-of position for a Black man, but Howard was in no way intimidated. Indeed, by this time he was a nationally and internationally known figure, identified by every-one—including *Life* magazine—as one of the great preachers and pastors of his era.

Howard and Sue saw the Boston University opening as a chance to expand the ministry they had developed at Fellowship Church. Moreover, they loved students, and the period at Marsh Chapel was a most rewarding one for them. (Martin Luther King, Jr., was in his last year of residence as a doctoral student at the university when the Thurmans arrived, and at one of their informal sessions at the house Sue tried to make a case for the young minister-philosopher to take Howard's place at Fellowship. But King had set his face to-ward the South.) The B.U. period also allowed the Thurmans to make a long-desired pilgrimage to Africa. As usual, Howard went in search not only of his own fully appreciated roots but also of the common ground that might be available to all humankind through the proper appropriation of indigenous African religions.

In 1965 Howard Thurman formally retired from Boston Uni-versity, having gradually withdrawn from active leadership over a two-year period to provide for a smooth transition. He and Sue returned to San Francisco, a city he loved and the site of the Howard Thur-man Educational Trust they had established. The trust was a base for them, but just as important, the gifts received by the trust from friends and supporters enabled Howard to continue and expand his career-long pledge to help young people seeking an education, just as he had been helped many times along the way. Meanwhile, he tried to meet some of the demands from across the country for his presence as lecturer, counselor, preacher, and teacher, and he or-ganized a series of small seminars for younger leaders. All the while, Sue kept reminding him that he was not the young man of the 1930s and 1940s any more. Sometimes he listened. Sometimes his body, especially his lungs, forced him to change pace.

It was during that post–Boston University period that I first met Howard Thurman (although I sometimes feel I have never not known him). He came to speak in Atlanta while I was teaching at Spelman College, and I went to visit with him, for I had long known and appreciated his work, initially through *Jesus and the Disinherited*. From that first encounter in the mid-1960s, my family and I found the Howard Thurman who had watered so many lives in deep, deep places.

I remember the times in his San Francisco study or living room, especially after our time of mourning for our mutual loss of Martin King. I recall how carefully and sympathetically he questioned me about the Black Power/Black Identity movement. "What are the young people doing, what are they thinking, where do you think they're going?" Critical, compassionate, hopeful, and eager to understand— he was all of these things as we talked into the night. Often his great eyes would be filled with mischievousness, and he'd have an appropriate story to tell—and he always enjoyed the stories at least as much as anyone else. Sometimes his stocky frame would shake with laughter. This was an earthy mystic, filled with pranks and jokes, ever ready to laugh at himself, at life, and at anything else close at hand. This was a perambulating mystic, tiring out younger folks on his walks up and down the hilly streets of San Francisco.

I remember going to him in times of deep personal need, some-times talking by phone, sometimes face to face. He was always sol-idly present, listening, understanding, admonishing when necessary, sharing silence, surrounding and undergirding me with prayers, doing whatever else seemed helpful. We could feel Howard and Sue keep-ing our entire family in a special place of love and meditation be-tween them.

I remember our silences. They were filled with his wisdom and compassion. Indeed, it may be that he was the wisest and most com-passionate man I have ever known.

Oh yes, I remember, too, how he encouraged me to finish my book about the Black experience in America, *There Is a River,* and when I took so long that some publishers were saying that Blackness had gone out of style, I remember Howard. He put on his suit, took the bus downtown, and went to see his longtime friend Dr. Daniel Collins of Harcourt Brace Jovanovich. He told Dan that I had a manuscript that he ought to read and that Mr. Jovanovich ought to read, too. It was done.

Howard Thurman opened doors, and the doors to publishers' offices were among the least important of them. Many of us have become more fully human because of Howard's opening love. Many of us have been challenged by his life to do our own moving, deep into the heart of our own "spiritual idiom," thereby drawing nearer to the "inside [of] all peoples, all cultures, all faiths."

When Howard changed the form of his movement in 1981 and passed on, we were saddened, but not desperate. We remembered

how Sue used to say, "Howard has a way of leading people home."
Now we are deeply aware of his continuing presence, his opening
of the way, and we understand more fully than ever before the
meaning of the words of an African poet who declared:

> Those who are dead are never gone,
> they are there in the thickening shadow.
> The dead are not under the earth:
> they are in the tree that rustles,
> they are in the wood that groans,
> they are in the water that runs,
> they are in the water that sleeps,
> they are in the hut, they are in the crowd,
> the dead are not dead.

He is not dead. He lives in these printed words, in thousands
of lives, "in the water that runs," in the opening doors. Never gone.
Deep river, moving on.

VINCENT HARDING
Denver, Colorado
Autumn 1983

ACKNOWLEDGMENTS

My father and I began this collection during the early days of his final illness. We discussed and roughly sketched its outline. When his health worsened, our preliminary work had to stop, but it was understood between us that I would complete the project alone.

A year after his death I was able to return to the book. Soon I discovered that the structure and organization fell easily into place, that passages I had forgotten came back as familiar old friends, that in fact I was not alone. We finished the book as we had begun—together.

For additional help I am indebted to my mother, Sue Bailey Thurman, whose loving encouragement and support never failed; to my friend Dr. Luther E. Smith, the eminent Thurman scholar, of Emory University, Atlanta; and to the staff of the Howard Thurman Educational Trust.

A. S. T.
San Francisco, California
January 1984

CONCERNING
DISCIPLINES
OF THE SPIRIT

Life and Order

MIRACLES IN THE SPIRIT

"There are miracles in the spirit of which the world knows nothing." Such is the testimony that comes to us from the lips of George Fox. Our lives are surrounded day by day and night after eventful night by the stupendous revelations of what man is discovering about the world around him. Each day we seem to penetrate more deeply into the process of nature. Thousands of men and women with utter devotion give themselves to the pursuit of secret disclosures from the chamber of mysteries of which they themselves are a part and from which they have come forth. It is as if there is a mighty collective and individual effort to remember what they were before the mind became mind and the body became flesh and blood. So successful has been the appropriation of the knowledge of the mysteries of air and wind and earth that what a decade ago would have startled and frightened the most mature adult is today taken for granted by the simplest child. We speak of going to the moon not as denizens of the shadows where unrealities tumble over one another in utter chaos. Rather we speak of going to the moon and back again with voices that are brimming over with an arrogance that even a god may not command.

3

But let one arise in our midst to speak of secrets of another kind. Let one say that the world of the spirit has vast frontiers which call to us as our native heath. At once the deep split in our spirits reveals itself. Out of our eyes, as we listen, there leaps the steady glow of recognition while our lips speak of superstition and delusion. Can the miracles in the spirit be real, true? Because they seem always to be personal and private, does this not add to their unreality?

The miracles in the spirit? What are they? The resolving of inner conflict upon which all the lances of the mind have splintered and fallen helplessly from the hand; the daring of the spirit that puts to rout the evil deed and the decadent unfaith; the experiencing of new purposes which give courage to the weak, hope to the despairing, life to those burdened by sin and failure; the quality of reverence that glows within the mind, illumining it with incentive to bring under the control of Spirit all the boundless fruits of knowledge; the necessity for inner and outer peace as the meaning of all men's striving; the discovery that the "Covenant of Brotherhood" is the witness of the work of the Spirit of God in the life of man and the hymn of praise offered to Him as Thanksgiving and Glory!

THE CONSCIENTIOUS DEMAND

Years and years ago—farther back than the records of history reveal—early man learned how to use a club in self-defense and thus to extend his control over an area farther than his arm unaided could reach. When he learned to throw this club with precision and power, it meant that the control of his environment was farther extended. So the story goes; as man developed—extending his arm through club, bow and arrow, gun powder, gasoline engine, through various kinds of vehicles and machines up to and including the jet-propelled plane and the atomic bomb—he required a complete adjustment of his mind and spirit to his new power. He has been forced to fit his new powers, with each development, into a scheme of life that would keep him from destroying himself. Difficult as this adjustment has been for man's mind, it has been infinitely more difficult for his spirit and conscience. A bow-and-arrow conscience finds itself paralyzed

4

in the presence of the cannon and the rifle. A sense of social responsibility in the use of the arrow finds itself paralyzed by the tremendous moral demands of gun powder. The dilemma of modern man is to match spiritual and moral maturity with the amazing power created by his mastery over nature. He has learned a part of the sector of energy by unlocking the door of the atom, and yet he continues to be moved by prejudice, greed and lust. He has devised a machine that can keep pace with the speed of the earth through the heavens, and yet he has not learned how to walk the earth in the midst of his fellows with simple reverence and grace. Today we stand on the verge of a brave, startling era which can yield the end of poverty, of war, and of all the breeds of hate that have made the earth a hell for countless millions. Oh, for how many years, by our deeds, shall we curse God and die, when we could reflect Him and live?

WE SPREAD OUR LIVES BEFORE THEE

The story of our lives is the old story of man. There is the insistent need to separate ourselves from the tasks by which our days are surrounded. The urgency within us cries out for detachment from the traffic and the complexities of our involvements. There is the ebb and flow of anxiety within us because always there seems to be so little time for withdrawal, for reflection. These are the thoughts which find their way into our spirits when at last the Time of Quiet is our portion.

It is no ordinary experience to spread our lives before the honest scrutiny of our own selves, but there is no escape from such a necessity. The obvious things in our lives we pass over, taking them for granted; this may be a source of weakness and despair. Deeply are we aware of limitations in many dimensions of our lives. We are conscious of the ways in which and by which we have undermined the Light, the Truth, that is within; sometimes we do call good things bad and bad things good.

There are some things in our lives which we have not looked at for a long, long time. We make as an act of sacrament the lifting and exposing of these things before God, with tenderness and compassion. There are some things within us that are so far beneath the surface of our movements and our functioning that we are unmindful not only of their presence but also of the quality of their influence in our decisions, our judgment, and our behavior. In the quietness we will their exposure before God, that they may be lifted to the center of our focus, that we may know what they are and seek to deal with them in keeping with our health and our innermost wisdom.

All of the involvements of our lives in family, in primary community relations, in our state and country, and in the far-flung reaches of the things that we affect, and the things that affect us in our world; all of the concern that is ours for various aspects of the things that affect us and that we affect—these we spread before our own eyes and before the scrutiny of God.

THE GROWING EDGE

Look well to the growing edge. All around us worlds are dying and new worlds are being born; all around us life is dying and life is being born. The fruit ripens on the tree, the roots are silently at work in the darkness of the earth against a time when there shall be new lives, fresh blossoms, green fruit. Such is the growing edge! It is the extra breath from the exhausted lung, the one more thing to try when all else has failed, the upward reach of life when weariness closes in upon all endeavor. This is the basis of hope in moments of despair, the incentive to carry on when times are out of joint and men have lost their reason, the source of confidence when worlds crash and dreams whiten into ash. The birth of the child—life's most dramatic answer to death—this is the growing edge incarnate. Look well to the growing edge!

Commitment

A STRANGE FREEDOM

It is a strange freedom to be adrift in the world of men without a sense of anchor anywhere. Always there is the need of mooring, the need for the firm grip on something that is rooted and will not give. The urge to be accountable to someone, to know that beyond the individual himself there is an answer that must be given, cannot be denied. The deed a man performs must be weighed in a balance held by another's hand. The very spirit of a man tends to panic from the desolation of going nameless up and down the streets of other minds where no salutation greets and no friendly recognition makes secure. It is a strange freedom to be adrift in the world of men.

Always a way must be found for bringing into one's solitary place the settled look from another's face, for getting the quiet sanction of another's grace to undergird the meaning of the self. To be ignored, to be passed over as of no account and of no meaning, is to be made into a faceless thing, not a man. It is better to be the complete victim of an anger unrestrained and a wrath which knows no bounds, to be torn asunder without mercy or battered to a pulp by angry violence, than to be passed over as if one were not. Here at least one is dealt with, encountered, vanquished, or overwhelmed—

but not ignored. It is a strange freedom to go nameless up and down the streets of other minds where no salutation greets and no sign is given to mark the place one calls one's own.

The name marks the claim a man stakes against the world; it is the private banner under which he moves which is his right whatever else betides. The name is a man's water mark above which the tides can never rise. It is the thing he holds that keeps him in the way when every light has failed and every marker has been destroyed. It is the rallying point around which a man gathers all that he means by himself. It is his announcement to life that he is present and accounted for in all his parts. To be made anonymous and to give to it the acquiescence of the heart is to live without life, and for such a one, even death is no dying.

To be known, to be called by one's name, is to find one's place and hold it against all the hordes of hell. This is to *know* one's value, for one's self alone. It is to honor an act as one's very own, it is to live a life that is one's very own, it is to bow before an altar that is one's very own, it is to worship a God who is one's very own.

It is a strange freedom to be adrift in the world of men, to act with no accounting, to go nameless up and down the streets of other minds where no salutation greets and no sign is given to mark the place one calls one's own.

SADDLE YOUR DREAMS

"Saddle your dreams before you ride them." It is the nature of dreams to run riot, never to wish to contain themselves within limitations that are fixed. Sometimes they seem to be the cry of the heart for the boundless and the unexplored. Often they are fashioned out of longings too vital to die, out of hankerings fed by hidden springs in the dark places of the spirit. Often they are the offspring of hopes that can never be realized and longings that can never find fulfillment. Sometimes they are the weird stirrings of ghosts of dead plans and the kindling of ashes in a hearth that has long since been deserted. Many and fancy are the names by which dreams are called— fantasies, repressed desires, vanities of the spirit, will-o'-the-wisps. Sometimes we seek to dismiss them by calling their indulgence daydreaming, by which we mean taking flight from the realities of our own world and dwelling in the twilight of vain imaginings.

All of this may be true. But all their meaning need not be exhausted by such harsh judgment. The dreams belong to us; they come full-blown out of the real world in which we work and hope and carry on. They are not impostors. They are not foreign elements invading our world like some solitary comet from the outer reaches of space which pays one visit to the sun and is gone never to come again. No! Our dreams are our *thing*. They become *other* when we let them lose their character. Here is the fatal blunder. Our dreams must be saddled by the hard facts of our world before we ride them off among the stars. Thus, they become for us the bearers of the new possibility, the enlarged horizon, the great hope. Even as they romp among the stars they come back to their place in our lives, bringing with them the radiance of the far heights, the lofty regions, and giving to all our days the lift and the magic of the stars.

THE NARROW RIDGE

For some men there can be no security in life apart from being surrounded by the broad expanse of a country in which all landmarks are clear and the journey is along a well-worn path. Day after day they must be able to look up at any moment and know exactly where they are. Their lives feed on the familiar tidbits concerning those to whom one long adjustment has been made, and the possibility of the sudden shift in temperament or behavior almost never occurs. There is a strange comfort in the assurance of the commonplace and familiar. Everything is in its place and all things are arranged in a neat pattern of stability. The one great fear is the fear of change, the one great dread is the dread of strangeness.

Of course there is strength in this kind of security. Living can become routinized and reduced to the dignity of the behavior pattern. Thus the shock of the sudden encounter has a constant absorption. It is as if one's life were lived behind a sure and continuous windbreak. Days come and go and each one is as the one before. At length the monotony folds its wings and stirs no more. There is not even the pith of endurance, only the settling in and the dimming of all lights.

Buber says that life for him is at its very best when he is living on what he calls "the narrow ridge." It is a way of life that generates zest for each day's round because it is lived with anticipation.

There is the full recognition of the necessity for routines and even the inner provisions for the simple monotony which is a part of all human experience. The commonplace remains the commonplace and the ordinary remains the ordinary—but this does not exhaust the meaning of the days. Each day's length is rimmed round with a margin of the joy of the unexpected, the anticipation of the new and the significant. It is to give to living a whiff of ammonia. The accent, the bias, of such a life is on the side of the margin, the overtone, rather than a mere acceptance of the commonplace and the ordinary. If such is one's prevailing attitude, then even the commonplace becomes infused with the kind of vitality that gives it a new meaning. This is not merely a matter of temperament or special gift. Such a possibility lies within reach of every man. It stems out of a conviction about the meaning of life as a whole, a faith that affirms that Life can be trusted to fulfill itself in the big Moment *and* the ordinary event, that what a man demands of life must never be more than what he is willing to believe about life. In each of us there is a "Cascade Eagle," a bird that is higher when soaring in the gorge than the highest soarer above the plains—because the gorge is in the mountains. To give this eagle wings is the call to every man.

KNOWLEDGE . . . SHALL VANISH AWAY

"Whether there be knowledge, it shall vanish away. . . ."

A ceaseless search like the ebb and flow of oceans
Marks all man's days:
For him no rest, no rest;
The fever in the blood
Is answer to the temper of the mind.

When Time was young, just learning how to walk,
It placed its stamp on the single cell
Which gave a slant to all that lives
Today or yesterday, no matter when.
A ceaseless search like the ebb and flow of oceans
Marks all man's days.

Is there some point, some place of rest
To bring an end to all man's quest?
Something that does not fail?
Something that lasts beyond all things that pass
When shadows thicken and the lights grow dim?
Some worldly hope that gives retreat
From all the winds that beat upon the world?
Some sure attachment to another's life
That stands secure against all change of mind or heart?
Some private dream where only dwells
The purest secrets of desire?
All these must fade,
All these must pass away.

There is a sense of wholeness at the core of man
That must abound in all he does;
That marks with reverence his ev'ry step;
That has its sway when all else fails;
That wearies out all evil things;
That warms the depth of frozen fears
Making friend of foe,
Making love of hate,
And lasts beyond the living and the dead,
Beyond the goals of peace, the ends of war!
This man seeks through all his years:
To be complete and of one piece, within, without.

COMES THAT WHICH IS PERFECT

"But when that which is perfect is come, that which is in part shall
be done away."

Of all the stories Jesus told,
There is none more deadly where it strikes
Than what he said about the man
Who came to feast with wedding guests
Without the proper dress.

One precious moment all his own, to bring to life
His only gift.
Nameless, unclaimed, the moments come and go,
The smooth unfolding of each passing
Weans the life from earlier dreams,
Dulls the sharp edges of the mind.
Days are but days, and nights but interludes
Before the sound begins again.
And then one moment, unlike all the rest,
Descends upon his world.
It comes unheralded, but it bears his name!
The one desire which all his years have sought
Stands ripe for plucking before his startled eyes;
The one great vision from the heights
That launched him on his way when life was young;
The perfect love to make his life complete . . .
But always the fatal flaw.
The refrain's the same;
The wedding feast is on;
Down the long banquet hall, the King appears.
He sees the careless dress, the half-brushed hair,
In the wary eyes the slow chagrin.
Excuses, fears, or alibis can find no voice.
An awful stillness freezes everything.
The Moment burns itself away
Then passes even as it came.
And what is left? Stark despair
Where nothing lives;
The Dream has died.

THE MEANING OF COMMITMENT

· 1 ·

The meaning of commitment as a discipline of the spirit must take into account that mind and spirit cannot be separated from the body in any absolute sense. It has been wisely said that the time and the place of man's life on earth is the time and the place of his body, but the meaning of his life is as significant and eternal as he wills to make it. While he is on earth, his mind and spirit are domiciled in his body, bound up in a creature who is at once a child of nature and of God. Commitment means that it is possible for a man to yield the nerve center of his consent to a purpose or cause, a movement or an ideal, which may be more important to him than whether he lives or dies. The commitment is a self-conscious act of will by which he affirms his identification with what he is committed to. The character of his commitment is determined by that to which the center or core of his consent is given.

This does not mean, necessarily, that the quality and depth of a man's commitment are of the same order as what he is committed to. There is a dynamic inherent in commitment itself which seems to be independent of what the commitment is focused on. This is an important distinction, always to be borne in mind. Here again we encounter the same basic notion discovered above: there seems to be a certain automatic element in commitment, once it is set in motion. There are a mode of procedure and a sense of priority—one might say, an etiquette and a morality—that belong automatically to this kind of experience, once it becomes operative. In other words, once the conditions are met, energy becomes available in accordance with what seems a well-established pattern of behavior. What is true for plants and animals other than man seems to be true for man. There are many complexities introduced as we observe the pattern at the level of mind, but they must not confuse the basic, elemental fact. When the conditions are met, the energy of life is made available.

In the larger sense, something amoral seems to be at work here. It is as if the law of life were deeper than the particular expression of self-consciousness in man. It is clear, for instance, that there is no difference between the basic conditions that cause strawberries to grow and the basic conditions that cause poison ivy to grow. Whatever the prerequisites for each, once they are met, the energy of life begins to flow with creative results. The fact that strawberries are a delight to the taste, and nutritious, while poison ivy is irritating and disturbing to man, is beside the point. It is rightly observed that life does not take consequences into account. Each plant meets the conditions for life, and each is supported and sustained.

Serious problems arise when the same principle operates in the conscious activities of man. There is a sense, alas, in which it is true that the wicked do prosper. When a man who has an evil heart gives the nerve center of his consent to evil enterprise, he does receive energy and strength. The most casual observation confirms this in human experience. There is a vitality in the demonic enterprise when it becomes the fundamental commitment of a life. However, the Christian view insists that ultimately the evil enterprise will not be sustained by life, for the simple reason that it is *against* life. What is against life will be destroyed by life, for what is against life is against God. Nevertheless, there is a time interval when nothing is in evidence that can distinguish the quality or integrity of an evil commitment from a good one. This is at least one of the important insights in the Master's parable of the wheat and the tares. There is a period in their growth when they cannot be distinguished or separated from each other. Ultimately the wheat bears fruit proper to itself, and the tares are only tares. But meanwhile the issue is not clear, not clear at all. Again, the Master says that God "makes his sun rise on the evil and the good, and sends rain on the just and the unjust." We seem to be in the presence of a broad and all-comprehending rhythm. There is a logic and an order in the universe in which all living things, at least, are deeply involved.

It remains now to examine the bearing of this fundamental trait of the life process on the meaning of commitment—the act by which the individual gives himself in utter support of a single or particular end. Energy and vitality are apparently not spread around on the basis of a general gratuity; over and above what is given for the mere manifestation of life, there are conditions inherent in the process. When these are met, something happens, energy starts moving, pulsing, becoming manifest in accordance with the form of life that has fulfilled the conditions. In the experience of mankind, the attitude or act that triggers this release of fresh vigor and vitality is singleness of mind. This means surrendering the life at the very core of one's self-consciousness to a single end, goal, or purpose. When a man is able to bring to bear upon a single purpose all the powers of his being, his whole life is energized and vitalized. This is the same principle we have already seen in operation. It shows itself wherever life is manifest. We may expect to find it at work in man's religious experience. In fact, it is my view that the general insight becomes profoundly particularized in religious commitment and that the "general law" reaches its apotheosis in man's religious experience, in the surrender of his life to God. This is the focal point to which all the other manifestations of the insight quietly call attention.

In Christianity there is ever the central, inescapable demand of surrender. The assumption is that this is well within the power of the individual. If the power is lacking, every effort must be put forth to find out what the hindrance is. No exception is permissible. "If the eye is a hindrance, pluck it out . . . if the arm is a hindrance, cut if off." Whatever stands in the way of the complete and full surrender, we must search it out and remove it. If a bad relationship is a hindrance, one must clean it up. In other words, whatever roadblocks appear, the individual must remove them. The yielding of the very nerve center of one's consent is a private, personal act in which a human being, as sovereign, says "Yes." The ability to do this, to say "Yes," is not the result of any special talent, gift, or endowment. It is not the product of any particular status due to birth, social definition, race, or national origin. It is not a power one can exercise only if given the right by one's fellows. It is not contingent upon wealth or poverty, sickness or health, creed or absence of creed. No, the demand is direct and simple: Surrender your inner consent to God—this is your sovereign right—this is your birthright privilege. And a man can do it directly and in his own name. For this he needs no special sponsorship. He yields *his* heart to God and in so doing experiences for the first time a sense of coming home and of being at home.

Here we look squarely into the face of the demand of the Master concerning the Kingdom of God and the meaning of discipleship. It is expressed thus:

> And a scribe came up and said to him, "Teacher, I will follow you anywhere"; Jesus said to him, "Foxes have holes, wild birds have nests, but the Son of Man has nowhere to lay his head." . . . Another of the disciples said to him, "Lord, let me go and bury my father first of all"; Jesus said to him, "Follow me, and leave the dead to bury their own dead."
>
> MATT. 9:19–22

> For where your treasure lies, your heart will lie there too. The eye is the lamp of the body: so, if your Eye is generous, the whole of your

body will be illumined, but if your Eye is selfish, the whole of your
body will be darkened. And if your very light turns dark, then—what
a darkness it is! No one can serve two masters: either he will hate one
and love the other, or else he will stand by the one and despise the
other—you cannot serve both God and Mammon. . . . Seek God's
Realm and his goodness, and all that will be yours over and above.

MATT. 6:21–24, 33

Oswald McCall gives an exciting dimension to the concept in
these words:

Be under no illusion, you shall gather to yourself the images you love.
As you go, the shapes, the lights, the shadows of the things you have
preferred will come to you, yes, inveterately, inevitably as bees to their
hives. And there in your mind and spirit they will leave with you their
distilled essence, sweet as honey or bitter as gall . . .

Cleverness may select skillful words to cast a veil about you, and
circumspection may never sleep, yet you will not be hid. No.

As year adds to year, that face of yours, which once lay smooth
in your baby crib, like an unwritten page, will take to itself lines, and
still more lines, as the parchment of an old historian who jealously
sets down all the story. And there, more deep than acids etch the steel,
will grow the inscribed narrative of your mental habits, the emotions
of your heart, your sense of conscience, your response to duty, what
you think of your God and of your fellowmen and of yourself. It will
all be there. For men become like that which they love, and the name
thereof is written on their brows.*

· 2 ·

Now we are ready to deal with the working paper of commitment:
this is a living world; life is alive, and as expressions of life we, too,
are alive and sustained by the characteristic vitality of life itself. God
is the source of the vitality, the life, of all living things. His energy
is available to plants, to animals, and to our own bodies if the conditions are met. Life is a responsible activity. What is true for our
bodies is also true for mind and spirit. At these levels God is immediately available to us if the door is opened to Him. The door is
opened by yielding to Him that nerve center where we feel consent

---

*Oswald McCall, *The Hand of God* (New York: Harper & Brothers, 1957), pp. 122–23. Reprinted by permission of Harper & Row, Publishers, Inc.

or the withholding of it most centrally. Thus, if a man makes his deliberate self-conscious intention the offering to God of his central consent and obedience, then he becomes energized by the living Spirit of the living God.

Let me hasten to point out that this principle does not exhaust all the possibilities. There seem to be occasions, or better, persons, who have the gift of the Spirit where there is no awareness of any act of commitment initiating it. They are the "once born" souls. Their openness to God is one with their own self-consciousness—to share His life and be flooded by His presence is natural to them.

There is another consideration that must be borne steadily in mind. The working principle we are thinking of has nothing to do with the question of merit or demerit. When the conditions are met, the individual does not "merit" the energizing strength of the life of God. No, the point is that man's relation to life occurs within a responsible framework—he lives and functions in an orderly context, an essential milieu in which order and not disorder is characteristic. The vast creative mood of existence *is* creative, not chaotic. There is an essential harmony in all existence, and the life of every living thing shares in it. Man co-operates with the Spirit of God by making himself open and available to it. And this fact is crucial. A man may elect not to do this and thereby create for himself many problems of inner chaos and confusion; these may or may not be assessed as such.

The autonomy of the individual must not be denied. It would seem to follow, then, that if the individual meets the conditions, the results ensue automatically. Let us take a look at Meister Eckhart's idea. If we reduce commitment to a mechanical process, there is a denial of other prerogatives and aspects of personality. Commitment viewed in such exclusive terms becomes a manipulative device rather than the door through which man enters into a *good* relationship with God. The yielding of the deep inner nerve center of consent is not a solitary action, unrelated to the total structure or context of the life. It is not a unilateral act in the midst of other unilateral acts on the part of the individual. It is, rather, an ingathering of all the phases of one's being, a creative summary of the individual's life—it is a saturation of the self with the mood and the integrity of assent. Something total within the man says "Yes." It is a unanimous vote and not a mere plurality. It is the yielding of mind, yet more than

mind; it is the agreement of the self, expressed in an act of will—
yet more than will; it is the sensation of all the feeling tones—yet
more than emotions. Despite this ramification, the act of commitment may pinpoint a certain moment in time, or a certain encounter
in given circumstances, or a place, or an act of decision that stands
out boldly on the horizon of all one's days—the roots spread out in
all dimensions of living.

WHEN KNOWLEDGE COMES

The setting is the Garden of Eden. Adam and Eve are the central figures in an idyllic surrounding. All is peaceful. All is innocent. They are told by God that they are free to do anything except one thing. They are forbidden to eat the fruit of the tree of knowledge which grows in the midst of the garden. For if they eat of the fruit they shall be driven from the garden and from that day forward they shall be responsible for their own lives. They eat of the fruit; they are driven out of the garden; they become responsible for their own lives. With the coming of knowledge, they have lost their innocence.

The transition from innocence to knowledge is always perilous and fraught with hazard. There is something very comforting and reassuring about innocence. To dwell in innocence is to inhabit a region where storms do not come and where all the breezes are gentle and balmy. It is to live in the calm of the eye of the hurricane. It is to live in a static environment which makes upon the individual no demands other than to *be*. All else is cared for, is guaranteed.

But when knowledge comes, the whole world is turned upside down. The meaning of things begins to emerge. And more importantly, the relations between things are seen for the first time. Questions are asked and answers are sought. A strange restlessness comes over the spirit and the enormity of error moves over the horizon like a vast shadow. Struggle emerges as the way of life. An appetite is awakened that can never be satisfied. A person becomes conscious of himself; the urge to know, to understand, to find answers, turns inward. Every estimate of others becomes a question of self-estimate, every judgment upon life becomes a self-judgment. The question of the meaning of one's self becomes one with the meaning of life.

This process of moving from innocence to knowledge is never finished. Always there is the realm of innocence, always there is the realm of knowledge. Always there is some area of innocence untouched by knowledge. The more profound the growth of knowledge, the more aware the individual becomes of the dimensions of innocence. Pride in knowledge is always tempered by the dominion of innocence. Often we do not become aware of innocence until we experience knowledge.

The setting is the Garden of Eden. Adam and Eve are the central figures in an idyllic surrounding. All is peaceful. All is innocent. They are told by God that they are free to do anything except one thing. They are forbidden to eat the fruit of the tree of knowledge which grows in the midst of the garden. For if they eat of the fruit they shall be driven from the garden and from that day forward they shall be responsible for their own lives. They eat of the fruit; they are driven out of the garden; they become responsible for their own lives.

NO EXPERIENCE
CONTAINS ALL

There is something strange and awesome about the quality of mind that keeps it from coming to rest within any single idea, or any single experience. No deed which we have experienced, however good and wonderful it may be, can quite contain all that we meant by the thing we have done. No word that we have ever uttered can express fully and adequately what we were trying to say. No goal that we have ever set before us and achieved is ever capable of containing all that we were seeking. There always remains a residue that does not ever get itself contained by any vessel we may use, whether it be a thought, an idea, a deed, a goal, a dream, or even a life. The *something more* cries out for expression and the expression does not ever quite come off.

In the entire gamut of our relationship with one another this experience of man is written large. There is a time when we dream of the perfect relationship—the perfect union, the perfect friendship, the perfect love. Standing in the first full flush of the newness of love, we are often so overcome by the vast release of life and joy that we are convinced that what others have felt only dimly is ours in all its glory and completeness. This is good! This is wonderful! There is more to our feelings than we are expressing, there is more in our vision of love than we are experiencing—however slowly something else begins to emerge. We cannot escape the sure persistent sense of inadequacy—however hard we try. Even when our offering of the self is completely accepted and we are to another person far more than he ever dreamed that anyone would or could ever be to him, the fact remains that what we are giving is only partial, what we are sharing is less, much less, than is our desiring.

Therefore, to put into the deed less than the best; to give to the relationship only a shadow of the self; to put at the disposal of the dream only that which is fragmentary and ineffective is to spénd one's days stumbling through the darkness. If a man's best is never quite within his grasp, the less than best is woefully inadequate. There is ever the hope that what the mind searches for today, but does not quite succeed in finding, will be its strength and stay tomorrow and tomorrow and tomorrow.

A C C E P T   O U R   F A C T

Often it is most difficult to accept our fact. Such acceptance means to say "yes" to that which is our own bill of particulars. It does not begin with embracing in some grand manner the great world of which we are a part—even though it may include that, ultimately. It does not mean the recognition of our membership in the human race— although it may include that, ultimately. It means being very specific about ourselves. This is our face, not another's; it will always be our face, exhibiting a countenance that reveals all the laughter and all the tears of our years of living. Whatever a face means in the history of the human race, all the face-meaning which is uniquely ours is ours as utterly as if there were no face on earth except our own. No substitute can be found for it—go where we will, knock at every door, our face remains our face. This is an item of our bill of particulars.

Our situation is uniquely our own. True, we may be victims of circumstances. The operation of forces that did not take our needs into account may have marred our lives and twisted our personalities out of harmony with our intent and our dream. All of this may be an accurate description of our experience of life. If there had been some hand to raise itself in our behalf at the moment of crisis, how different would our whole world be. But there was no hand. There was only we and the cutting edge of the moment with nothing between. All through the years the scar tissue has marked the place. We cannot forget. Our situation is uniquely our own.

Often more difficult than to *accept* our fact is to learn how to *deal* with our fact. It is here that the resources of our lives are brought to bear. It may be that we reject all resources as of no avail and we abandon ourself to our fact, taking refuge in bitterness and despair. Our heart grows cold and life becomes a great and unyielding weariness.

Or we may draw upon all skills and understandings outside of and beyond ourselves, seeking always to alter our fact in ways that are both creative and redemptive. This may happen after we have exhausted our own inner vitalities to that end. If all of these fail then we must learn how to live with our fact, to domesticate it and make of it a friend. In all ages men have found in religion access to God who companions them in such struggles, giving not only comfort and reassurance, but also strength and courage. To discover this is to say "yes" to Life and to our life.

LIFE MUST BE EXPERIENCED

In many ways modern man lives his life as a bystander. Again and again we are several steps removed from the primary experiences of living. When a person becomes critically ill, under most circumstances he is taken from the bosom of his family to a hospital. Here he is given the kind of care and treatment that would be impossible in the home. And this is good. But it means that all of the experience of tenderness that comes from having to care for the sick is denied us. We have little of the winnowing of character that exposes life to the elemental nobility of human nature at bay. The care of the sick often purges the life of self-centeredness and hardness of heart.

When there is death in the family, the body is removed to the funeral establishment. It is no longer the shared responsibility of the members of the family to prepare the body for burial. Many persons live their entire lives without ever seeing a human being die. There is available to us no primary contact with the experience of death as a part of the common life. The great and tragic exception occurs during vast violences like war or the kinds of disaster mentioned in bills of lading as Acts of God. Life and death are seen more and more as two separate entities; we cling to one and fear the other.

All of this adds up to a profound distrust of life itself. Life is seen then as being something to conquer, to struggle with and against. Life is the enemy. It is not to be embraced, to be lived. Hence we creep through our days, reacting to our world as if our faith were in magic, rather than in life. Man must experience life; he must feel it run through his whole being that life belongs to him and he to life. The experience *of* life, not *in* life, will teach a man not to fear life but to love life. He discovers that the test of life in him is to be found in the amount of pain, of frustration, he can absorb without spoiling his joy in living. To keep alive an original sense of aliveness is to know that life is its own restraint and a man is able to stand anything that life can do to him. This is what religion means by faith in God. "O men, how little you trust God."

THE SELF-ENCOUNTER

When have you last had a good session with yourself? Or have you ever had it out with *you*?

Most often you are brought face to face with yourself only when such an encounter is forced upon you. Usually it is in connection with a crisis situation. There is a death in the immediate circle of close family or friends with the result that definite changes must be made in your way of living and thinking. You must accustom yourself to living without the active relationship of the departed one. Or it may be that there is the quickening discovery that your parents are old and can no longer relate to you at the point of your needs but you must relate to them at the point of their need.

There may be other causes of self-confrontation. A chance remark from a friend may bring you quickly to face the fact that you are a pretender in your relations with others, that you have never faced up to your own lack of integrity in word and in act. In a time of temper you may say things of which you are deeply ashamed, not so much because you said them—that is bad enough—but because you were capable of thinking them. You may discover that in trying to make a decision involving a course of action, you are utterly incompetent to do so because you have never claimed your mind as your own. All through the years you have drifted from one position to another, letting your meaning be determined by your response to others or their demands—not determined by how you felt, really, nor what you personally thought. Now you look for some clue outside yourself and there is none to be found. *You* must decide and abide.

Whatever may be the occasion, there comes a deep necessity which leads you finally into the closet with yourself. It is here that you raise the real questions about yourself. The leading one is, What is it, after all, that I amount to, ultimately? Such a question cuts through all that is superficial and trivial in life to the very nerve center of yourself. And this is a religious question because it deals with the total meaning of life at its heart. At such a moment, and at such a time, you must discover for yourself what is the *true* basis of your self-respect. This is found only in relation to God, whose Presence makes itself known in the most lucid moments of self-awareness. For all of us are His children and the most crucial clue to a knowledge of Him is to be found in the most honest and most total knowledge of the self.

THE TEMPTATION TO POSTPONE

The temptation to postpone living until some future time is very subtle—that is, to postpone living significantly. Such a temptation is apt to present itself at any time and to any person. There is the person who says, "When my ship comes in . . ." or "When my luck changes . . ." or "When I get a certain job, then I'll come into my own and begin to live." When we are very young we are apt to think that all our youth is but preliminary to the real business of living. Of course this is true but not altogether. In terms of vocational preparation or in terms of certain broad social responsibilities that are the inevitable accompaniment to adulthood, such is the case. Sometimes because of a sudden or radical reversal in circumstances, an individual may suspend all meaningful living, devoting his time and energy completely to the rugged business of recouping his position or fashioning an immediate technique of survival. Everything has to wait until the situation is in hand and normalcy is restored. Sometimes everything is held up because of a decision which someone else must make, and for a short or long interval life hangs in the balance. At such a time no plans can be made, no decisions determined; waiting, waiting, waiting—this seems to be all that can be managed.

Nevertheless, to postpone living significantly in the present is a serious blunder. Life does not stop being life because we are experiencing reverses or because we are young or because we are preparing ourselves vocationally or because certain important decisions that are in the hands of others have not been made. All of this is to give a purely quantitative character to life, to measure it exclusively in terms of the episode, the event, the circumstance. It is important to cultivate a "feeling for significance" in living and thus to give the quality of aliveness to the experience of living moment by moment. This means seeking ever for fullness, keenness, and zest as the open sesame to experienced life in the living of life. What is lived deeply is securely one's own and nothing can ever take it away—neither circumstance, nor age, nor even Death itself.

> The life that I have lived,
>   so full, so keen,
> Is mine! I hold it firm
>   beneath thy [Death] blow
> And, dying, take it with me
>   where I go.*

*From "Life I Lived" by Ernest Raymond, *The New York Times Magazine*, September 27, 1959. © 1959 by The New York Times Company. Reprinted by permission.

STRENGTH TO BE FREE

"Give me the strength to be free." The thought of being free comes upon us sometimes with such power that under its impact we lose the meaning that the thought implies. Often, "being free" means to be where we are not at the moment, to be relieved of a particular set of chores or responsibilities that are bearing heavily upon minds, to be surrounded by a careless rapture with no reminders of costs of any kind, to be on the open road with nothing overhead but the blue sky and whole days in which to roam. For many, "being free" means movement, change, reordering.

To be free may not mean any of these things. It may not involve a single change in a single circumstance, or it may not extend beyond one's own gate, beyond the four walls in the midst of which all of one's working hours and endless nights are spent. It may mean no surcease from the old familiar routine and the perennial cares which have become one's persistent lot. Quite possibly, your days mean the deepening of your rut, the increasing of your monotony and the enlarging of the areas of your dullness. All of this, and more, may be true for you.

"Give me the strength to be free." Often, to be free means the ability to deal with the realities of one's situation so as not to be overcome by them. It is the manifestation of a quality of being and living that results not only from understanding of one's situation but also from wisdom in dealing with it. It takes no strength to give up, to accept shackles of circumstance so that they become shackles of soul, to shrug the shoulders in bland acquiescence. This is easy. But do not congratulate yourself that you have solved anything. In simple language, you have sold out, surrendered, given up. It takes strength to affirm the high prerogative of your spirit. And you will find that if you do, a host of invisible angels will wing to your defense, and the glory of the living God will envelop your surroundings because in you He has come into His own.

OUR LITTLE LIVES

Our little lives, our big problems—these we place upon Thy
altar!
The quietness in Thy Temple of Silence again and again
rebuffs us:
For some there is no discipline to hold them steady in the
waiting
And the minds reject the noiseless invasion of Thy Spirit.
For some there is no will to offer what is central in the
thoughts—
The confusion is so manifest, there is no starting place to
take hold.
For some the evils of the world tear down all concentra-
tions
And scatter the focus of the high resolves.

War and the threat of war has covered us with
heavy shadows,
Making the days big with forebodings—
The nights crowded with frenzied dreams and
restless churnings.
We do not know how to do what we know to do.
We do not know how to be what we know to be.

Our little lives, our big problems—these we place upon Thy
altar!
Brood over our spirits, Our Father,
Blow upon whatever dream Thou hast for us
That there may glow once again upon our hearths
The light from Thy altar.
Pour out upon us whatever our spirits need of shock, of
lift, of release
That we may find strength for these days—
Courage and hope for tomorrow.
In confidence we rest in Thy sustaining grace

Which makes possible triumph in defeat, gain in loss, and
  love in hate.
We rejoice this day to say:
Our little lives, our big problems—these we place upon Thy
  altar!

R E S E R V O I R   O R   C A N A L

Are you a reservoir or are you a canal or a swamp? The distinction
is literal. The function of a canal is to channel water; it is a device
by which water may move from one place to another in an orderly
and direct manner. It holds water in a temporary sense only; it holds
it in transit from one point to another. The function of the reservoir
is to contain, to hold water. It is a large receptacle designed for the
purpose, whether it is merely an excavation in the earth or some
vessel especially designed. It is a place in which water is stored in
order that it may be available when needed. In it provisions are made
for outflow and inflow.

A swamp differs from either. A swamp has an inlet but no outlet. Water flows into it but there is no provision made for water to
flow out. The result? The water rots and many living things die.
Often there is a strange and deathlike odor that pervades the atmosphere. The water is alive but apt to be rotten. There is life in a
swamp but it is stale.

The dominant trend of a man's life may take on the characteristics of a canal, reservoir, or swamp. The important accent is on
the dominant trend. There are some lives that seem ever to be channels, canals through which things flow. They are connecting links
between other people, movements, purposes. They make the network by which all kinds of communications are possible. They seem
to be adept at relating needs to sources of help, friendlessness to
friendliness. Of course, the peddler of gossip is also a canal. If you
are a canal, what kind of things do you connect?

Or are you a reservoir? Are you a resource which may be drawn
upon in times of others' needs and your own as well? Have you developed a method for keeping your inlet and your outlet in good
working order so that the cup which you give is never empty? As a
reservoir, you are a trustee of all the gifts God has shared with you.
You know they are not your own.

Are you a swamp? Are you always reaching for more and more, hoarding whatever comes your way as your special belongings? If so, do you wonder why you are friendless, why the things you touch seem ever to decay? A swamp is a place where living things often sicken and die. The water in a swamp has no outlet. Canal, reservoir, or swamp—*which?*

N O   O N E   E V E R   W I N S
A   F I G H T

"No one ever wins a fight"—thoughtfully, and with eyes searching the depths of me, my grandmother repeated the words. I was something to behold. One eye was swollen, my jacket was ripped with all the buttons torn from their places, and there was a large tear in the right knee of my trousers.

It was a hard and bitter fight. I had stood all I could, until at last I threw discretion to the winds and the fight was on. The fact that he was larger and older and had brothers did not matter. For four blocks we had fought and there was none to separate us. At last I began to gain in power; with one tremendous effort I got him to the ground and, as the saying went, "made him eat dirt." Then I had come home to face my grandmother. "No one ever wins a fight," were her only words as she looked at me. "But I beat him," I said. "Yes, but look at you. You beat him, but you will learn someday that nobody ever wins a fight."

Many years have come and gone since that afternoon in early summer. I have seen many fights, big and little. I have lived through two world wars. The wisdom of these telling words becomes clearer as the days unfold. There is something seductive about the quickening sense of power that comes when the fight is on. There is a bewitching something men call honor, in behalf of which they often do and become the dishonorable thing. It is all very strange. How often honor is sacrificed in defense of honor. Honor is often a strange mixture of many things—pride, fear, hate, shame, courage, truth, cowardice—many things. The mind takes many curious twistings and turnings as it runs the interference for one's survival. And yet the term survival alone is not quite what is meant. Men want to survive, yes, but on their own terms. And this is most often what is meant by honor.

"No one ever wins a fight." This suggests that there is always some other way; or does it mean that man can always choose the weapons he shall use? Not to fight at all is to choose a weapon by which one fights. Perhaps the authentic moral stature of a man is determined by his choice of weapons which he uses in his fight against the adversary. Of all weapons, love is the most deadly and devastating, and few there be who dare trust their fate in its hands.

FATE AND DESTINY

It may seem to be splitting hairs to say that Destiny is what a man does with his fate. Fate is given; Destiny is won. Fate is the raw materials of experience. They come uninvited and often unanticipated. Destiny is what a man does with these raw materials.

A man participates in his fate almost as a spectator or perhaps as a victim; he does not call the tunes. It is important to make clear that this is only an aspect of human experience. To ignore the margin of experience that seems to be unresponsive to any private will or desire is disastrous. To ascribe responsibility for all the things that happen to one to some kind of fate is equally disastrous.

It is quite reasonable to say that there are forces in life that are set in motion by something beyond the power of man to comprehend or control. The purpose of such forces, their significance, what it is that they finally mean for human life, only God knows. The point at which they touch us or affect us cannot be fully understood. Why they affect us as they do, what they mean in themselves, we do not know. Sometimes they seem like trial and error, like accidents, like blind erratic power that is without conscience or consciousness, only a gross aliveness. To say that those forces are evil or good presupposes a knowledge of ends which we do not have. The point at which they affect our lives determines whether we call them good or evil. This is a private judgment that we pass upon a segment of our primary contact with the forces of life. Out of this contact we build our destiny.

We determine what we shall do with our circumstances. It is here that religion makes one of its most important contributions to life. It is a resource that provides strength, stability, and confidence as one works at one's destiny. It gives assurance of a God who shares in the issue and whose everlasting arms are always there.

I know not where His islands lift
Their fronded palms in air.
I only know I cannot drift
Beyond His love and care.

WE MUST DARE

Olive Schreiner attaches a significant footnote to her discussion on "Parasitism" in her volume entitled *Women and Labor*. It is the story of an old mother duck who brought her latest brood of ducklings down beside what had been a pond. Since her previous ducklings were born, the pond had become baked mud. The duck urged her little brood to go in and swim around, to eat worms and chickweed, where no water, no worms, and no chickweed were; while they with their fresh young instincts smelled the chickweed and heard the water way up the dam. They left their mother beside her old pond to go in quest of water and of food, perhaps to get lost on the way or perhaps to find it. To their old mother they said, "Can't you see that the world has changed? You can't bring the water back into the dried-up pond. It may have been better and pleasanter when it was there, but now it is gone forever. Would you and yours swim again, it must be in other waters."

There is an element of grave risk in all adventure. On the cover of a pacifist magazine published in England before World War II, there appeared this striking sentence: "It is madness to sail a sea that has never been charted before; to look for a land, the existence of which is in question; if Columbus had reflected thus, he would never have weighed anchor, but with this madness he discovered a New World." The reassurance of a secure income, the quiet glow of working with a safe and respected institution in conventional ways, the sense of well-being that comes from being accepted by everyone because one's thinking is "sensible" and safe, all of this makes for a certain kind of deep tranquility. But there is apt to be no growing edge and very little of the tang and zest of aliveness that only the adventurous spirit knows. It is not an accident that the messengers of the gods were symbolized as human beings with wings, ages before men thought of the possibility of flying through the air. The God of life is an adventurer and those who would affirm their fraternity must follow in His train.

Growing Under Pressure

C H A I N S   O F   G O L D

"Chains of gold are no less chains than chains of iron."

This line is taken from one of the letters of Fénelon. He goes on to suggest that the person who is in chains is quite naturally the object of pity to anyone who is without chains. But the serious question is, Who is there that is without chains?

Chains are of various kinds and we need not be involved in the waste of equating them in terms of gold or iron. There are the chains that are ours because of the accidents of birth. It may be that if we had had a choice of parents we would have selected other parents. But would we? All that marked the lives of our parents before they were our parents may be directly reflected in how we were taught and in the atmosphere of our homes. These things influenced our lives deeply and in some strange way, perhaps, decided the limitations (chains) under which we live all our days.

There are the limitations owing to the experiences of our childhood beyond the ken of family and friends: the particular teacher in grade school whose life touched ours at a time and in a way that set in motion certain attitudes that can never quite leave us. These limitations sit in on all our subsequent decisions and leave the long trail of their consequences in everything we do.

There are habits which we formed at a time when we were scarcely aware that they were habits and what they would mean in the wide expanse of the years. They seemed so innocuous at the time—we did not know what they would be like when youth was far behind and all the full-blown demands of maturity would be upon us. These too are chains.

A little later in his letter Fénelon speaks of the comfort that comes from the realization that our chains may be fashioned by Providence. Here he is making no reference to fate or accident or tragedy but rather to the fact that one who is committed to God finds that he is no longer at liberty to do what he would be free to do if he were not so committed. He cannot hate another man even though to hate would be to pass on to another what would seem to be his just desert. He cannot throw his life away by living to no purpose because he is committed to follow a path which is His path wherever it takes him. ". . . After all, the consolation of knowing that you are where you are through God's Providence is quite inexhaustible; while you have that, nothing can matter. Well is it for those whom God cuts off from their own will, that they may follow Him."

THE DAILY TEMPEST

It is a commonplace remark that our lives are surrounded with so much movement, so many pressures, so many demands, that our spirits are often crowded into a corner. As soon as we awaken in the morning we are taken over by the ruthlessness of our daily routine. In some important ways this is good. It means that there is a regularity and a structure to our days that make it possible for us to accomplish tasks which would be impossible otherwise.

But there is another aspect of the matter of daily time tables— an oppressive aspect. We are made prisoner by time tables. We become busy—note the words: not, we are busy, but we *become* busy. Within ourselves we develop an inner sense of *rush* and *haste*. There is a kind of anxiety that is like the sense of impending doom that comes into the life when the spirit is crowded by too much movement.

It is true that for many people the demands upon their lives are so great that only careful planning in terms of a workable time table can see them through. Even where the demands are not great and overwhelming, the economy, the efficiency of an established way of functioning, is undeniable. The purpose of such a pattern is not merely to accomplish more work and with dispatch, but it is to increase the margin of one's self that is available for the cultivation of the inner life. It takes time to cultivate the mind. It takes time to grow in wisdom. It takes time to savor the qualities of living. It takes time to feel one's way into one's self. It takes time to walk with God.

THE DECISION TO ACT

It is a wondrous thing that a decision to act releases energy in the personality. For days on end a person may drift along without much energy, having no particular sense of direction and having no will to change. Then something happens to alter the pattern. It may be something very simple and inconsequential in itself but it stabs awake, it alarms, it disturbs. In a flash one gets a vivid picture of one's self— and it passes. The result is decision, sharp, definitive decision. In the wake of the decision, yes, even as a part of the decision itself, energy is released. The act of decision sweeps all before it and the life of the individual may be changed forever.

In the act the individual has a sense of personal stake. Once the decision is made all other options are frozen and in their place is compulsion. There is something so irrevocable about the act— perhaps that is why the tendency to dally and to postpone is ever present. A man may be sorry for the act, he may wish that he could undo it, he may long for the wheels of time to reverse themselves so that he could start again. He may try to redeem the act by some other act which counteracts what he has done. He may do all of these things, but he cannot alter the finality of the act itself.

It is good that this is so, for it means that the integrity of the act is private, personal, inescapable. Whatever may be the pressure to which a person yields, whatever may be the fears and anxieties which push him to the point of decision from which his act flows, whatever may be the reasons out of which his decision arises, when he acts, his responsibility for the act is uniquely his own.

 The moving finger writes, and having writ
Moves on,

Nor all your piety nor wit
Can call it back to cancel half a line
Nor all your tears wash out a word of it.

Here at last is the place where a person may discover what manner of man he is—here he may sense the independence of the self—here he may stand in his own right as a person—here Life claims him as a part of its vast creative power. It may be that in the integrity of the act a man knows for himself that he is created in the image of God, the Father of all that lives. Shrink not from your heritage by holding back when your *time* comes to *act*—for to act is to claim your true sonship.

A SEED UPON THE WIND

"Man without God is a seed upon the wind." What a picture! A tiny, living thing awaiting its moment of fulfillment, caught up in the movement of tremendous energy, is at the mercy of forces that are not responsive to its own ends! There is a grand unconscious vitality unfolding with mounting energy its impersonal purpose. In the grip of something like this, what is a tiny seed—no more than a particle of dust, a nameless nothing. Here is the abandonment of all purpose, stark helplessness without mooring or anchor. The fact that there is locked within the seed a private world of pattern and design makes no difference to the fierce velocities that sweep it on the reckless, relentless way.

"Man without God is a seed upon the wind." He is a victim of the currents of life that carry him where they will with a bland unmindfulness of purposes and ends which belong to him as a living, thinking, feeling creature. It means that such a man has no sense of center. He takes his clue to all meaning and values from the passing moment, the transitory event, the immediate issue of his day. He is at home nowhere because he is not at home "somewhere." The Master speaks of this in his direct question: "What would a man give in exchange for his soul?"

But there is a sense in which a man *with* God is a seed upon the wind—the man who has made the primary surrender, the commitment, the yielding to God at the core of his being. He is one who has relaxed his will to exercise and hold firm the initiative over his own life. This does not come without exacting struggle of the soul. One by one the outposts of his spirit are captured, retaken and lost again through hours, months, even years of warfare, until at last the very citadel of his spirit is under siege and he is subjected to an utter yielding. There follows often the long silence when nothing stirs. Then out of the quiet of his vanquished spirit something stirs and a new life emerges that belongs more to God than to self. The movement now rests with Purposes that are beyond the little purposes, with Ends that transcend the private ends, the Purposes and Ends of God. There is a sense in which a man *with* God is a seed upon the wind.

N O N E   N E E D   B E   A L O N E

For some there awaits along the way always the vision bright to cheer the path and lift the load aloft. The glory of the shining light surrounds the simplest deed, the hardest choice, the heaviest care. Theirs is not the lot to be in doubt, to wander lost amidst the shadows of their hills. They know not how it comes, nor whence; they only know the look expectant and the grand surmise.

There are some who know the vision and its fearful cost in deep despair and rugged quest. There are no forerunners of the light to come, no stirring of the inward parts to alert the heart and calm the wind. Wrestling, struggling, searching, seeking; for them this is the only way by which surcease is found. Sometimes a sharp resentment of their *fact* darts along the channels of the mind, tearing the tender tendrils of their hopes in bitter threads. Aghast, they watch the question form: Why must it always be like this for me?

There are some to whom the vision never comes and long ago they learned that such is not their way. For them the road is never rough, nor smooth; the light is never bright, nor does it quite go out. The long silent path reveals no sudden turns, no glad surprise. Anchored to a sure monotony, they gather strength just sufficient for the daily need—no more, no less. They only see with little eyes, they seem supported by little strengths, they move along with little hopes.

TWO KINDS OF IDEALS

Two kinds of ideals are always at work in the lives of men. There are those ideals that are ultimate and in a very real sense always far out beyond anything that can be achieved. Or as one person put it, they are like far-off lighthouses whose glow is far away in the distance. They belong to the realm of the absolute and are never marred by the sordidness of the surroundings in which men work and struggle. They are perfect in all their structure and the vision of them quickens the pulse and kindles the desire for the real but the unattainable. They are very important in the life of the race because they keep alive a perennial hope that the best may yet sometime come to be in fact what it is in fancy. Life would be very poor and wretched without them. What creates them is ever a mystery; they belong to life and yet they are something other than life.

There are also those ideals that seem to be created out of the stubborn realities, in the midst of which men work and live. They belong essentially to the stuff of life, the very raw materials of experience. They are never separate from what a man knows to be the character of his daily living. Always they are close at hand, a part of the immediate possibility, always being achieved but never quite fully achieved. With reference to these latter ideals a man is never disillusioned, he knows deep within himself that they belong to his world, to his striving. Always they seem to float just above the ebb and flow of all his moments. Their chief characteristic is that they belong. As long as a man is alive, though he may fail again and again, he is sure they are a part of all his striving.

It is well within the range of possibility that these two kinds of ideals will in time prove to be of one piece. The present ever-achieving ideal is seen as the nearer end of the far-reaching and ultimate ideal. When this happens, a man experiences the integration of his life. He becomes deeply assured that what he is striving for in his little world is suddenly a part of the larger whole. He is no longer alone in his striving. If he be religious, what he strives for at his best, what he seeks where he is, when he is almost himself, is what God is seeking in the great ends that guide ultimately the destiny of all of life. Such a man finds a place which is uniquely his place and most naturally seeks the strength of God to stabilize him in his most commonplace striving.

KEEP ALIVE THE DREAM IN THE HEART

As long as a man has a dream in his heart, he cannot lose the significance of living. It is a part of the pretensions of modern life to traffic in what is generally called "realism." There is much insistence upon being practical, down to earth. Such things as dreams are wont to be regarded as romantic or as a badge of immaturity, or as escape hatches for the human spirit. When such a mood or attitude is carefully scrutinized, it is found to be made up largely of pretensions, in short, of bluff. Men cannot continue long to live if the dream in the heart has perished. It is then that they stop hoping, stop looking, and the last embers of their anticipations fade away.

The dream in the heart is the outlet. It is one with the living water welling up from the very springs of Being, nourishing and sustaining all of life. Where there is no dream, the life becomes a swamp, a dreary dead place and, deep within, a man's heart begins to rot. The dream need not be some great and overwhelming plan; it need not be a dramatic picture of what might or must be someday; it need not be a concrete outpouring of a world-shaking possibility of sure fulfillment. Such may be important for some; such may be crucial for a particular moment of human history. But it is not in these grand ways that the dream nourishes life. The dream is the quiet persistence in the heart that enables a man to ride out the storms of his churning experiences. It is the exciting whisper moving through the aisles of his spirit answering the monotony of limitless days of dull routine. It is the ever-recurring melody in the midst of the broken harmony and harsh discords of human conflict. It is the touch of significance which highlights the ordinary experience, the common event.

The dream is no outward thing. It does not take its rise from the environment in which one moves or functions. It lives in the inward parts, it is deep within, where the issues of life and death are ultimately determined. Keep alive the dream; for as long as a man has a dream in his heart, he cannot lose the significance of living.

THE GREAT EXPOSURE

Sometimes there is only a sixty-second divide between youth and maturity, childhood and adulthood, strength and weakness, life and death. That life is vulnerable is the key to its longevity. We are surrounded every day by the exposure to sudden and devastating calamity. Despite all efforts to the contrary, there is no device by which we may get immunity from the "slings and arrows of outrageous fortune." Here is a man in the full prime of active life, with all the strength and vigor of a rounded maturity—disease strikes, he withers and dies quickly, without warning and often without premonition. Here is a carefree happy child surrounded by all the love that wise devotion and careless rapture can give—a plane crash, both parents perish and what at ten o'clock was a child becomes, at ten-one, a desolate creature shunted across the Great Divide that separates hope from hopelessness, dependence from independence. Thus it goes in one vein.

Or here is a person for whom all the lights had long since gone out, the way ahead is no way—a sharp, sudden turn in the road or a chance encounter in the darkness and everything is changed. Life is vulnerable—always there is the exposed flank.

Sometimes much energy is spent in a vain attempt to protect one's self. We try to harden our fiber, to render ourselves safe from exposure. We refuse to love anyone because we cannot risk being hurt. We withdraw from participation in the struggles of our fellows because we must not get caught in the communal agony of those around us. We take no stand where fateful issues are at stake because we dare not run the risk of exposure to attack. But all this, at long last, is of no avail. The attack from without is missed and we escape only to find that the life we have protected has slowly and quietly sickened deep within because it was cut off from the nourishment of the Great Exposure. It is the way of life that it be nourished and sustained by the constant threat, the sudden rending.

Then,

> Welcome each rebuff
> That makes life's smoothness, rough.

COURAGE AND COWARDICE

There is ever a thin line which separates courage from cowardice. Sometimes the distinction between courage and cowardice is not easy to make. Here is a man who seems always to manifest bravery. Even before the issues are clearly defined, he takes his stand, lest he be regarded by himself or others as being a coward. Or, it may be that he moves into a situation with utter recklessness, unmindful of any clear estimate of what is involved, lest his deliberateness might be construed as a fearful hesitance. As a boy he was ever one to take a dare, because he did not want to seem "chicken." He is always first to sense a moment when an issue seems to be side-stepped and is ever eager to grasp the nettle while others wait for reinforcement. He enjoys the reputation of being forthright, direct, and unafraid. This estimate of his fellows may be well deserved. But it may not be; for his seeming courage may be but his defense against a deep inner uncertainty and creeping fear. What he has not discovered is that of which true courage consists.

Courage is not a blustering manifestation of strength and power. Sometimes courage is only revealed in the midst of great weakness and greater fear. It is often the ultimate rallying of all the resources of personality to face a crucial and devastating demand. And this is not all. There is a quiet courage that comes from an inward spring of confidence in the meaning and significance of life. Such courage is an underground river, flowing far beneath the shifting events of one's experience, keeping alive a thousand little springs of action. It has neither trumpet to announce it nor crowds to applaud; it is best seen in the lives of men and women who do their work from day to day without hurry and without fever. It is the patient waiting of the humble man whose integrity keeps his spirit sweet and his heart strong. Wherever one encounters it, a lift is given to life and vast reassurance invades the being. To walk with such a person in the daily round is to keep company with angels, to have one's path illumined by the "Light that lighteth every man that cometh into the world."

WHEN THE STRAIN IS HEAVIEST

At times when the strain is heaviest upon us,
And our tired nerves cry out in many-tongued pain
Because the flow of love is choked far below the deep re-
  cesses of the heart,
We seek with cravings firm and hard
The strength to break the dam
That we may live again in love's warm stream.
We want more love; and more and more
Until, at last, we are restored and made anew!
Or, so it seems.

When we are closer drawn to God's great Light
And in its radiance stand revealed,
The meaning of our need informs our minds.
"More love," we cried; as if love could be weighed, mea-
  sured, bundled, tied.
As if with perfect wisdom we could say—to one, a little
  love; to another, an added portion;
And on and on until all debts were paid
With no one left behind.

But now we see the tragic blunder of our cry.
Not for more love our hungry cravings seek!
But more power to love.
To put behind the tender feeling, the understanding heart,
The boundless reaches of the Father's Care
Makes love eternal, always kindled, always new.
This becomes the eager meaning of the aching heart
The bitter cry—the anguish call!

THE WORLD IS TOO MUCH WITH US

The problem of the religious man's attitude toward the world is persistent and perennial. One reaches a conclusion about it only to discover that it becomes unresolved again. Perhaps the most direct attempt toward a solution is to seek withdrawal from the world. "The world is too much with us" is a common feeling. When one seeks withdrawal from the world, it is admission that the world is fundamentally and completely "other than" that which is congenial to the things of the spirit; or the individual who seeks withdrawal is convinced that, for his highest spiritual growth, he must not be involved in the entanglements which are the common lot. If it is the former, the inescapable conclusion is that the contradictions of experience are in themselves final and binding. There is ever a recognition of the necessity of temporary withdrawal from the world and its insistences. This is a part of the very rhythm of life. We live by alternations. The religious man is no exception. He withdraws from the world, and then he attacks the world; he retreats and he advances.

Or the religious man may summarize all that the world means in terms of negations into one single manifestation. He may decide that all evil, for instance, is reduced to a single entity. It may be alcohol, or tobacco, or war, or greed. If such is his conclusion then it follows that all energies must be bent toward a single end. Such a solution to the problems of the world is, perhaps, a radical oversimplification. It says that, from within the confines of a particular manifestation of the world, the total solution to the problem of life must be sought and may be found. Obviously, such a solution is inadequate. Both religion and life are too complex.

Or the religious man may recognize that all the world is made up of raw materials which stand in immediate candidacy for the realization of the kingdom, the rule of God. This is a very far-reaching insight with profound radical implications. The idea is inherent in the suggestion to Peter in *The Acts of the Apostles* that nothing that God made should be regarded as unclean. If God is the Creator of life in its totality, then all things are in candidacy for the achievement of the high and holy end. This is not to say that evil has no meaning, but it is to say that, once the evilness of evil is removed, resolved, uprooted, then the total character is thoroughly altered. The religious man who takes this position is never afraid of life, nor does he shrink from vicissitudes. He seeks at every point the emergence of the will and the mind of God from within himself and within the stuff of life itself. What is revealed in life is one with that which transcends life.

THE SEED OF
THE JACK PINE

In response to a letter of inquiry addressed to a Canadian forester concerning the jack pine, which abounds in British Columbia, the following statement was received: "Essentially, you are correct when you say that jack pine cones require artificial heat to release the seed from the cone. The cones often remain closed for years, the seeds retaining their viability. In the interior of the province, the cones which have dropped to the ground will open at least partly with the help of the sun's reflected heat. However, the establishment of the majority of our jack pine stands has undoubtedly been established following forest fires. Seldom do the cones release their seed while on the tree."

The seed of the jack pine will not be given up by the cone unless the cone itself is subjected to sustained and concentrated heat. The forest fire sweeps all before it and there remain but the charred reminders of a former growth and a former beauty. It is then in the midst of the ashes that the secret of the cone is exposed. The tender seed finds the stirring of life deep within itself—and what is deepest in the seed reaches out to what is deepest in life. The result? A tender shoot, gentle roots, until, at last, there stands straight against the sky the majestic glory of the jack pine.

It is not too far afield to suggest that there are things deep within the human spirit that are firmly imbedded, dormant, latent, and inactive. These things are always positive, even though they may be destructive rather than creative. But there they remain until our lives are swept by the forest fire. It may be some mindless tragedy, some violent disclosure of human depravity, or some moment of agony in which the whole country or nation may be involved. The experience releases something that has been locked up within all through the years. If it be something that calls to the deepest things in life, we may, like the jack pine, grow tall and straight against the sky!

CONCERNING THE YUCCA

A very kind friend sent me a letter a few days ago from which I quote the following: "I learned a truth about the yucca . . . that its huge seed-pod cluster must never be disturbed until the pods are empty of seed . . . otherwise the seeds will be spilled on the rock and hard soil and be eaten by birds or mice. Only the terrific lashing and tearing of winter storms can rightly thrash out these seeds and smash them or their pods down among the rocks and thus blow or wash the seeds into crevices—where they can safely germinate, root, and find sufficient water and depth in their short growing season before the summer drought sets in, thus to carry over the young plant."

It is ever a dangerous thing to draw analogies. Nevertheless, the fact is inescapable that there are qualities that seem to be hidden deep within the very texture of the human spirit that can only be laid bare, that they may grow and be fruitful, by the most terrific flailings of a desperate adversity. There are not only such qualities as endurance but also such qualities as tenderness, gentleness, and boundless affection. It seems that these qualities emerge in their fullest glory only when there is nothing more that adversity can do. There is a strange halo surrounding great tribulation which shines in a transcendent glory. This radiance is the basis of the moral appeal always inherent in profound suffering. In addition, there is a starkness which suggests that an ultimate something has been reached which is eternal.

The prophet on the isle of Patmos, in his vision, speaks of those who have gone through great tribulation, that God shall wipe away every tear from their eyes. It is the revelation of a dimension of the human spirit that only becomes available when everything else has been torn away. It is true that in the process everything may be swept away, but the testimony of countless persons in all ages is that it is possible for a man to stand anything that life can do to him. In those to whom such a disclosure is made, the light of the eternal burns steadily and undimmed. They have won the right, and theirs is the glory!

✦ I WILL NOT GIVE UP

It was above the timber line. The steady march of the forest had stopped as if some invisible barrier had been erected beyond which no trees dared move even in single file. Beyond was barrenness, sheer rocks, snow patches, and strong untrammeled winds. Here and there were short tufts of evergreen bushes that had somehow managed to survive despite the severe pressures under which they had to live. They were not lush, they lacked the kind of grace of the vegetation below the timber line, but they were alive and hardy.

Upon close investigation, however, it was found that these were not ordinary shrubs. The formation of the needles was identical with that of the trees farther down; as a matter of fact, they looked like branches of the other trees. When one actually examined them, the astounding revelation was that they *were* branches. For, hugging the ground, following the shape of the terrain, were trees that could not grow upright, following the pattern of their kind. Instead, they were growing as vines grow along the ground, and what seemed to be patches of stunted shrubs were rows of branches of growing, developing trees.

What must have been the tortuous frustration and the stubborn battle that had finally resulted in this strange phenomenon! It is as if the tree had said, "I am destined to reach for the skies and embrace in my arms the wind, the rain, the snow, and the sun, singing my song of joy to all the heavens. But this I cannot do. I have taken root beyond the timber line, and yet I do not want to die; I must not die. I shall make a careful survey of my situation and work out a method, a way of life, that will yield growth and development for me despite the contradictions under which I must eke out my days. In the end I may not look like the other trees, I may not be what all that is within me cries out to be. But I will not give up. I will use to the full every resource in me and about me to answer life with life. In so doing, I shall affirm that this is the kind of universe that sustains, upon demand, the life that is in it."

I wonder if I dare to act even as the tree acts. I wonder! I wonder! Do you?

THE PRESSURE OF CRISIS

When Lloyd George, the British statesman, was a boy, one of his family responsibilities was to collect firewood for warmth and for cooking. He discovered early that always after a very terrific storm, with high winds and driving rain, he had very little difficulty in finding as much, and more, wood than he needed at the time. When the days were beautiful, sunny, and the skies untroubled, firewood was at a premium. Despite the fact that the sunny days were happy ones for him, providing him with long hours to fill his heart with delight, nevertheless, in terms of other needs which were his specific responsibilities, they were his most difficult times.

Many years after, he realized what had been happening. During the times of heavy rains and driving winds, many of the dead limbs were broken off and many rotten trees were toppled over. The living things were separated from the dead things. But when the sun was shining and the weather was clear and beautiful, the dead and the not dead were undistinguishable.

The experience of Lloyd George is common to us all. When all is well with our world, there is often no necessity to separate the "dead" from the "not dead" in our lives. Under the pressure of crisis when we need all available vitality, we are apt to discover that much in us is of no account, valueless. When our tree is rocked by mighty winds, all the limbs that do not have free and easy access to what sustains the trunk are torn away; there is nothing to hold them fast.

It is good to know what there is in us that is strong and solidly rooted. It is good to have the assurance that can only come from having ridden the storm and remained intact. Far beside the point is the why of the storm. Beside the point, too, may be the interpretation of the storm that makes of it an active agent of redemption. Given the storm, it is wisdom to know that when it comes, the things that are firmly held by the vitality of the life are apt to remain, chastened but confirmed; while the things that are dead, sterile, or lifeless are apt to be torn away.

THE MOMENTS
OF HIGH RESOLVE

Keep fresh before me
The moments of my high resolve.

Despite the dullness and barrenness of the days that pass, if I search with due diligence, I can always find a deposit left by some former radiance. But I had forgotten. At the time it was full-orbed, glorious, and resplendent. I was sure that I would never forget. In the moment of its fullness, I was sure that it would illumine my path for all the rest of my journey. I had forgotten how easy it is to forget.

There was no intent to betray what seemed so sure at the time. My response was whole, clean, authentic. But little by little, there crept into my life the dust and grit of the journey. Details, lower-level demands, all kinds of crosscurrents—nothing momentous, nothing overwhelming, nothing flagrant—just wear and tear. If there had been some direct challenge—a clear-cut issue—I would have fought it to the end, and beyond.

In the quietness of this place, surrounded by the all-pervading Presence of God, my heart whispers: Keep fresh before me the moments of my High Resolve, that in fair weather or in foul, in good times or in tempests, in the days when the darkness and the foe are nameless or familiar, I may not forget that to which my life is committed.

Keep fresh before me
The moments of my high resolve.

GOD RESTORETH MY SOUL

The ravages of time are at work in me. I remember when to do the wrong thing brought sharp and swift judgment to my mind and to my spirit. Then there followed a period when much in me that was sensitive to error grew dull and numb. There was no marked and dramatic change—simply the quiet wearing away of the sharp and pointed consciousness of wrong. Until, at last, there were the dead places, the barren spots. It may have been some passing remark from a thoughtful friend, or a flash of light from a forgotten moment of searching prayer, or a challenge to sympathy to which my mind alone responded but of which my feelings were unaware. Then I knew how far I had drifted, and in the wake of that awareness God moved with the swiftness of the eagle in the hunt. The miracle had happened—He had restored my soul.

The drain on my spirit from so much of hardship, the tearing of the brambles in my path, have taken their toll. All the energies seem to spend themselves merely in keeping going. The excuses of weariness and exhaustion seemed ever at hand and anxious to serve. Again and again, the words flowed into me—It takes too much effort to go the second mile—Why should I care so much, no one else seems to be bothered—It is all I can do to handle the necessities of my own life and that I do poorly . . . on and on the stream flowed unchecked.

Then, somewhere along the way, all seemed wrong. I took time aside for checking before God. I told Him all about my increasing dullness, wearisome detail after wearisome detail. When I finished, I was spent. While I waited in my exhaustion, Strength and Renewal were at work in me. Weakness made strong—exhaustion transformed into energies. Deep within there was born the declaration that this risk I must not ever run again. I know now that God restoreth the soul moment by moment, if the door is not held tightly against Him or if it is not permitted to jam by too much of cares and weariness.

God restoreth my soul!

A T I M E O F S N O W

The Apostle Paul writes to his young friend Timothy, saying, "Do thy diligence to make thy voyage before winter." I would like to add a line to the injunction, taken from a speech I heard many years ago: "There is a time of snow in all adventure." If the two sentences are connected by the simple word "because," a suggestive idea is revealed. The revised passage would read, "Do thy diligence to make thy voyage before winter because there is a time of snow in all adventure." The temptation to put off the important decision, the crucial conversation, the beginning of the exacting task, and the living of life seriously is ever present.

When we are young, it is easy to say that we cannot begin to take on our responsibilities until we are older. The fatal words are, "There is always time." What has happened about that important book you were going to read? What about that friend who misunderstood you? Weeks and months ago you were planning to sit down and talk it through, but you have not done it. There is that letter you were going to write when first you heard that an acquaintance of other years had fallen on evil times, but it has been a year and a half now, and it seems too late to write the letter.

The time of snow has set in. Sometimes, in private conversation or in a meeting, an opportunity appears to say the right word, to save a situation, or to bring about a new and creative attitude toward an old problem, or to protect a defenseless absent person; and we let the opportunity pass by default. After that, we may discover that there is little if anything that can be done. There is a time of snow in all adventure, and we forget it to our peril. This injunction is radically important in preparation for tasks to be done. When our preparation is superficial, or careless, the real significance shows up when we go into production, and then it is apt to be too late—the season of snow is upon us. How long must have been the preparation before a beautiful thing like a rose could appear! What travail must be borne before the earth is peopled with whole, integrated persons!

Growing With a Sense of Values

I WANT TO BE BETTER

The concern which I lay bare before God today is my need
to be better:

I want to be better than I am in my most ordinary day-by-
day contacts:
    With my friends—
    With my family—
    With my casual contacts—
    With my business relations—
    With my associates in work and play.

I want to be better than I am in the responsibilities that
are mine:
    I am conscious of many petty resentments.
    I am conscious of increasing hostility toward certain
        people.
    I am conscious of the effort to be pleasing for effect,
        not because it is a genuine feeling on my part.
    I am conscious of a tendency to shift to other shoul-
        ders burdens that are clearly my own.

5 0

I want to be better in the quality of my religious experience:
>I want to develop an honest and clear prayer life.
>I want to develop a sensitiveness to the will of God in
>>my own life.
>I want to develop a charitableness toward my fellows
>>that is far greater even than my most exaggerated
>>pretensions.
>I want to be better than I am.

I lay bare this need and this desire before God in the quietness of this moment.

I NEED COURAGE

The concern I lay bare before God today is my need for
courage:

I need courage to be honest—
>Honest in my use of words
>Honest in accepting responsibility
>Honest in dealing with myself
>Honest in dealing with my fellows
>Honest in my relations with God

I need courage to face the problems of my own life—the
problems of personal values:
>They are confused
>They are often unreal
>They are too exacting for comfort

The problems of my job:
>Perhaps I am working at cross-purposes with my own
>>desires, ambitions, equipment.
>Perhaps I am arrogant instead of taking pride in doing
>>work well.
>Perhaps I am doing what I am doing just to prove a
>>point—spending a lifetime to prove a point that is
>>not worth proving after all.

Perhaps I have never found anything that could challenge me, and my life seems wasted.

Here in the quietness I lay bare before God my need for
courage, for the strength to be honest, for the guidance
to deal effectually with the problems of my own life.

O God, thou wilt not despise!

I   C O N F E S S

The concern which I lay bare before God today is:

My concern for the life of the world in these troubled times.
I confess my own inner confusion as I look out upon the
world.
There is food for all—many are hungry.
There are clothes enough for all—many are in rags.
There is room enough for all—many are crowded.
There are none who want war—preparations for
conflict abound.

I confess my own share in the ills of the times.
I have shirked my own responsibilities as a citizen.
I have not been wise in casting my ballot.
I have left to others a real interest in making a public
opinion worthy of democracy.
I have been concerned about my own little job, my
own little security, my own shelter, my own
bread.

I have not really cared about jobs for others, security for others, shelter for others, bread for others.
I have not worked for peace; I want peace, but I
have voted and worked for war.
I have silenced my own voice that it may not be
heard on the side of any cause, however right, if
it meant running risks or damaging my own little
reputation.

Let Thy light burn in me that I may, from this moment
on, take effective steps within my own powers, to live
up to the light and courageously to pay for the kind of
world I so deeply desire.

DO NOT RELEASE
YOUR HOLD

It is a source of constant wonder how trees seem to take the measure of the climate and make of their existence a working paper on
life. Along some parts of the coast where there is a steady wind from
the sea, there is a general recognition of the fact that it is extremely
difficult for trees to grow tall and straight against the sky. Yet they
do. They bend with the wind and ride out every storm, yielding only
enough to guarantee themselves against destruction. It is a very fine
art, this bending with the wind and keeping on.

Of course, the winds leave their mark. The trees are not upright as if they have never known the relentless pressure of many
winds through many days. One sees, sometimes, trees that have grown
in a community of trees where there is mass protection of many trunks
for those not on the outer rim. Such trees have flattened tops. The
trunk may be tall and straight, gaining every available inch of shelter all the way up, until at last there is the point where the topmost
branch feels the pull of the sun and the sky to go its way alone.
Here there is no single branch. Doubtless many have tried, but in
the process have been snapped off, leaving their bleeding stumps as
a mute testimony to heroic worth.

The tree soon learns its lesson: within the resources available
to it, a little canopy of branches inch their way above the protecting
wall of other trees. They are young and supple, they bend with the
wind, always sustained by the sturdy growth from which they have
come. Unless the wind is able to sever them from the main body of
the tree, their continued growth is guaranteed. The tree seems to
say to the branches, "Bend with the wind but do not release your
hold, and you can ride out any storm." To the trees that did not
learn how to bend with the wind but preferred rather to remain
straight and defiant against the sky and are now dead and rotting in
the earth, it was a great moment when they came crashing to the
ground with a certain sense of triumph: "Ah, it took the concen-

trated violence of all the winds of heaven to bring me low. Such is
the measure of my strength and my power."

There is a strange, naked glory in the majesty of so grand a
homecoming. All through the life of man on the planet, there have
been sun-crowned men like that, and around them movements for
the healing of the nations have arisen. And yet man, in the mass,
has continued to survive because he has learned to bend with the
wind.

THE KINGDOM OF VALUES

It is a truth recognized over and over again in various guises that
the key to the meaning of life is found deep within each one of us.
When Jesus insists that the Kingdom of God is within, he is affirming that which is a part of the common experience of the race. In-
cidentally, this is one of the unique things about Jesus: he calls
attention again and again to that which is so utterly a part of the
deep commonplace experience of life.

There is a story told of the musk deer of North India. In the
springtime, the roe is haunted by the odor of musk. He runs wildly
over hill and ravine with his nostrils dilating and his little body
throbbing with desire, sure that around the next clump of trees or
bush he will find musk, the object of his quest. Then at last he falls,
exhausted, with his little head resting on his tiny hoofs, only to discover that the odor of musk is in his own hide.

The key to the meaning of life is within you. If you have a glass
of water out of the ocean, all the water in the ocean is not in your
glass, but all the water in your glass is ocean water. This is a characteristic of life. The responsibility for living with meaning and dignity can never be finally taken away from the individual. Of course,
there is the fact of limitations of heredity and the like, which may
circumscribe decidedly the area of awareness within the individual
life; there is the total sphere of accidents which may alter the mind
and the spirit by some deadly seizure. But the fact remains that the
judgment which the individual passes upon life and by which life
weighs him in the balance, finds its key within the individual and
not outside of him. It is the great and crowning dignity of human
life.

Man rates the risk that life takes by resting its case within his own spirit. How good God is to trust the Kingdom of Values to the discernment of the mind and spirit of man!

GOD, I NEED THEE

God, I need Thee.
    When morning crowds the night away
    And tasks of waking seize my mind;
    I need Thy poise.

God, I need Thee.
    When love is hard to see
    Amid the ugliness and slime,
    I need Thy eyes.

God, I need Thee.
    When clashes come with those
    Who walk the way with me,
    I need Thy smile.

God, I need Thee.
    When the path to take before me lies,
    I see it . . . courage flees—
    I need Thy faith.

God, I need Thee.
    When the day's work is done,
    Tired, discouraged, wasted,
    I need Thy rest.

STRIKE THE ROCK ARIGHT

    . . . There's magic all around us
    In rocks and trees, and in the minds of men,
    Deep hidden springs of magic.
        He who strikes
        the rock aright, may find them where he will.*

*From "Watchers of the Sky" from *Collected Poems in One Volume* by Alfred Noyes (J. B. Lippincott Company). Copyright 1922, 1950 by Alfred Noyes. Reprinted by permission of Harper & Row, Publishers, Inc.

It is very easy to assume an attitude of indifference toward the ordinary commonplace aspects of life. This is natural because constant exposure to experiences tends to deaden one's sensitiveness to their meaning. Life does grow dingy on one's sleeve unless there is a constant awareness of the growing edge of one's experience. The mood of arrogance toward the ordinary person and the tendency to grovel in the presence of the high and powerful beset us all. This is due to the deep quest of the human spirit for status, for position, for security-rating.

I remember once meeting a most extraordinary man on a college campus where I was giving a series of lectures in religion. Each morning he sat in the front seat. He was disabled—he walked suspended between two huge crutches. At the close of the last lecture, he came up to me. "Mr. Thurman, you have been very kind to me during this week. I want to give you something. Will you come to my room this evening when you are through with your work?"

It was agreed.

In the interval I asked one of the students about him. I was told that he was an old fellow who earned his living by repairing shoes in a shop on top of the hill. Some of the students referred to him simply as "Old Crip." When I entered his room in the late evening, he was standing behind a chair supporting himself very deftly. "Mr. Thurman, do you like Shakespeare? What is your favorite play?" *"Macbeth,"* I replied; then, without further ado, he read for me from memory the entire first act of *Macbeth.* And at my dictation, for over an hour, he read scene after scene from Shakespearean tragedies. He was just an old man earning his living by repairing shoes for college men who thought nothing of him.

There is magic all round us. It may be that the person with whom you live every day or with whom you work has, locked deep within, the answer to your own greatest need if you know how to "strike the rock aright."

Growing Into Self-Fulfillment

RESULTS NOT CRUCIAL

In one of the parables Jesus tells the story of a certain nobleman who went abroad to obtain power for himself and then return. Before he left he called his ten servants, giving them each a twenty-dollar bill, and telling them, "Trade with this until I come back." When he returned, he ordered his servants to be brought before him for their report.

The first man said, "Sir, your twenty dollars have made one hundred."

"Fine," said the nobleman.

The second man said, "Sir, your twenty dollars have made fifty dollars."

"Excellent," said the nobleman.

The third man was the only one who made a speech. He said, "Sir, here is your twenty dollars. I kept it safe in a napkin, for I was afraid of you. Perhaps you do not know this, but you have a reputation of being a very hard man. You pick up what you have never put down. You reap where you have not sown, you gather into barns what you have not planted!"

The nobleman was incensed. He ordered the servant cast off his place into "outer darkness."

Here I make an end of the story. The unfortunate servant was not "cast off" because he did not realize any profit for the nobleman. No. He was cast off because he did not "work at it."

We are never under obligation to achieve results. Of course, results are important and it may be that that is the reason effort is put forth. But results are not mandatory. Much of the energy and effort and many anxious hours are spent over the probable failure or success of our ventures. No man likes to fail. But it is important to remember that under certain circumstances, failure is its own success.

To keep one's eye on results is to detract markedly from the business at hand. This is to be diverted from the task itself. It is to be only partially available to demands at hand. Very often it causes one to betray one's own inner sense of values because to hold fast to the integrity of the act may create the kind of displeasure which in the end will affect the results. However, if the results are left free to form themselves in terms of the quality and character of the act, then all of one's resources can be put at the disposal of the act itself.

There are many forces over which the individual can exercise no control whatsoever. A man plants a seed in the ground and the seed sprouts and grows. The weather, the winds, the elements, cannot be controlled by the farmer. The result is never a sure thing. So what does the farmer do? He plants. Always he plants. Again and again he works at it—the ultimate confidence and assurance that even though his seed does not grow to fruition, seeds do grow and they do come to fruition.

The task of men who work for the Kingdom of God, is to *work* for the Kingdom of God. The result beyond this demand is not in their hands. He who keeps his eyes on results cannot give himself wholeheartedly to his task, however simple or complex that task may be.

NO LIFE WITHOUT WAR AND AFFLICTION

"For whatsoever plans I shall devise for my own peace, my life cannot be without war and affliction."

It is natural to have a plan for one's life. The mind is always trying to make sense out of experience. This is true even when there does not seem to be a pattern or plan on the basis of which an individual lives his life. There are some people who by temperament are so orderly that no action is contemplated by them in the absence of a well-defined plan. If such a person is making a simple journey, careful attention is given to every detail of schedule and of events in which he is likely to be involved. For him each day is ordered between the hours of waking and of sleeping.

There are others for whom planning comes hard. They put off every detail until the last minute and move through life in a kind of breathless confusion. They depend upon chance and the particular circumstance to determine what must or must not be done. There is a sense in which their lives are lived in a state of extended crisis.

But whether one falls into one or the other category or somewhere in between, there is a sense in which one's life moves within the structure of pattern and plan. Particularly is this true of one's life as a whole. There are things that one finds meaningful and things that one likes or dislikes. There are goals that are kept before one— vocation, personal fulfillment in family life, status, position, prestige. In such contemplation of goals, there is a normal tendency to exclude the things that would make for conflict and turmoil and to include the things that will make for peace and tranquillity.

Thomas à Kempis reminds us that it is the nature of life, and man's experience in it, that there be what he calls "war and affliction." This is not a note of pessimism and futility—it is rather a recognition that conflict is a part of the life process. Whatever may be the plan which one has for one's life, one must *win* the right to achieve it. Again and again in the struggle a man may experience failure, but he must know for himself that even though such is his experience, the final word has not been spoken. Included in his plan must be not only the possibility of failure but also the fact that he will not escape struggle, conflict, and war. Mr. Valiant-for-Truth in *Pilgrim's Progress* says, "My sword I give to him that shall succeed me in my pilgrimage, and my courage and skill to him that can get it. My marks and my scars I carry with me, to be a witness for me that I have fought His battle who will be my rewarder."

FRIENDS WHOM I
KNEW NOT

Thou hast made known to me friends whom I knew not.
Thou has brought the distant near and made a brother of the stranger.

The strength of the personal life is often found in the depth and intensity of its isolation. The fight for selfhood is unending. There is the ever-present need to stand alone, unsupported and unchallenged. To be sure of one's self, to be counted for one's self *as* one's self, is to experience aliveness in its most exciting dimension. If there is a job of work to be done that is impossible, if there is a need to be met that is limitless, if there is a word to be said that can never be said, the spirit of the whole man is mustered and in the exhaustive effort he finds *himself* in the solitariness of strength renewed and courage regained.

Below the surface of all the activity and functioning in which life engages us, there is a level of disengagement when the individual is a private actor on a lonely stage. It is here that things are seen without their outer garbs—the seedlings of desires take quiet root, the bitter waters and the sweet springs find their beginnings, the tiny stirrings that become the raging tempests are seen to shimmer in the semidarkness—this is "the region," "the place," "the clime" where man is the lonely solitary guest in the vast empty house of the world.

But this is not all of a man's life, this is not the full and solid picture. The strands of life cannot be so divided that each can be traced to a separate source. There is no mine, there is no thine. When there is that which I would claim as my very own, a second look, a subtle strangeness, something, announces that there can never be anything that is my very own. Always moving in upon a man's life is the friend whose existence he did not know, whose coming and going is not his to determine. The journeyings take many forms— sometimes it is in the vista that opens before his mind because of lines written long before in an age he did not know; sometimes it is in a simple encounter along the way when before his eyes the unknown stranger becomes the sharer of tidings that could be borne only by a friend. Sometimes a deep racial memory throws into focus an ancient wisdom that steadies the hand and stabilizes the heart. Always moving in upon a man's life is the friend whose existence he did not know, whose coming and going is not his to determine. At last, a man's life is his very own *and* a man's life is never his, alone.

THE NEED FOR PERIODIC REST

The need for periodic rest is not confined to mechanisms of various kinds. Rest may be complete inactivity when all customary functioning is suspended and everything comes to a pause. Rest may be a variation in intensity, a contrast between loud and soft, high and low, strong and weak, a change of pace. Rest may be a complete shifting of scenery by the movement of objects or the person. All things seem to be held in place by the stability of a rhythm that holds and releases but never lets go.

Under this same necessity lives the mind as well. There is an inner characteristic of mind that shares profoundly in the rhythm that holds and releases but never lets go. Rest for the mind takes many forms: it may come in the change of material upon which it works; it may be ranging widely and irresponsibly over strange areas of thought; it may be tackling a tough problem with more than the customary intensity; it may be daydreaming, that strange and wonderful fairyland of sugar plums and candies; it may be the experience of being swept to a perilous height by a sudden gale that rushes in from some distant shore or of being caught in the churning spiral of a water spout that moves up from some hidden depth; it may be all, any, or none of these but something else again. Rest for the mind may be a part of its activity! Thus working and resting are a single thing. Perhaps this is true because the mind takes its energy neat, in a manner direct and immediate.

Under the same necessity lives the spirit as well. There is no clear distinction between mind and spirit, but there is a quality of mind that is more than thought and the process of thought: this quality involves feelings and the wholeness in which the life of man has its being. There is no need to tarry over the correctness of definition or even over the preciseness of meaning. What is being considered is what a man means totally when he says, "I am." This "self" shares profoundly in the rhythm that holds and releases but never lets go. There is the rest of detachment and withdrawal when the spirit moves into the depths of the region of the Great Silence, where world weariness is washed away and blurred vision is once again prepared for the focus of the long view where seeking and finding are so united that failure and frustration, real though they are, are no longer felt to be ultimately real. Here the Presence of God is sensed as an all-pervasive aliveness which materializes into the concreteness of communion: the reality of prayer. Here God speaks without words and the self listens without ears. Here at last, glimpses of the meaning of all things and the meaning of one's own life are seen with all their strivings. To accept this is one meaning of the good line, "Rest in the Lord—O, rest in the Lord."

THE EXPERIENCE OF GROWING UP

Always the experience of growing up teaches the same lesson:

The hard way of self-reliance—the uneasy tensions of self-confidence.
What there is to be done in accordance with the persistent desire,
Each must do for himself.
Often by trial and error, by fumblings and blunderings,
Here a little, there a little more,
Step, by uncertain step, we move in the direction of self-awareness:
Gathering unto ourselves a personal flavor, a tang of uniqueness.
In this strength of intimate disclosure, each person faces his world,
Does battle with nameless forces,
Conquers and is defeated, wins or loses, waxes strong or weak.
Always experience says, "Rely on your own strength, hold fast to your own resources, desert not your own mind."

In the same sure moment, the same voice whispers, "Upon
    your own strength, upon your own resource, upon your
    own mind,
At long last you cannot rely.
Your own strength is weakness
Your own mind is shallow
Your own spirit is feeble."
The paradox:
All experience strips us of much except our sheer strength
    of mind, of spirit.
All experience reveals that upon these we must not finally
    depend.
Brooding over us and about us, even in the shadows of the
    paradox, there is something more—
There is a strength beyond our strength, giving strength
    to our strength.
Whether we bow our knee before an altar or
Spend our days in the delusions of our significance,
The unalterable picture remains the same;
Sometimes in the stillness of the quiet, if we listen,
We can hear the whisper in the heart
Giving strength to weakness, courage to fear, hope to
    despair.

"WHATSOEVER A MAN SOWETH . . ."

I watched him for a long time. He was so busily engaged in his task
that he did not notice my approach until he heard my voice. Then
he raised himself erect with all the slow dignity of a man who had
exhausted the cup of haste to the very dregs. He was an old man—
as I discovered before our conversation was over, a full eighty-one
years. Further talk between us revealed that he was planting a small
grove of pecan trees. The little treelets were not more than two and
a half or three feet in height. My curiosity was unbounded.

    "Why did you not select larger trees so as to increase the pos-
sibility of your living to see them bear at least one cup of nuts?"

    He fixed his eyes directly on my face, with no particular point of focus, but with a gaze that took in the totality of my features. Finally he said, "These small trees are cheaper and I have very little money."

"So you do not expect to live to see the trees reach sufficient maturity to bear fruit?"

"No, but is that important? All my life I have eaten fruit from trees that I did not plant, why should I not plant trees to bear fruit for those who may enjoy them long after I am gone? Besides, the man who plants because he will reap the harvest has no faith in life."

Years have passed since that sunny afternoon in LaGrange, Georgia, when those words were said. Again and again, the thought has come back ro me, "Besides, the man who plants because he will reap the harvest has no faith in life." The fact is that much of life is made up of reaping where we have not sown and planting where we shall never reap. And yet this is not all the story. There is a reaping of precisely what we have sown, with the extra thrown in, guaranteed by the laws of growth. Thus the insight from the scriptures: "Be not deceived, God is not mocked, for whatsoever a man soweth that shall he also reap." The good and the not-good alike. All of life is a planting and a harvesting. No man gathers merely the crop that he himself has planted. This is another dimension of the brotherhood of man.

THE WILL TO LIVE

There is much that has been written and even more that has been said about "the will to live," in life in general, in human life in particular. It is described as a quality inherent in life, an instinct with uncanny power to seek that which feeds and sustains it, however precariously. It is a wide and deep urgency with what seems to be a consciousness all its own. You have seen trees growing out of sheer rock; or roots, finding no soil below or being unable to penetrate the rocky substance of the earth, spread themselves, fan shape, on the surface, sending their tendrils into every crevice and cranny where hidden moisture and soil fragments accumulate. You have seen human beings with their bodies reduced to mere skeletons and all the vestiges of health wiped out—yet for interminable periods they continue breathing, as if to breathe were life.

Sometimes this will to live takes other forms. Suddenly faced with some terrible moment of devastation, all the lights of the mind are turned out—one blacks out. It is like coasting a car; the motor is turned off but it continues to move because of a cumulative momentum. Sometimes we escape into pain when not to escape seems to us to spell destruction. Again, the will operates in reverse: we escape into health. There is a real illness with which we cannot cope without disintegration, and we take refuge in the pose of health which, viewed from within, is not a fiction but a fact of experience.

In the history of the religious experience of the race, doctrines of immortality are expressions of this will to live. They are not counsels of despair but deep affirmations of the core of life, declaring that life is continuous, permanent, timeless, eternal. What a tremendous boon, what a glorious outreach of the human spirit! The will to live says that life *is,* and it is not predicated upon any other factors. While life cannot be thought of as pure existence, yet it seems always to be *more than* that through which it expresses itself. Thank God for the will to live; it is His signature in the midst of the changing scene of experience and fact.

THE VALUE OF STRUGGLE

It was a beautiful little garden just outside the dining room window. With the simplicity characteristic of him, my friend gave me the names and explained the habits of life of various plants growing there. I was struck by what was said about a little bush which grew near the steps.

"This plant is called daphne. It is not doing well here because it is too comfortably situated. The soil is too rich, and it gets too much protection. This plant tends to go to wood and leaves with very, very poor blossoms if it is placed where it does not have to struggle. The aim of all plants is to reproduce themselves by making seeds. Poor soil challenges this particular plant, making it conserve its strength and concentrate it on the main business, the production of blossoms which in turn become seeds: the guarantee of the perpetuation of its kind."

Then the silence fell while my mind took wings. An easy life devoid of challenge (too much protection) scatters the energy, dissipates the resources, works against singleness of mind, without which, there can be no real fulfillment. Most of us do not voluntarily seek the difficult thing, the hard job, and the stubborn task. There are some people who are born with such singleness of mind that instinctively they gravitate toward the tough assignment. There are always those to whom we turn automatically if there is something to be done that requires unusual courage, patience, or concentrated effort. These persons, by their temperaments and will-to-do, contribute deeply to our own delinquency and weakness. There are others who are afflicted with a morbid sense of martyrdom and who seem perpetually to be atoning for some hidden sin by volunteering to do the unpleasant thing, by taking upon themselves responsibilities which in the end merely deepen their own sense of guilt or self-mortification. It is wisdom so to understand oneself that one will not accept the role within one's range of choices that causes one to "go to wood and leaves."

We are not like the daphne plant. Sometimes within very wide limits, often within extremely narrow limits, we have the privilege of choice. Some things we know contribute to our weaknesses, to our tendency to grow flabby and soft; some things we know toughen our fiber and cause us to pool all our resources in the effort to achieve singleness of mind, of purpose, and of will. Wood and leaves, or the blossom of fulfillment—which?

Life Is Its Own Restraint

TO HIM THAT WAITS

"To him that waits, all things reveal themselves, provided that he has the courage not to deny in the darkness what he has seen in the light."

Waiting is a window opening on many landscapes. For some, waiting means the cessation of all activity when energy is gone and exhaustion is all that the heart can manage. It is the long slow panting of the spirit. There is no will to will—"spent" is the word. There is no hope, no hopelessness—there is no sense of anticipation or even awareness of a loss of hope. Perhaps even the memory of function itself has faded. There is now and before—there is no after.

For some, waiting is a time of intense preparation for the next leg of the journey. Here at last comes a moment when forces can be realigned and a new attack upon an old problem can be set in order. Or it may be a time of reassessment of all plans and of checking past failures against present insight. It may be the moment of the long look ahead when the landscape stretches far in many directions and the chance to select one's way among many choices cannot be denied.

For some, waiting is a sense of disaster of the soul. It is what

Francis Thompson suggests in the line: "Naked I wait Thy love's uplifted stroke!" The last hiding place has been abandoned because even the idea of escape is without meaning. Here is no fear, no panic, only the sheer excruciation of utter disaster. It is a kind of emotional blackout in the final moment before the crash—it is the passage through the Zone of Treacherous Quiet.

For many, waiting is something more than all of this. It is the experience of recovering balance when catapulted from one's place. It is the quiet forming of a pattern of recollection in which there is called into focus the fragmentary values from myriad encounters of many kinds in a lifetime of living. It is to watch a gathering darkness until all light is swallowed up completely without the power to interfere or bring a halt. Then to continue one's journey in the darkness with one's footsteps guided by the illumination of remembered radiance is to know courage of a peculiar kind—the courage to demand that light continue to be light even in the surrounding darkness. To walk in the light while darkness invades, envelops, and surrounds is to wait on the Lord. This is to know the renewal of strength. This is to walk and faint not.

THE IDOL OF TOGETHERNESS

"If thy soul is a stranger to thee, the whole world is unhomely."

The fight for the private life is fierce and unyielding. Often it seems as if our times are in league with the enemy. There is little rhythm of alternation between the individual and the others. Land values are so high that breathing space around the places where we live is cut away. We flee from the crowded city to the quiet of the countryside. But the countryside becomes jammed with the sounds, the noises, the sights, the pressures which were left behind. Sometimes we escape into the city from the country.

Because of the disintegration of the mood of tenderness that has overtaken us, we falter in our understanding of one another. There is a certain kind of understanding abroad—it is understanding that invades, snoops, threatens, and makes afraid or embarrasses. The craftsmen of the public taste move in upon us, seeking to determine the kind of food we eat, the soap we use, the make of car we drive, and the best way to brush our teeth. What has become of the person, the private wish?

We have made an idol of togetherness. It is the watchword of our times, it is more and more the substitute for God. In the great huddle we are desolate, lonely, and afraid. Our shoulders touch but our hearts cry out for understanding without which there can be no life and no meaning. The Great Cause, even the Cause of Survival, is not enough! There must be found ever-creative ways that can ventilate the private soul without blowing it away, that can confirm and affirm the integrity of the person in the midst of the collective necessities of our times.

There is within reach of every man a defense against the Grand Invasion. He can seek deliberately to become intimately acquainted with himself. He can cultivate an enriching life with persons, enhancing the private meaning and the personal worth. He can grow in the experience of solitude, companioned by the minds and spirits who, as Pilgrims of the Lonely Road, have left logs of their journey. He can become at home, within, by locating in his own spirit the trysting place where he and his God may meet; for it is here that life becomes *private* without being *self-centered,* that the little purposes that cloy may be absorbed in the Big Purpose that structures and redefines, that the individual comes to himself, the wanderer is home, and the private life is saved for deliberate involvement.

THE QUIET MINISTRY
OF THE SPIRIT

It is good to experience the quiet ministry of the living spirit of the living God. Again and again there are the little healings of silent breaches which sustain us in our contacts with the world and with one another. We are stunned by the little word, the unexpected silence, the smile off key; without quite knowing why, the balance is recovered and the rhythm of the hurt is stopped in its place. There is the sense of estrangement which overtakes the happiest human relations and the experience of recovery that makes the heart sing its old song with a new lilt. There are days when everything seems difficult, when the ordinary tasks become major undertakings, when one is sensitive and every moment is threatened by an explosion that does not quite come to pass; then without apparent cause, the whole picture changes and the spirit can breathe again with ease, the spring in the step comes back again. It is good to experience the quiet ministry of the living spirit of the living God.

Sometimes we are catapulted into disaster with a suddenness that paralyzes the mind and leaves the exposure to fear unshielded by courage or by strength. If there had been some warning, some intimation of what was to come, the wisdom of the years could have buttressed the life with a measured protection. But no, this was not the case. Often even before the full awareness of what has taken place can be felt, the realignment of one's powers begins to work and recovery is on the way. There are problems that meet us head-on in our journey. The issue of our spirit and the thing that confronts us is joined—we are engulfed in the great silence of fateful struggle. It seems that nowhere, in no place, can an answer be found. In vain we seek a clue, a key, even a little thing to give a fleeting respite, a second wind. Again and again it is apt to happen: the miracle of relief; a chance word from a casual conversation; a sentiment or a line in a letter; the refrain of an old song; an image from the past; a paragraph from a printed page; a stirring of prayer in the heart—the miracle of relief and we are released. The danger is past, the conflict is over. It is good, so very good, to experience the quiet ministry of the living spirit of the living God.

A GOOD DEATH

"I want to die easy when I die." This is a line from an old song which belonged to another period and another age. There is no gruesome note here, not a single morbid or depressing overtone. We are not face to face with something that is grim and foreboding. But we are faced with a grand conception of death that gathers in its sweep all the little fears and anxieties that condition the personal view and the private contemplation of the end of life. It is a Trumpet Call to human dignity.

The madder the world seems, the more the rumors of lethal devices reach our ears, the more we are desirous of finding and clinging to a few simple values: things that can be felt and held and owned; a bit of economic security, transitory though it be, that will give a few rare moments free of the immediate necessity of working for that day's bread; the experience of love, however fleeting, and perchance a family as a primary defense against not being wanted and not belonging. So strenuous is our pursuit of these things that it is difficult even to grasp the great concept which the line presents to the human spirit—"I want to die easy when I die."

Life and death are felt as a single respiration—the ebb and flow of a single tide. Death is not the invasion of an alien principle, it is not an attack upon life by an enemy. Death is not the Grim Reaper, the black-cowled skeleton with blazing eyes, galloping on a white horse. No! Life and death are identical twins. Therefore it is man's privilege and wisdom to make a good death, even as it is to make a good life.

A good death is made up of the same elements as a good life. A good life is what a man does with the details of living if he sees his life as an instrument, a deliberate instrument in the hands of Life, that transcends all boundaries and all horizons. It is this *beyond dimension* that saves the individual life from being swallowed by the tyranny of present needs, present hungers, and present threats. This is to put distance *within* the experience and to live the quality of the beyond even in the intensity of the present moment. And a good death—what is it? It has the same quality and character as a good life. True, the body may be stripped of all defenses by the ravages of disease; there may remain no surface expression of dignity and self-respect as the organism yields slowly to the pressure of change monitored by death. These are all secondary. The real issue is at another depth entirely. It is at the place where Life has been long since accepted and yielded to, where the private will has become infused with the Great Will, where the child of God realizes his sonship. This is the knowledge that the son has of the Father and the Father of the son—this is to know God and to abide in Him forever.

No One Escapes

THE INNOCENT ONES

One of the characters in Margaret Kennedy's novel *The Feast* suggests that the entire human race is tolerated for its innocent minority. There is a strange and aweful vitality in the suffering of the innocent. It does not fall within any category. The mind moves very easily in the balance of the swinging pendulum. We are accustomed to equating things in terms of the order of equilibrium. Our values are defined most easily as merit and demerit, reward and punishment. There is great sustenance for the spirit in the assurance that reverses can somehow be balanced by the deeds which brought them about. Many men find the depths of contentment in their suffering when they remember that their pain is deserved, their payment is for a just and honest debt. Of course there may be a full measure, pressed down and overflowing, but the hard core of the pain is for acknowledged wrong done; the essence of the hardship is atonement for evil done. All of this falls into a simple pattern of checks and balances, of sowing and reaping, of planting and harvesting.

But where the pain is without apparent merit, where innocence abounds and no case can be made that will give a sound basis for the *experience of the agony*, then the mind spins in a crazy circle.

Always there must be an answer, there must be found some clue to the mystery of the suffering of the innocent. It is not enough to say that the fathers have eaten sour grapes and their children's teeth are set on edge. This is not enough. It is not enough to say that the individual sufferer is a victim of circumstances over which he is unable to exercise any controls. There is apt ever to be an element of truth in such assertions. But the heart of the issue remains untouched. The innocent do suffer; this is the experience of man.

Margaret Kennedy's idea is an arresting one. It is that mankind is protected and sustained by undeserved suffering—that swinging out beyond the logic of antecedent and consequence, of sowing and reaping, there is another power, another force, supplementing and restoring the ravages wrought in human life by punishment and reward. The innocent ones are always present when the payment falls due—they are not heroes or saints, they are not those who are the conscious burden-bearers of the sins and transgressions of men. They are the innocent ones—they are always there. Their presence in the world is the stabilizing factor, the precious ingredient that maintains the delicate balance preventing humanity from plunging into the abyss. It is not to be wondered at that in all the religions of mankind there is ever at work the movement to have the word *made* flesh, without being *of* the flesh. It is humanity's way of *affirming* that the innocent ones *hold* while all that evil men do exacts its due.

> Their shoulders hold the sky suspended,
> They stand, and earth's foundations stay.

THE NIGHT VIEW
OF THE WORLD

"Upon the night view of the world, a day view must follow." This is an ancient insight grounded in the experience of the race in its long journey through all the years of man's becoming. Here is no cold idea born out of the vigil of some solitary thinker in lonely retreat from the traffic of the common ways. It is not the wisdom of the book put down in ordered words by the learned and the schooled. It is insight woven into the pattern of all living things, reaching its

7 3

grand apotheosis in the reflection of man gazing deep into the heart of his own experience.

That the day view follows the night view is written large in nature. Indeed it is one with nature itself. The clouds gather heavy with unshed tears; at last they burst, sending over the total landscape waters gathered from the silent offering of sea and river. The next day dawns and the whole heavens are aflame with the glorious brilliance of the sun. This is the way the rhythm moves. The fall of the year comes, then winter with its trees stripped of leaf and bud; cold winds ruthless in bitterness and sting. One day there is sleet and ice; in the silence of the nighttime the snow falls soundlessly—all this until at last the cold seems endless and all there is seems to be shadowy and foreboding. The earth is weary and heavy. Then something stirs—a strange new vitality pulses through everything. One can feel the pressure of some vast energy pushing, always pushing through dead branches, slumbering roots—life surges everywhere within and without. Spring has come. The day usurps the night view.

Is there any wonder that deeper than idea and concept is the insistent conviction that the night can never stay, that winter is ever moving toward the spring? Thus, when a man sees the lights go out one by one, when he sees the end of his days marked by death—his death—he *senses,* rather than knows, that even the night into which he is entering will be followed by day. It remains for religion to give this ancient wisdom phrase and symbol. For millions of men and women in many climes this phrase and this symbol are forever one with Jesus, the Prophet from Galilee. When the preacher says as a part of the last rites, "I am the Resurrection and the Life . . . ," he is reminding us all of the ancient wisdom: "Upon the night view of the world, a day view must follow."

THE IDEA AND
THE REALITY

Between the idea
And the reality
Between the motion

And the act
Falls the shadow.*

This quotation from T. S. Eliot's "The Hollow Men" puts into crisp words one of the oldest problems of the human spirit. There is always the riding frustration to all human effort that makes it fall short of the intent, the clear-cut purpose. Sometimes it is very difficult for the idea or the plan to be clearly defined. It is hard to make up one's mind about goals because motives are often confused. To know precisely what it is that we want is often a very torturous process.

And yet, the great frustration is not at the point of the elusive and indefinable goal or purpose. It is rather at the point of determining how to span the gulf that lies between the goal and its fulfillment, the purpose and its realization. The gulf is deep and wide between the dream and the implementation. Look at any achievement of your life, however simple or elaborate! There is one judgment that you can pass upon it: it is so much less than you had in mind. As the dream lay nestled in your mind untouched by the things that sully or corrupt, you were stirred to the deep places within by its rightness, by its beauty, by its truth. Then the time of birth was upon you—the dream took its place among the stuff of your daily round. Looking upon it now, it is so much less than what it seemed to be before. It is ever thus.

A man sees the good and tries to achieve it in what he thinks, says, and does. With what results? You know your answer. How often have you felt: the good I see I do not, or the good I see I achieve only in such limited, inadequate ways that I wonder even about the vision itself. Always there is the shadow. Always there is the wide place between the dream and its fulfillment.

T O   B E   F R E E   F R O M   C A R E

There is natural longing for a life that is free from carking care. The important thing is not that we want to live in the empty monotony of sameness but that what we want is to be relieved of the

*From "The Hollow Men" in *Collected Poems 1909–1962* by T. S. Eliot, copyright 1936 by Harcourt Brace Jovanovich, Inc.; copyright © 1963, 1964 by T. S. Eliot. Reprinted by permission.

pressure of anxiety that comes from finding no escape from the things that make life hard. There is an insistent urgency of the unpleasant task or the handicap of mind or body that clings within our enthusiasm and seems ever abiding. For many there is the fear that a disease that has been put to flight will return in full force, laying waste the body and despoiling all the dreams of a lifetime. In fine we want to be rid of the things that encumber, that make more difficult the journey which is set before us. . . . Persistent anxieties, time-wearied weaknesses, uncontrollable and explosive tempers; scar tissues from old injuries, the troubled feeling that we can never quite define owing to our intimate reaction to the impact of the age of violence in which we live . . .

In our times of quiet, of meditation, either alone or in the midst of a congregation, we come to grips with what to us is our tragic fact, our private predicament. Patiently we seek to detach ourselves and take a long look in two dimensions—one at our lives free of our burden, the other at our lives underneath our load. It is then that we give wings to our longings. As we wait in the silence, sometimes clearly, sometimes feebly, an answer comes.

With fumbling words we give ourselves to prayer:

Our Father, we want to be rid of that which comes between us and Thy vision. Teach us how. We are but little children stumbling in the darkness. Do not reject even our weakness, O God, but accept us totally as we are. Work over us, knead us, and fashion us until at last we take on the character which is Thy Spirit and the mind which is Thy Mind. We trust Thee to do Thy Things in us, O God, God the Father of our spirits. Amen.

TWILIGHTS AND ENDLESS LANDSCAPES

The intimate and gentle blanket of twilight had covered the desert with a softness highlighted by the restrained radiance of the disappearing sun. All the fears of war, the terrible bitterness of the marketplace, the deep insecurities of modern life, seemed far removed from the surrounding quiet.

Long before the coming of cities, long before the coming of men, there were twilights, radiant and glowing skies and endless landscapes. It may be that long after the earth has reclaimed the cities and the last traces of man's fevered life have been gathered into the Great Quiet, there will be twilights, radiant and glowing skies and endless landscapes.

It is not because man and his cities are not significant that they cannot outlast the twilights, the radiant and glowing skies and the endless landscapes. But their significance is of another kind. Man and his cities spring out of the earth, they are the children of the Great Womb that breathes through twilights, radiant and glowing skies and endless landscapes. Man and his cities, caught in the web their dreams inspire, manage to push the twilights out of mind. They wear themselves out and they forget from whence they come and in what at long last they find their strength. Their dreams become nightmares, their hopes become fears, and the same story repeats itself; they are claimed in the end by the twilights, the radiant and glowing skies and endless landscapes.

The more hectic the life of the cities, the more greedy and lustful the heart and mind of man, the more he forgets the meaning of the twilights, the radiant and glowing skies and endless landscapes. It is not too late. Man and his cities may yet be saved. There is still time to remember that there is twilight, the creative isthmus joining day with night. It is the time of pause when nature changes her guard. It is the lung of time by which the rhythmic respiration of day and night are guaranteed and sustained. All living things would fade and die from too much light or too much darkness, if twilight were not. In the midst of all the madness of the present hour, twilights remain and shall settle down upon the world at the close of day and usher in the nights in endless succession, despite bombs, rockets, and flying death. This is good to remember.

Even though they look down upon the ruin of cities and the fall of man, radiant and glowing skies will still trumpet their glory to the God of Life. Death and destruction cannot permanently obscure their wonder or drown their song. To remember this is to safeguard each day with the margin of strength that invades the soul from the radiant and glowing skies. These declare the glory and the tenderness of God.

THE CREATIVE EBB

There is a fallow time for the spirit when the soil is barren because of sheer exhaustion. It may come unannounced like an overnight visitor "passing through." It may be sudden as a sharp turn-in on an unfamiliar road. It may come at the end of a long, long period of strenuous effort in handling some slippery in-and-out temptation that fails to follow a pattern. It may result from the plateau of tragedy that quietly wore away the growing edge of alertness until nothing was left but the exhausted roots of aliveness. The general climate of social unrest, of national and international turmoil, the falling of kingdoms, the constant, muted suffering of hungry men and starving women and children on the other sides of the oceans, all these things may so paralyze normal responses to life that a blight settles over the spirit, leaving all the fields of interest withered and parched.

It is quite possible that spreading oneself so thin with too much going "to and fro" has yielded a fever of activity that saps all energy, even from one's surplus store, and we must stop for the quiet replenishing of an empty cupboard. Perhaps too much anxiety, a too-hard trying, a searching strain to do by oneself what can never be done that way, has made one's spirit seem like a water tap whose washer is worn out from too much pressure. But withal there may be the simplest possible explanation: the rhythmic ebb and flow of one's powers, simply this and nothing more. Whatever may be the reasons, one has to deal with the fact. Face it! Then resolutely dig out dead roots, clear the ground, but don't forget to make a humus pit against the time when some young or feeble plants will need stimulation from past flowerings in your garden. Work out new designs by dreaming daring dreams and great and creative planning. The time is not wasted.

The time of fallowness is a time of rest and restoration, of filling up and replenishing. It is the moment when the meaning of all things can be searched out, tracked down, and made to yield the secret of living. Thank God for the fallow time!

The Broken Harmony

A NEW HEAVEN AND A NEW EARTH

We are in varied ways concerned about welfare and well-being—our own and that of others. Rare indeed is the man who looks at his own life, who examines his personal position, and is assured that he is in no need of improvement. The place where a man stands is never quite the place that marks the limit of his powers and the resting point for all his dreams. This is the way of life.

It is easier to be more concerned about the welfare and well-being of the world than about our own. Few can escape the urge to join in the general chorus of the age that we have fallen upon evil days. There seems to be a strange, weary comfort in taking one's place against the wailing wall. There is a searching danger ever present in all anxiety, whether personal or social. It can so easily become a substitute for thoughtful planning and action. One is constantly placed in jeopardy by this possibility. Have you ever said with real feeling, "I must do something about drinking so much coffee" or "I am alarmed over the fact that I can't seem to get down to business with my own personal life"? Of the great number of people who feel outraged over what seems to be a terrible miscarriage of justice, how many do something concrete about it? All the energy is exhausted in such remarks: "How awful"—"What a tragedy"—"Something ought to be done"—"What a shame."

Again, our emotional reaction to situations causes us to adopt measures that bring quick and temporary relief from the immediate pressures on us but do not have much effect on the situations themselves. The real purpose is to relieve only ourselves. Somehow we must find that which is big enough to absolve us from artificial and ineffective methods for increasing welfare and well-being. This means the large view, the great faith, which will release the vast courage capable of sustaining us in the long pull toward a valid increase in welfare and well-being. It is for this reason that a religious faith about life and its meaning becomes a necessity for all who would work for a new heaven and a new earth, the achievement of which is literal fact.

HUMAN ENDURANCE

There often seems to be a clearly defined limit to human endurance. Everyone has had the experience of exhaustion. If you cannot get to bed you are sure that you will go to sleep standing. Then something happens. It may be that a friend comes by to see you, a friend whose path has not crossed yours in several years. It may be that there are tidings of good news or of tragedy. At any rate, something happens in you, with the result that you are awake, recovered, even excited. A few minutes before, the weariness was closing in like a dense fog. But now it is gone.

Of course, knowledge about the body and mind gives an increasingly satisfying explanation of this kind of experience. The important thing, however, is the fact that beyond the zero point of endurance there are vast possibilities. The precise limitations under which you live your particular life cannot be determined. Usually the stimulus, the incentive must come from the outside—be brought to you on the wings of external circumstance. This means that the power available to you in great demand is not yours to command. I wonder!

This simple fact of revitalizing human endurance opens a great vista for living. It cannot be that what is possible to the body and nervous system by way of tapping the individual resource on demand is denied the spirit. The spirit in man is not easily vanquished. It is fragile *and* tough. You may fail again and again and yet something will not let you give up. Something keeps you from accepting "no" as a final answer. It is this quality that makes for survival of values when the circumstances of one's life are most against decency, goodness, and right. Men tend to hold on when there seems to be no point in holding on, because they find that they *must.* It is often at such a point that the spirit in man and the spirit of God blend into one creative illumination. This is the great miracle. The body and the nervous system know.

YOUR NEIGHBOR'S LANDMARKS

"Think twice before you move your neighbor's landmarks."

There is an ancient wisdom in this timely caution. Curious indeed is the form of arrogance that causes a man to feel that it is his peculiar right to set the whole world in order—to close all open things, to make all crooked paths straight. Such an attitude says that all knowledge, all virtue, all truth can be contained in a single vessel. This is a great sacrilege.

It is important to remember that one man is never quite in a position to see what it is that another man sees. What one man may never know is precisely how an event, an act, or a thing is experienced by another man. We are uninformed about the content that a man brings to the events of his life. We do not know what was at work in a man when he staked his claim on an aspect of life.

In the long way that we take, in our growing up, in the vicissitudes of life by which we are led into its meaning and its mystery, there are established for us, for each one of us, certain landmarks. They represent discoveries sometimes symbolizing the moment when we became aware of the purpose of our lives; they may establish for us our membership in the human frailty; they may be certain words that were spoken into a stillness within us, the sound thereof singing forever through all the corridors of our being as landmarks; yes, each one of us has his own. No communication between people is possible if there is not some mutual recognition of the landmarks.

There are no reverences that bind us together as people that can be meaningful if the landmarks are profaned. To understand a man is not merely to know his name and the number of his thoughts, to be acquainted with how he acts or what he does. To know a man is to know, somewhat, of his landmarks. For these are his points of referral that stand out beyond and above all the traffic of his life, advising and tutoring him in his journey through life and beyond. In the language of religion, these are the places where the Eternal has been caught and held for a swirling moment in time and years. "Think twice before you move your neighbor's landmarks."

MAKING A GOOD LIFE

There is much conversation about making a good life. Deep within the human spirit is a concern that insists upon perfection. The distinction must be made between perfection in a particular activity, in a particular skill, and the central concern of the human spirit for perfection as a total experience. The former can be measured in terms of standards and concrete goals. I know a man who is most meticulous about many things that have their place but are inconsequential. He is so insistent about the temperature of his coffee that he neglects simple courtesy to the person who serves it.

Sometimes the attitude is more comprehensive. It has to do with staking out an area and covering it in a certain way with a satisfactory structure. It has to do with plans and their fulfillment—ends and the means by which the ends are secured. This kind of perfection often makes for arrogance of spirit and unbearable snobbery. It says to all and sundry: There is but one way to do a thing and this is that way. It does not always follow that arrogance is the result; there may be a simple pride in the beauty and the wholeness of the flawless. To behold a lovely thing in all its parts, be it a deed, a well-rounded idea, a clear, beautiful, and perfect phrase or a way of performing, is to experience a moment of glory and sheer delight.

But the central concern for perfection lies outside of all manifestations and all deeds. It is more than, and other than, all expressions of every kind, and yet it informs the ultimate character of all expressions of every kind. It is the image which the sculptor sees in the block of marble; the dream in the soul of the prophet and the seer; the profound sense of life in the spirit of the dying; the picture of the beloved in the eyes of the lover; the hope that continues when all rational grounds for confidence have been destroyed. It is what remains when all doors have finally closed and all the lights have gone out, one by one. Here at last we are face to face with what man is in his literal substance: the essence of his nobility and dignity. In religion it is called the image of the Creator and is the authentic "for instance" of the givenness of God. To be aware of this is the source of all man's confidential endurance through the vicissitudes of his living. This is to sit in judgment on every deed, however good and perfect it may be within itself—to move with reverence through all of life, always seeking and finding, always building and rebuilding, always repenting, always rejoicing. This is to walk with God.

REMAIN AT PEACE

"Accustom yourself to remain at peace in the depth of your heart, in spite of your restless imagination."

Peace anywhere seems to be wishful thinking during the days of turmoils within and violences without. Peace of mind, peace of heart, peace of home, peace of country, peace of world, peace of cosmos—it does not matter which, the same sense of pinpoint unreality pervades. There seems to be a vast stirring of energy, malignant and unstructured, that catapults to the surface all kinds of disharmonies, conflicts, and disorders. The Middle East, the Far East, South Africa, North Africa, West Africa, Hungary, Poland, France, Germany, Russia, the Indian Nations of the Americas, the continental United States viewed by section, state, or city—always there is present the turbulent quality, the out-of-hand aspect, of the common life.

Years ago a free-lance writer visited Dr. M. W. Locke, the famous Canadian physician. The technique he used in treatment of bodily ills had to do with foot manipulation. A little crippled girl sat in the chair before the doctor. Very gently he began massaging her crippled limb—then he gave the foot a sudden manipulation. The girl screamed! A shudder went through the people waiting their turn. In the afternoon, the writer saw the father of the little girl and offered sympathy.

"Thank you very much," said the father. "But you do not understand. When my daughter first came here several weeks ago, the doctor could do anything to her foot and she could not feel it. When I heard her cry aloud this morning I said, 'Thank God, life is in her foot at last.' "

The stirring of energy in myriad forms of unstructured malevolences may well be the spirit of Life, of God at work in behalf of new life and perhaps a new creation on this planet. We must find our place in the areas of the new vitalities, the place where the old is breaking up and the new is being born. What a moment to be alive and, more importantly, to be aware! Of course, this we cannot do unless we are able to gather unto ourselves the wise caution of Fénelon, "Accustom yourself to remain at peace in the depth of your heart, in spite of your restless imagination." God grant this for each of us.

THE LIGHT OF HIS SPIRIT

In many ways beyond all calculation and reflection, our lives have been deeply touched and influenced by the character, the teaching, and the spirit of Jesus of Nazareth. He moves in and out upon the horizon of our days like some fleeting ghost. At times, when we are least aware and least prepared, some startling clear thrust of his mind is our portion—the normal tempo of our ways is turned back upon itself and we are reminded of what we are, and of what life is. Often the judgment of such moments is swift and silencing: sometimes his insight kindles a wistful longing in the heart, softened by the muted cadence of unfulfilled dreams and unrealized hopes. Sometimes his words stir to life long forgotten resolutions, call to mind an earlier time when our feet were set in a good path and our plan was for holy endeavor. Like a great wind they move, fanning into flame the burning spirit of the living God, and our leaden spirits are given wings that sweep beyond all vistas and beyond all horizons.

There is no way to balance the debt we owe to the spirit which he let loose in the world. It is upon this that we meditate now in the gathering quietness. Each of us, in his own way, finds the stairs leading to the Holy Place. We gather in our hands the fragments of our lives, searching eagerly for some creative synthesis, some wholeness, some all-encompassing unity capable of stilling the tempests within us and quieting all the inner turbulence of our fears. We seek to walk in our own path which opens up before us, made clear by the light of His Spirit and the radiance which it casts all around us. We join Him in the almighty trust that God is our Father and we are His children living under the shadow of His Spirit.

Accept the offering of our lives, O God; we do not know quite what to do with them. We place them before Thee as they are, encumbered and fragmented, with no hints, no suggestions, no attempts to order the working of Thy Spirit upon us. Accept our lives, our Father—work them over. Correct them. Purify them. Hold them in Thy focus lest we perish and the spirit within us dies. Amen.

WHO, OR WHAT, IS TO BLAME?

The desire to be one's true self is ever persistent. Equally persistent is the tendency to locate the responsibility for failure to be one's true self in events, persons, and conditions—all of which are outside and beyond one's self. Often a person says, "I would be the kind of person I desire to be," or "I would do the thing that I have always wanted to do *if*—." The list is endless: if I had been born a boy rather than a girl; if I had been tall and strong rather than short and weak; if I had been given the diet proper for a growing child; if my parents had been understanding and sympathetic rather than cold and impersonal; if I had lived in a different kind of community, or had grown up on the right side of the tracks; if my parents had not separated when I was a child and made me the victim of a broken home; if I had not been taught the wrong things about sex, about religion, about myself; if I had been of a different racial or national origin—and on and on. The interesting fact is that in each "if" there is apt to be, for the person who uses it, a significant element of truth. This element of truth is seized upon as the complete answer to the personal problem, as the single source of all the individual's maladjustments.

There is more to the story than is indicated. Often, not always, the person who feels most completely defeated in fulfillment is the one who has been unable or unwilling to exploit resources that were close at hand. There is a curious inability to take personal responsibility for what one does or fails to do, without a sense of martyrdom or heroics. Religion is most helpful in developing in the individual a sense of personal responsibility for one's action and thus aiding the process of self-fulfillment. It is helpful in two ways primarily: There is the insistence upon the individual's responsibility to God for his own life. This means that he cannot escape the scrutiny of God. If he is responsible to God, the basis of that responsibility has to be in himself. If it is there, then the area of alibis is definitely circumscribed. The assumption is that the individual is ever in immediate candidacy to get an "assist" from God—that he is not alone in his quest. Through prayer, meditation and singleness of mind, the individual's life may be invaded by strength, insight, and courage sufficient for his needs. Thus he need not seek refuge in excuses but can live his life with ever-increasing vigor and experience . . . an ever-deepening sense of fulfillment.

EVERY MAN MUST DECIDE

The ability to know what is the right thing to do in a given circumstance is a sheer gift of God. The element of gift is inherent in the process of decision. Perhaps gift is the wrong word; it is a quality of genius or immediate inspiration. The process is very simple and perhaps elemental. First, we weigh all the possible alternatives. We examine them carefully, weighing this and weighing that. There is always an abundance of advice available—some of it technical, some of it out of the full-orbed generosity of those who love us and wish us well. Each bit of it has to be weighed and measured in the light of the end sought. This means that the crucial consideration is to know what is the desirable end. What is it that I most want to see happen if the conditions were ideal or if my desire were completely fulfilled?

Once this end is clearly visualized, then it is possible to have a sense of direction with reference to the decision that must be made. If it becomes clear that the ideal end cannot be realized, it follows that such a pursuit has to be relinquished. This relinquishment is always difficult because the mind, the spirit, the body desires are all focused upon the ideal end. Every person thinks that it is his peculiar destiny to have the ideal come true for him. The result is that, with one's mind, the ideal possibility is abandoned but emotionally it is difficult to give it up. Thus the conflict.

The resources of one's personality cannot be marshaled. A man finds that he cannot work wholeheartedly for the achievable or possible end because he cannot give up the inner demand for the ideal end. Oftentimes precious months or years pass with no solution in evidence because there is ever the hope that the ideal end may, in some miraculous manner, come to pass. Then the time for action does come at last. There comes a moment when something has to be done; one can no longer postpone the decision—the definite act resolves an otherwise intolerable situation. Once the decision is made, the die is cast. Is my decision right or wrong, wise or foolish? At the moment, I may be unable to answer the question. For what is right in the light of the present set of facts may not be able to stand up under the scrutiny of unfolding days. I may not have appraised the facts properly. My decision may have been largely influenced by my desires which were at work at the very center of my conscious processes.

In the face of all the uncertainties that surround any decision, the wise man acts in the light of his best judgment illumined by the integrity of his profoundest spiritual insights. Then the rest is in the hands of the future and in the mind of God. The possibility of error, of profound and terrible error, is at once the height and the depth of man's freedom. For this, God be praised!

Concerning the
Presence of God

THE PATIENCE OF
UNANSWERED PRAYER

"Teach me the patience of unanswered prayer" is a line of the familiar hymn. It opens up before the mind the wide intensity of unfulfilled hopes, broken dreams, and anguished denials. Who is there that has not carried at a central place in his concerns the persistent hunger, sometimes dull and quiet, sometimes feverish and angry, for something that has not come to pass. The hunger moves in the background of all the days like the rumble of distant thunder or the far-off roar of the sea. Sometimes it is so close that all of life seems summarized in its urgency and its denial, the denial of life itself.

The general overtones of anguish created by the unfulfilled need often send the soul searching for some clue, some key to unlock the door of the treasure house. All sorts of things are tried. Often there is the searching of one's own way of life to see if in the intricacies of the personal behavior pattern may not stand revealed the reason for the unmet need. Often there is the subtle intimation of some weakness in the character that takes no overt form but turns up as limitations in understanding or blind spots in perception. Often there is the sure knowledge that one has been hurt, crippled by the actions of others and no care exercised in the healing process, with the result that growth was out of line and twisted. But despite all of the meaning of all of the possible clues, the persistent hunger works away deep within. It remains unfulfilled and unmet.

Slowly it may dawn upon the spirit that there is a special ministry of unfulfillment. It may be that the persistent hunger is an Angel of Light, carrying out a particular assignment in life. With the coming of this possibility into consideration, slowly, tensions are relaxed and the center of emphasis is shifted from the hunger itself to what it has meant to deal with it through all the years. Slowly at first, the words are shaped and the pattern of them shows itself. At last, a man may say, "I know now that there is present in my life a quality that is only mine because the hunger is mine. Thus, at last, I come to the door and seek entrance where is gathered the great community. I know the password: 'Teach me the patience of unanswered prayer.' "

BUT THEN FACE TO FACE

"For now we see through a glass, darkly; but then face to face. . . ."

It is the judgment scene.
The climax of man's life has come at last;
The oriental despot sits enthroned.
Before him come the peoples of the earth.
Here are no men, no women, boys or girls
Struggling for rank, wealth, class, or power.
No race or tribe has standing here.
All walls that separate, divide,
By the moving drama are pushed aside.
Each life is freed of all pretense,
Each shadowy seeming swept away
By the mighty spread of ceaseless light.
   "I was sick, comfortless;
   I was hungry and desperate;
   I was lonely, wretched;
   I was in prison, forsaken . . ."
Strange awful words from Him;

Words more searching followed after:
"I know your tasks were manifold;
Unyielding claims consumed your thoughts.
There was no time to be at ease with deeds,
To give yourself beyond your creed.
Oh, I know about your temperament, your health,
Somehow you could not manage all your chores,
Excuses came to reinforce the empty feeling of your
    heart.
I know how hard it was for you.
You did not want to be an easy touch!
Beyond all else, your ties of blood;
Charity must begin at home.
Besides,
You did not know, but are you sure?
Do you recall the flashes of concern
That held you in your place that day?
I see you do remember well.
Again they came and then again,
Until at last they came no more;
Only the hollow darkness of the self cut off
From all the pain and pathos of the world.
No word of mine can alter what your days have done."
The story of your life is what the judge reveals.
From the relentless judgment, is there no appeal?

H E   P R A Y E D
F O R   H I S   F R I E N D S

In the final chapters of the Book of Job there appears a very searching sentence introduced into the drama by the author. The sentence: God turned the captivity of Job when he prayed for his friends.
He is suggesting that God was unable to find a resting place in the
heart, in the life of Job, until he, Job, altered fundamentally his attitude toward his friends. There seems to be a special rancor re-
served for friends when disaffection arises.

It seems simple, sometimes, to deal charitably with those who
may be regarded as enemies. There is something rather flattering

and condescending about extending grace to one who is beyond the pale. To pray for one's enemies can be a very superior role. But to pray for one's friends—that is another matter. Always there is the implication that one's friends should know better than to behave as they have done. It is hard to forgive one's friends for error in relationships, because each error is regarded as betrayal.

Job's experience is instructive. His friends had come to comfort him, to do the gracious act at a moment of deep distress. He was glad that they remembered him. But when they came, their words were full of judgment. They dealt with Job's predicament, but they did not deal with Job himself. What he needed most desperately was to be understood by them, to be able to place reaction to his tragedy in their responsive hands and find rest. When they were unable to do this for him and with him, he felt betrayed. He was embittered by his experience. Out of his distress, he could understand the Chaldeans who had raided his flocks; he could grasp the helplessness of man in the midst of tantrums of nature which in his case had been destructive of his children. But his friends were in another category. To pray for his friends meant that he had forgiven them. He could not bring them before God unless this relationship was right. It was blasphemous to ask God to do for his friends what Job himself was unwilling to do. When Job was able to pray for his friends, he had solved the basic problem of his suffering and his rebellion. That is why the dramatist says that God turned the captivity of Job when Job prayed for his friends.

IF THOU STANDETH BESIDE ME

If Thou standeth beside me
Nothing can prevail against me.

"If Thou standeth beside me." There are times when the sense of aloneness is very acute. Often these are times of struggle where the odds are uneven. Curious indeed is it that the sense of not being alone is apt to be most acutely felt when the concentration upon the matter at hand is absorbing. This means that there is available, at the moment, no margin of me exposed to the Presence of God. To be aware that God is standing beside me calls for some measure of detachment from my own personal struggle and turmoil.

"If Thou standeth beside me." It is entirely possible that the Presence of God may be most acutely felt in and through the struggle and the turmoil. It is not something apart from my involvements but a quality of Presence that emerges from the midst of my tempests. Or more accurately, it becomes a quality of the tempest itself. Sometimes this identification becomes very confusing, causing me to say that God brings the struggle. It is sufficient for me to know that He is found in the midst of all that befalls me. Nothing can prevail against me. The affirmation is the result of the disclosure of the Presence of God in the midst of what befalls me. First, He is felt as being with, in, and among the struggling elements of my experience. Then, out of the midst of these, His Presence emerges and becomes One who stands by my side. It is then that I am lifted up and strengthened.

> If Thou standeth beside me
> Nothing can prevail against me.

THE ENDURANCE OF PERSONALITY

It is a matter of amazing significance that the Creator of life assumes that human beings are able to absorb most of the negative and destructive things that happen to them without disintegration and collapse. There is nothing more staggering to contemplate than the sheer endurance of personality. It is tender and tough. It is soft and hard. It is lucid and opaque. Even the human body exhibits staggering endurance. In a book like Cannon's *The Wisdom of the Body,* the significance of such a remark becomes clear. Almost all "well" people are fighting and winning in their bodies the battle of disease. Or consider the adjustment that one has to make to noise. Have you ever picked out the different noises heard on a busy city street? Every single sound takes its minor or major toll of energy from one's storehouse, and yet these sounds can be so absorbed that the emotional balance of the personality will not be thrown off.

Or think of what is required in making one's adjustment to all sorts of people with whom one is thrown into more or less direct contact. The people with whom one works and who may be mutually irritating, or the people with whom one lives, may require major adjustments in order to keep the emotional balance. Some years ago, a farmer gave two apples to a friend of mine, visiting in the State of Washington. Each apple had a deep scar extending from the stem halfway around the circumference. The scar was marked by shriveled apple flesh. The rest of the apple had grown rounded-out, but the dead place remained. The story the farmer told my friend was this: When the apples were very young on the trees, a hail storm bruised them deeply. The apples did not rot, they did not fall off the tree; they did live. It was as if they decided to absorb as much as possible of the violence of the hail storm and go on with the business of self-realization.

The world is full of people who are like the apples. It is the greatest tribute to personality that the Creator of life assumes that each manifestation of life will have enough inner strength to fight its battles with such simple tools as may be at its disposal. A part of the business of living is to get better tools and to increase the tool-technique, but the fundamental assumption remains.

H O W   G O O D
T O   C E N T E R   D O W N !

How good it is to center down!
To sit quietly and see one's self pass by!
The streets of our minds seethe with endless traffic;
Our spirits resound with clashings, with noisy silences,
While something deep within hungers and thirsts for the
    still moment and the resting lull.
With full intensity we seek, ere the quiet passes, a fresh
    sense of order in our living;
A direction, a strong sure purpose that will structure our
    confusion and bring meaning to our chaos.
We look at ourselves in this waiting moment—the kinds
    of people we are.
The questions persist: what are we doing with our lives?—
    what are the motives that order our days?

What is the end of our doings? Where are we trying to go?

Where do we put the emphasis and where are our values focused?

For what end do we make sacrifices? Where is my treasure and what do I love most in life?

What do I hate most in life and to what am I true?

Over and over the questions beat in upon the waiting moment.

As we listen, floating up through all the jangling echoes of our turbulence, there is a sound of another kind—

A deeper note which only the stillness of the heart makes clear.

It moves directly to the core of our being. Our questions are answered,

Our spirits refreshed, and we move back into the traffic of our daily round

With the peace of the Eternal in our step.

How good it is to center down!

WE YIELD TO THE LOVE OF GOD

We bare our lives to the scrutiny, to the judgment, to the love of God. There is so much that burdens the mind, that peoples the thoughts, that again and again we are confused even in the great quiet Presence of God.

We yield to Him our confusions: the chaos of our minds and spirits; the tensions that tame the glory of the love of God out of our lives.

We yield to Him our frailties and our limitations: our quiet physical pains and the long chain of anxieties they inspire; the fatigue of spirit, because with reference to our private burdens often we become so tired.

We yield the desires of our minds and hearts: the private intimate wishes by which again and again the springs of our activities are fed and kept alive.

We yield the desires of which we are ashamed: those desires that buffet our spirits and torture our minds and yet seem to cling to us with such tenacity.

We yield our joys: the joy in being alive; the joy in renewed friendships; the joy in reestablished and reconciled lives; the joy in the day's work and the night's rest; the sheer joy of being loved, of caring and being cared for.

We yield our concerns for the world where we are exposed to much that casts down and depresses, to little that uplifts and inspires: war and the threat of war; the long loneliness and the deathwatch which seems to stalk our culture and fill our civilization with deadly dry rot.

We yield our lives, the nerve centers of our consent: lest the mainsprings of all our values collapse and we become like shadows in the night.

All of this—and more than tongue can say and heart can feel and mind can think—all of this we yield to the scrutiny, to the judgment, to the love of God.

I   SEEK   ROOM   FOR   PEACE

I seek the enlargement of my heart that there may be room for Peace.

Already there is room enough for chaos. There is in every day's experience much that makes for confusion and bewilderment. Often I do not understand quite how my relations with others become frayed and chaotic. Sometimes this chaos is a positive thing; it means that something new, creative, and whole is beginning to pull together the tattered fragments of my relationship with a person and to fashion it into that which delights the spirit and makes glad the heart. Sometimes the chaos is negative, a sign of degeneration in a relationship once meaningful and good. There is room enough for chaos.

But the need of my heart is for room for Peace: Peace of mind that inspires singleness of purpose; Peace of heart that quiets all fears and uproots all panic; Peace of spirit that filters through all confusions and robs them of their power. These I seek *now*. I know that here in this quietness my life can be infused with Peace.

Therefore, before God, I seek the enlargement of my
heart at this moment, that there may be room for Peace.

LORD, LORD, OPEN UNTO ME

Open unto me—light for
my darkness.
Open unto me—courage for
my fear.
Open unto me—hope for
my despair.
Open unto me—peace for
my turmoil.

Open unto me—joy for
my sorrow.
Open unto me—strength for
my weakness.
Open unto me—wisdom for
my confusion.
Open unto me—forgiveness for
my sins.
Open unto me—tenderness for
my toughness.
Open unto me—love for
my hates.
Open unto me—Thy Self for
my self.

Lord, Lord, open unto me!

GOD KNOWS THE HEART

God who knows the heart's secrets
Understands the Spirit's intention.

Often we are reminded that the heart has secrets which it cannot
share with anyone, not even with itself. This is true because there
is in each one of us lingerings of desires that have long since spent
themselves in overt or direct action; there are the throbs of impulses

that have not become sufficiently articulate to define themselves; there are vague reactions to experiences that are so much a part of our very substance that we cannot distinguish them from our true selves. And yet, all these and much more are a part of the secrets of the heart.

The secrets of the heart are the raw material of the genuine spirit of the individual. They are the stuff of the Spirit that dwells deep within each one of us. When we pray, there is the word that is spoken, the thought that is clearly defined, the desire that is actively felt—and more! The "more" is the very essence of the life's deep intent, it is the crucial units of shapeless meanings that give to each life its quality and its flavor.

God knows the heart's secrets and deals with us at the level of the heart's profoundest hunger. Where there is fear or anxiety, these take precedence over the ebb and flow of the inward tides. In order for the deepest things in us to be touched and kindled, both fear and anxiety must be wiped away. This we can do for ourselves, sometimes, but not often. The one thing that they cannot abide is conscious exposure to the Love of God.

> God who knows the heart's secrets
> Understands the Spirit's intention.

"HAPPY IS HE WHO RELIES ON GOD..."

The prophet Jeremiah says, "A curse on him who relies on man, who depends upon mere human aid; for he is like some desert shrub that never thrives, set in a solitary place in the steppes. But happy is he who relies on God, who has God for his confidence, for he is like a tree planted beside a stream sending his roots down to the water. He has no fear of scorching heat, his leaves are always green. He goes on bearing fruit when all around is barren and looks out on life with quiet eyes."

Some years ago I read a most interesting account in the *National Geographic Magazine* concerning certain trees found growing in the Sahara Desert. These trees are not a part of any oasis but stand alone in the midst of the heat and wind, without obvious moisture. It seems that, hundreds of years ago, what is now the desert was a dank, luxurious growth. As the desert appeared, the vegetation was destroyed until, at last, there was nothing left of the past glory except an oasis here and there. But not all vegetation disappeared; for there were a few trees that had sent their roots so far down into the heart of the earth in quest of moisture and food that they discovered deep flowing rivers full of concentrated chemicals. Here the roots are fed so effectively that the trees far above on the surface of the earth are able to stand anything that can happen to them at the hands of desert heat and blowing sand.

This is the secret of those whose lives are fed by deep inner resources of life. To him who is sure of God, He becomes for him the answer to life's greatest demands and, indeed, to its most searching and withering vicissitudes.

THE LORD IS THE STRENGTH OF MY LIFE

The Lord is.
Is God an idea in my mind,
A rumor planted by old tales born of fear when life was young and death lurked behind every waiting bush?
Is God the desire in my heart,
A longing that goes always unfulfilled?
Is God the restlessness I feel after dreams have come to pass
And all my hopes have built themselves into facts?
Is God the indescribable tenderness that creeps in the voice unawares,
That steals into the fingers as they linger momentarily in the hand of a friend?
Is God the endless churning of the turbulent sea
Or the steady shining of the stars against the blackness of the sky?
Is God the quenchless aching of the conscience over sins committed
And the vast cleansing in the soul riding on the wave of forgiveness that sweeps all before it?

The Lord is!
　He is more than tongue can tell,
　Than mind can think, than heart can feel!
The Lord is my strength.
　When day is done and in weariness I lay me down to
　　sleep,
　When fear becomes a lump in my throat and an illness
　　in my stomach,
　When the waters of temptation engulf me and I strangle
　　beneath the waves,
　When I have thought myself empty and the solution to
　　my problem hides,
　Lurking in the shadows of my mind,
　When the disease of my body tightens its grip and my
　　doctor picks up the broken lances of his skill and
　　knowledge and takes his leave,
　When the tidings are of brooding clouds of war
　　And of marching feet and humming planes moving in
　　the awful rhythm of the dirge of death—
The Lord is the strength of my life.
　Of whom
　　and of what
　　　shall I be afraid?

Psalm 139

THOU HAST SEARCHED ME
AND KNOWN ME

In all places
    Where I have dallied in joyous abandon,
    Where I have responded to ancient desires and yielded
      to impulses old as life, blinded like things that move
      without sight;
    Where chores have remained chores, unfulfilled by la-
      ziness of spirit and sluggishness of mind;
    Where work has been stripped of joy by the ruthless
      pruning of vagrant ambition;
    Where the task has been betrayed by slovenly effort;
    Where the response to human need has been halfhearted
      and weak;
    Where the surge of strength has spent itself in great
      concentration and I have been left a shaking reed in
      the wind;
    Where hope has mounted until from its quivering height
      I have seen the glory and wonder of the new dawn of
      great awakening;

Where the quiet hush of utter surrender envelops me in
    the great silence of intimate commitment;
Thou hast known me!

When I have lost my way, and thick fog has shrouded
    from my view the familiar path and the lights of home;
When with deliberate intent I have turned my back on
    truth and peace;
When in the midst of the crowd I have sought refuge
    among the strangers;
When things to do have peopled my days with mounting
    anxiety and ever-deepening frustration;
When in loneliness I have sat in the thicket of despair
    too weak to move, to lift my head;
Thou hast searched for and found me!

I cannot escape Thy Scrutiny!
I would not escape Thy Love!

THOU ART ACQUAINTED WITH ALL MY WAYS

With all my ways,
Thou art acquainted:
    The silent coming together of all the streams
    Nourished by springs of Being
    Fountained in ancient sires
    Since Life began:
        The quiet shaping of patterns,
        That gave meaning and substance
        To all I know as mine:
            The nurture of mother,
            The molding of climate,
            The rending of heritage
            That stamped their mark in tender mind
                and growing limb;

The tutoring by playmates
  and those who instruct;
The sure hand of Spirit
  that held in keeping
    sensitive meanings of right and wrong . . .

With all my ways
Thou art acquainted:
  The making of plans far below the level
    of the daily mind
    that find their way to guide
    the movement of the deed—
  Habits that monitor the freshness
    in all spontaneity
    and tame the glory of the creative act;
  The unrestrained joy of impulse
    sweeping all before it in riotous rejoicing;
  The great tenderness called to life
    by that which invades the heart
    and circles all desires;
  The little malices;
  The big hostilities;
  The subtle envies;
  The robust greeds;
  The whimpering contrition;
  The great confession;
  The single resolve;
  The fearful commitment;
  The tryst with Death
    that broods over the zest for life
    like intermittent shadows
    from sunrise to sunset—

Thou art acquainted—
Thou art acquainted—
With all my ways.

T H O U   H A S T   B E S E T   M E
B E H I N D   A N D   B E F O R E

Thou hast beset me behind and before
And laid Thine hand upon me!

    The upward push of life awakes the egg,
        an inner stirring sends it forth
        to be in all its parts according to its law.
    The blossom opens wide its heart
        to wind and bee,
        then closes.
        Deep within its pulsing core
        the dream of fruit takes shape
        and life decrees what it must be!
    The little chick mingles sound with
        baby duck and goose,
        sharing each the common food,
        drinking from the single trough;
    Day after day breezes blow—
    Rains bring to one and all the glad
        refreshment from the summer's sun—
    Yet, each follows his appointed way,
        without an awkward turn;
    Each fulfills the pattern of his own design.
    From tiny cell or ripened fruit,
    From baby chick or mammoth oak
        the same refrain goes forth:

Thou hast beset me behind and before
And laid Thine hand upon me!

    Muscle by muscle,
    Bone by bone
    Adding to strength and height,
    This the journey from infancy to youth;

Growing by day, by night;
Growth makes an end.
Some order calls a halt!
Beset behind, before,
Growth gives way.
But life does not stop,
The twins keep pace:
    Joy, sorrow—
    Sickness, health—
    Success, failure—
    Hope, despair—
    Courage, fear—
    Peace, turmoil.
The tempo quickens:
Dreams long cherished fall apart;
Slumbering desires awaken in vital strength;
The good seems no longer good;
The evil allures and engulfs;
The will is weak, the path grows dim,
Doubts gather, confusion is confounded,
Endurance languishes,
The spirit holds—
Till life begins anew.

Thou hast beset me behind and before
And laid Thine hand upon me!

THOU KNOWEST IT ALTOGETHER

My words cry out to give their hearts away:
  Each has its story and comes from afar.
  Again and again I seek my way with them,
  To ring them round with well-kept secrets
  Known to me, to me alone.

Sometimes they are willing carriers of private ends
Spending their strength in missions not their own.
Sometimes they rebel against the quality of my need
And force their way into another's heart,
Betraying the secrets I would not share.
Sometimes the full sweep of urgency
Frightens all speech,
Leaving me bruised and shaken.

My words cry out to give their hearts away:
   The integrity of the word—
Where may it be found?
Is it meanings the word has gained from all
   its wanderings through the wilderness of sounds
   in many lands, in far-off places?
Is it the self-offering of the word to the honest
   seeker after truth
   that it may blend its secret with the deep resolve?
Is it something outside the word—
   some meaning a man would share beyond the word
     itself?
Is there only the integrity of the man?

To domesticate the word;
To safeguard its character;
To purge the violence from its face;
To allow no service that defiles, degrades;
To make it one with truth;
To fill it with the pure intent;
This is to make the word the Sacrament,
The *angelos* of God.
This is the breath of life that makes man, man.
For there is not a word in my tongue
But lo, Thou knowest it altogether.

WHITHER SHALL I GO FROM THY PRESENCE

Whither shall I go from Thy Presence?
From Thee is there some hiding place?

   The deed is a thing so private,
   So inside the perfect working of desire
   That its inward part seems known to me,
   To me alone.

   The ebb and flow of thoughts
   Within my hidden sea,
   The forms that stir within the channels of my mind,
   Keep tryst with all my hidden hopes and fears.

   The ties that hold me fast to those
   Whose life with mine makes one,
   The tangled twine that binds my life
   With things I claim as mine,
   Are held in place by folds
   Of my embrace.

   The sealéd stillness that walls around
   The heartaches and the pain,
   Is held against all else that would invade.

   Awe-filled contrition emptied clear
   Of violence and sin,
   Seeps slowly from the wilderness
   Of my deserted soul.

   Almighty joy mounts to the brim
   And overflows in wild array,
   With music only ears attuned can hear.

   And yet,
   Always I know that Another

Sees and understands—
Every vigil with me keeps watch—
The door through which He comes no man
Can shut—
He is the Door!

I cannot go from Thy Presence,
There is no hiding place from Thee.

IF I ASCEND
UP INTO HEAVEN,
THOU ART THERE!

If I ascend up into heaven, Thou art there!
  When my joy overflows and
  No words contain it;
  When the thing I sought was lost
  Only to reappear within the hollow of my hand;
  When the day seems interminable
  But at eventide the burdens lift
  And weariness is a far-off memory;
  When there opens before the vista of the mind
  The wonder of new regions, far-off places;
  When the gentle touch of a loved one
  Makes music heard only by the listening heart;
  When the doctor's word is the final word
  And deep within the hidden places of the life
  Healing waters stir, bringing wholeness in their wake—
  When the wanderer comes home
  And the wayward finds peace in the ancient fireside—
  When from the ashes of old dreams
  The fires of a new life are kindled—
  Thou art there!

If I make my bed in hell—behold—
  When night remains night
  And darkness deepens;
  When the evilness of evil is unrelieved
  And utter desolation makes mockery

Of all that was true and good;
When the open door of refuge
Closes in my face
And to turn back is of no avail;
When the firm grip of sanity trembles
And all balances tilt, leaving
The mind tortured and crazed;
When all around, worlds crash
And winds blow torrid
Over the parched and wasted
Places of my spirit;
When sin multiplies itself
Until at last all goodness
Seems swallowed up and devoured;
When the chuckle of death
Is the only sound to be heard in the land—
Thou art there!

If I make my bed in hell . . .
If I ascend up into heaven . . .
Behold!

IN THY BOOK ALL MY MEMBERS ARE WRITTEN

The organism! How rare a thing it is!

The miracle of Hand:
  Fingers and thumbs
  Caught up in single grasp,
  Holding, shaping, fashioning outward things,
  To make the dream a fact.
The miracle of Parts:
  A restless muscle sending blood day unto day
  To sustain the rhythm of lungs, in and out,
  To keep alive the cell and striding step;
  The measured growth of bone
  To make the wholesome balance, the upright stance;

Great network of nerves reaching everywhere
To alert, to caution,
To gather news on every hand
To keep the world in place,
That meaning may remain.
The vital Brain:
The Watchman on the Wall
Controlling, dispatching,
Interpreting, deciding,
Holding within its tiny folds
The private journey and the grooved way . . .
The miracle of Mind:
Everywhere felt,
Nowhere seen;
A thing, no thing;
Matter, no matter;
Fleeting in passage,
Ever unmoving;
The Master of the House,
The Servant of All;
Reflection and image
All in one!

Great God! How vast must be Thy Faith
To risk so much in such a tiny frame;
To bring to being and to teach to praise
A living threat to all Thy nourished dreams!
And yet, not so—
Upon each part, the holy stamp:
"In Thy Book all my members are written
which in continuance were fashioned
when as yet, there was none of them!"

HOW PRECIOUS ARE THY THOUGHTS UNTO ME, O GOD!

How precious are Thy thoughts!

The nerve of life abounds in all I see,
The kernel of the seed holds in its place a swinging door,
Through which the boundless energy of living sub-
    stance flows,
Forming itself in root and stalk, in branch and fruit.
The germ in the egg awaits
The pregnant moment:
A gentle tug, a brooding urge,
An unhurried push to full creation,
Then living form of chick, or bird, or child.

A whisper in the mind—
A voice floating in the hills
Calling to itself
Kindred thoughts from far-off places:
Ideas take shape and form,
Firming within their vital wall,
A strange insistence:
They pull, they push, they drive,
Command!
Until, at last, they are
The Master in the House;
And the whole course of man's life
Is channeled into regions he does not know,
Nor scarcely understands.

How precious are Thy thoughts!

The response to goodness, the urge to minister;
The quickened willingness to bless;
The deep rejection of the evil deed, revealed;
The pull of the clear thought, the honest desire;

An all-embracing tenderness cradling the kindly act;
The far-flung hope comprising myriad strands of all man's
    dreams;
The hard rebuff to all that mocks and scorns;
The whole surrender of the center of consent,
To lose life only to find it again.

How precious are Thy thoughts unto me, O God!
How great is the sum of them!

WHEN I AWAKE, I AM
STILL WITH THEE

In all the waking hours
The Tentacles of Time
Give channel to each living thing:
   The bird on wing;
   The mole moving in darkness underground;
   The cricket chanting its evening song;
   The primeval whale sporting in chilly seas,
     or floating noiselessly in turbulent waters;
   In mountain crevice or sprawling meadow
   The delicate beauty of color-stained flower or fragile leaf;
   High above the timber line
     The sprig of green dares wind and snow;
   In the barren parchness of desert waste
     The juiceless shrub and waterlogged cactus;
   High in the treetop the green-pearled fruit of olive mis-
     tletoe,
     and the soft gray stillness of creeping moss;
   The infant, the growing child,
   The stumbling adolescent, the young adult,
   The man full-blown or stooped with years;
   The Tentacles of Time
   Give channel to each living thing.

And beyond this?
   Thoughts that move with grace of being:
   Light thoughts that dance and sing

Untouched by gloom or shadow or the dark;
Weighty thoughts that press upon the road
   with tracks that blossom into dreams
   or shape themselves in plan and scheme;
Thoughts that whisper;
Thoughts that shout;
Thoughts that wander without rest,
   Seeking, seeking, always seeking;
Thoughts that challenge;
Thoughts that soothe;
The Tentacles of Time
Give channel to each living thing.

Out from the House of Life
All things come,
And into it, each returns again for rest.

When I awake,
I am still with Thee.

I H A T E   T H E M   W I T H
P E R F E C T   H A T E

There is a weary joy in all revenge!
When a man's rejoicing
Over the broken lances of his vanquished foe
Leaves him clean and fresh and free.
   Or so it seems.
   It matters not, the violence—
   The bitterness spewed out of his hating heart . . .
   Is there no law?
   The sowing and reaping—
   Are they ever one?
Can man escape the consequence?
Can it ever be true?
   The enemy caught in my vital wrath—
   Was he not reaping what was sown?
   The penalty of my revenge,

Was it but the operation of law?
He had piled deed upon deed upon deed,
Reckless of all returns;
Emptied each hour of all the good,
Ringing it round with deeds that hurt,
With things that kill.
Is that not so?
In what he did
Was he not enemy of good,
Of God?
In my response, was I but a living thing
In Holy Hands—
Carrying out the law
Of which I am a part?
My hatred then is perfect
And I am free of stain.
But am I?
The vengeance which I execute
Becomes fresh seeds of violence sown,
And I must reap;
Or all is void.
It matters not the cause—
The consequence remains

"Vengeance is mine," saith the Lord,
"I will repay."

I rest my soul at last in this
And find my peace.

TRY ME AND KNOW MY THOUGHTS

Judgment seems far removed from act and deed.
Trumpets from the Past sound warning notes:
   The Day of Judgment!
   Prepare to meet thy God!
Beyond the gates of modern life

Ancient myths couched in dogmas old
Mold and rot in silent gloom:
   The end of time,
God on His Throne to judge mankind,
And a man alone stands before
The Judgment Seat;
The sky, a canopy above,
Heavenly floats:
   Angels, archangels, in ceaseless flight
   Bathed in Eternal Light forever,
   Blazing forth from the Throne of God . . .
   Such is the ancient myth.

Now man is free
To live unmindful of impending doom;
   Or so it seems.
There is a timeless warning in the far-off word,
The bitter truth returns in many forms;
No deed, no act, stands by itself alone.
   In bone and blood,
   In nerve and cell,
   In all the imagery of mind,
   In sound of voice,
   In wrinkled brow,
   Standing, sitting,
   Waking, sleeping,
   Laughter, tears,
   Imprint of thought,
   Registry of deed
   Remain for all man's days.
   There is a tight circle
   In which man moves.
   Nothing escapes;
   Soon or late,
   Somewhere, somewhen,
   The doer and the deed
   Are face to face!
The ancient myth renews its truth:
And a man stands alone

Before the Judgment Seat!
Try me, O God, and know my thoughts

And see if there be any wicked way
Within me!

God Is . . .

Not only is faith a way of knowing, a form of knowledge, but it is also one of life's great teachers. At no point is this fact more clearly demonstrated than in an individual's growing knowledge of God. It is obvious that, in the last analysis, proof of the existence of God is quite impossible. A simple reason for this is the fact that, if there is that to which God may be finally reduced, then He is not ultimate. But let us not be led astray by this apparent abstraction. Faith teaches a man that God is.

The human spirit has two fundamental demands that must be met relative to God. First, He must be vast, limitless, transcendent, all-comprehensive, so that there is no thing that is outside the wide reaches of His apprehension. The stars in the universe, the great galaxies of spatial groupings moving in endless rhythmic patterns in the trackless skies, as well as the tiny blade of grass by the roadside, are all within His grasp. The second demand is that He be personal and intimate. A man must have a sense of being cared for, of not being alone and stranded in the universe. All of us want the assurance of not being deserted *by* life nor deserted *in* life. Faith teaches us that God is—that He is the fact of life from which all other things take their meaning and reality. When Jesus prayed, he was conscious that, in his prayer, he met the Presence, and this conscious-ness was far more important and significant than the answering of his prayer. It is for this reason primarily that God was for Jesus the answer to all the issues and the problems of life. When I, with all my mind and heart, truly seek God and give myself in prayer, I, too, meet His Presence, and then I know for myself that Jesus was right.

· 2 ·

The second thing that man's faith teaches him about God is that God is near. One of the sayings of Jesus discovered among the pa-pyri at Oxyrhynchus is this: "Jesus saith: 'Wheresoever they may be, they are not without God; and where there is one alone, even then I am with him. Raise the stone, and there thou shalt find Me; cleave the wood, and I am there.' " Isaiah gives a vivid picture of Jehovah, a vision which came to him during the year of the death of King Uzziah. He saw the Lord on a great white throne, high and lifted up, and His Glory filled all the temple. Jesus erected a pyra-mid out of the funded insights of all the prophets, scaled its heights and brought God down out of the clouds, and found Him to be an intimate part of the warp and woof of human experience and human struggle.

Very often, we find it difficult to think of God as a part of life because we associate Him rather exclusively with the supernatural, the miraculous, the unusual. He belongs in the *special services* divi-sion of human life, where only the rare and extraordinary aspects of life are to be found. It was this conception that Jesus sought to un-dermine in his day. If God be far away, then He comes to us only on rare occasions and in rare situations. Of course, there is a sense in which this is true; the high moment, the great experience, the supreme challenge, the poignant sense of great contrition, all these may mark a sense of special Presence. But we do not live in such rarefied atmosphere. What we most want to know about God is whether He is present in the commonplace experiences of ordinary living, available to ordinary people under the most garden variety of circumstances. That God is not far from any one of us is the es-sence of the Gospel which Jesus proclaimed. "Closer is He than breathing, nearer than hands or feet."

· 3 ·

Finally, faith teaches us that God is love. This is a very difficult affirmation for the human spirit at times, because of the overwhelming amount of human misery and suffering by which our days are surrounded. All over the world, at this very moment, there is agony deeper than any formula of expression, the dumb inarticulate throb of which can only be sensed by a sympathy and understanding infinite in quality and limitless in grasp. Too, so much of human misery is poured out upon the innocent and helpless that life seems to be possessed of a vast, hideous deviltry.

Of course, there has never been a completely satisfying answer to human suffering, particularly as to the *why* of it. It is clear that the profoundly significant reflection upon the misery of life must begin not with an idea of omnipotence but with the concept of love. But a step from the conception of God as the perfect Knower men come inescapably to the conception of God as perfect love. To know fully is to understand and to understand is to care. The reason for affirming that God is love is based upon the fact that, in human experience, men discover that love is the most inclusive and completely inexhaustible aspect of life. Again and again, men have found that they will do gladly, for someone for whom their love is vast, what no power in heaven or hell could make them do if they did not love. Where love is great, we do for the beloved things which would be completely revolting if love were not. At every level of human life around us, we see this in operation. Therefore, whatever else God is, He must be love. He must be one with the most completely all-embracing, all-inspiring experience of human life. It is for this reason that, when a man is sure of God, God becomes not only his answer to the deeper needs of life but also sustaining confidence as he moves out upon the highway of life to meet the needs of other men. Wherever such a person goes he *is* a benediction, breathing peace.

JESUS
AND THE
DISINHERITED

Jesus—An Interpretation

To some God and Jesus may appeal in a way other than to us: some may come to faith in God and to love, without a conscious attachment to Jesus. Both Nature and good men besides Jesus may lead us to God. They who seek God with all their hearts must, however, some day on their way meet Jesus.*

Many and varied are the interpretations dealing with the teachings and the life of Jesus of Nazareth. But few of these interpretations deal with what the teachings and the life of Jesus have to say to those who stand, at a moment in human history, with their backs against the wall.

To those who need profound succor and strength to enable them to live in the present with dignity and creativity, Christianity often has been sterile and of little avail. The conventional Christian word is muffled, confused, and vague. Too often the price exacted by society for security and respectability is that the Christian movement in its formal expression must be on the side of the strong against the weak. This is a matter of tremendous significance, for it reveals to what extent a religion that was born of a people acquainted with

*Heinrich Weinel and Alban G. Widgery, *Jesus in the Nineteenth Century and After* (Edinburgh: T. and T. Clark, 1914), p. 405.

persecution and suffering has become the cornerstone of a civilization and of nations whose very position in modern life has too often been secured by a ruthless use of power applied to weak and defenseless peoples.

It is not a singular thing to hear a sermon that defines what should be the attitude of the Christian toward people who are less fortunate than himself. Again and again our missionary appeal is on the basis of the Christian responsibility to the needy, the ignorant, and the so-called backward peoples of the earth. There is a certain grandeur and nobility in administering to another's need out of one's fullness and plenty. One could be selfish, using his possessions—material or spiritual—for strictly private or personal ends. It is certainly to the glory of Christianity that it has been most insistent on the point of responsibility to others whose only claim upon one is the height and depth of their need. This impulse at the heart of Christianity is the human *will to share* with others what one has found meaningful to oneself elevated to the height of a moral imperative. But there is a lurking danger in this very emphasis. It is exceedingly difficult to hold oneself free from a certain contempt for those whose predicament makes moral appeal for defense and succor. It is the sin of pride and arrogance that has tended to vitiate the missionary impulse and to make of it an instrument of self-righteousness on the one hand and racial superiority on the other.

That is one reason why, again and again, there is no basic relationship between the simple practice of brotherhood in the commonplace relations of life and the ethical pretensions of our faith. It has long been a matter of serious moment that for decades we have studied the various peoples of the world and those who live as our neighbors as objects of missionary endeavor and enterprise without being at all willing to treat them either as brothers or as human beings. I say this without rancor, because it is not an issue in which vicious human beings are involved. But it is one of the subtle perils of a religion which calls attention—to the point of overemphasis, sometimes—to one's obligation to administer to human need.

I can count on the fingers of one hand the number of times that I have heard a sermon on the meaning of religion, of Christianity, to the man who stands with his back against the wall. It is urgent that my meaning be crystal clear. The masses of men live with their backs constantly against the wall. They are the poor, the disinherited, the dispossessed. What does our religion say to them? The issue is not what it counsels them to do for others whose need may be greater, but what religion offers to meet their own needs. The search for an answer to this question is perhaps the most important religious quest of modern life.

In the fall of 1935 I was serving as chairman of a delegation sent on a pilgrimage of friendship from the students of America to the students of India, Burma, and Ceylon. It was at a meeting in Ceylon that the whole crucial issue was pointed up to me in a way that I can never forget. At the close of a talk before the Law College, University of Colombo, on civil disabilities under states' rights in the United States, I was invited by the principal to have coffee.

We drank our coffee in silence. After the service had been removed, he said to me, "What are you doing over here? I know what the newspapers say about a pilgrimage of friendship and the rest, but that is not my question. What are *you* doing over here? This is what I mean.

"More than three hundred years ago your forefathers were taken from the western coast of Africa as slaves. The people who dealt in the slave traffic were Christians. One of your famous Christian hymn writers, Sir John Newton, made his money from the sale of slaves to the New World. He is the man who wrote 'How Sweet the Name of Jesus Sounds' and 'Amazing Grace'—there may be others, but these are the only ones I know. The name of one of the famous British slave vessels was 'Jesus.'

"The men who bought the slaves were Christians. Christian ministers, quoting the Christian apostle Paul, gave the sanction of religion to the system of slavery. Some seventy years or more ago you were freed by a man who was not a professing Christian, but was rather the spearhead of certain political, social, and economic forces, the significance of which he himself did not understand. During all the period since then you have lived in a Christian nation in which you are segregated, lynched, and burned. Even in the church, I understand, there is segregation. One of my students who went to your country sent me a clipping telling about a Christian church in which the regular Sunday worship was interrupted so that many could join a mob against one of your fellows. When he had been caught and done to death, they came back to resume their worship of their Christian God.

"I am a Hindu. I do not understand. Here you are in my country, standing deep within the Christian faith and tradition. I do not wish to seem rude to you. But, sir, I think you are a traitor to all the darker peoples of the earth. I am wondering what you, an intelligent man, can say in defense of your position."

Our subsequent conversation lasted for more than five hours. The clue to my own discussion with this probing, honest, sympathetic Hindu is found in my interpretation of the meaning of the religion of Jesus. It is a privilege, after so long a time, to set down what seems to me to be an essentially creative and prognostic interpretation of Jesus as religious subject rather than religious object. It is necessary to examine the religion of Jesus against the background of his own age and people, and to inquire into the content of his teaching with reference to the disinherited and the underprivileged.

We begin with the simple historical fact that Jesus was a Jew. The miracle of the Jewish people is almost as breathtaking as the miracle of Jesus. Is there something unique, some special increment of vitality in the womb of the people out of whose loins he came, that made of him a logical flowering of a long development of racial experience, ethical in quality and Godlike in tone? It is impossible for Jesus to be understood outside of the sense of community which Israel held with God. This does not take anything away from him; rather does it heighten the challenge which his life presents, for such reflection reveals him as the product of the constant working of the creative mind of God upon the life, thought, and character of a race of men. Here is one who was so conditioned and organized within himself that he became a perfect instrument for the embodiment of a set of ideals—ideals of such dramatic potency that they were capable of changing the calendar, rechanneling the thought of the world, and placing a new sense of the rhythm of life in a weary, nerve-snapped civilization.

How different might have been the story of the last two thousand years on this planet grown old from suffering if the link between Jesus and Israel had never been severed! What might have happened if Jesus, so perfect a flower from the brooding spirit of God in the soul of Israel, had been permitted to remain where his roots would have been fed by the distilled elements accumulated from Israel's wrestling with God! The thought is staggering. The Christian Church has tended to overlook its Judaic origins, but the fact is that Jesus of Nazareth was a Jew of Palestine when he went about his Father's business, announcing the acceptable year of the Lord.

Of course it may be argued that the fact that Jesus was a Jew is merely coincidental, that God could have expressed himself as easily and effectively in a Roman. True, but the fact is he did not. And it is with that fact that we must deal.

The second important fact for our consideration is that Jesus was a poor Jew. There is recorded in Luke the account of the dedication of Jesus at the temple: "And when the days of her purification according to the law of Moses were accomplished, they brought him . . . to the Lord; and to offer a sacrifice according to that which is said in the law of the Lord, a pair of turtledoves, or two young pigeons." When we examine the regulation in Leviticus, an interesting fact is revealed: "And when the days of her purifying are fulfilled, for a son, . . . she shall bring a lamb of the first year for a burnt offering, and a young pigeon, or a turtledove, for a sin offering. . . . And if she be not able to bring a lamb, then she shall bring two turtles, or two young pigeons; the one for a burnt offering and the other for a sin offering." It is clear from the text that the mother of Jesus was one whose means were not sufficient for a lamb, and who was compelled, therefore, to use doves or young pigeons.

The economic predicament with which he was identified in birth placed him initially with the great mass of men on the earth. The masses of the people are poor. If we dare take the position that in Jesus there was at work some radical destiny, it would be safe to say that in his poverty he was more truly Son of Man than he would have been if the incident of family or birth had made him a rich son of Israel. It is not a point to be labored, for again and again men have transcended circumstance of birth and training; but it is an observation not without merit.

The third fact is that Jesus was a member of a minority group in the midst of a larger dominant and controlling group. In 63 B.C. Palestine fell into the hands of the Romans. After this date the gruesome details of loss of status were etched, line by line, in the sensitive soul of Israel, dramatized ever by an increasing desecration of the Holy Land. To be sure, there was Herod, an Israelite, who ruled from 37 to 4 B.C.; but in some ways he was completely apostate. Taxes of all kinds increased, and out of these funds, extracted from the vitals of the people, temples in honor of Emperor Augustus were built within the boundaries of the holy soil. It was a sad and desolate time for the people. Herod became the symbol of shame and humiliation for all of Israel.

In Galilee a certain revolutionary, whose name was Judas, laid siege to the armory at Sepphoris and, with weapons taken there, tried to reestablish the political glory of Israel. How terrible a moment! The whole city of Sepphoris was regarded as a hostage, and Roman soldiers, aided by the warriors of King Aretas of Arabia, reduced the place to whited ash. In time the city was rebuilt—and perhaps Jesus was one of the carpenters employed from Nazareth, which was a neighboring village.

It is utterly fantastic to assume that Jesus grew to manhood untouched by the surging currents of the common life that made up the climate of Palestine. Not only must he have been aware of them; that he was affected by them is a most natural observation. A word of caution is urgent at this point. To place Jesus against the background of his time is by no means sufficient to explain him. Who can explain a spiritual genius—or any kind of genius, for that matter? The historical setting in which Jesus grew up, the psychological mood and temper of the age and of the House of Israel, the economic and social predicament of Jesus' family—all these are important. But they in themselves are unable to tell us precisely the thing that we most want to know: Why does he differ from many others in the same setting? Any explanation of Jesus in terms of psychology, politics, economics, religion, or the like must inevitably explain his contemporaries as well. It may tell why Jesus was a particular kind of Jew, but not why some other Jews were not Jesus. And that is, after all, the most important question, since the thing which makes him most significant is not the way in which he resembled his fellows but the way in which he differed from all the rest of them. Jesus inherited the same traits as countless other Jews of his time; he grew up in the same society; and yet he was Jesus, and the others were not. Uniqueness always escapes us as we undertake an analysis of character.

On the other hand, these considerations should not blind us to the significance of the environmental factors and the social and religious heritage of Jesus in determining the revolutionary character of some of his insights. One of the clearest and simplest statements of the issues here raised, and their bearing upon the character and teaching of Jesus, is found in Vladimir Simkhovitch's *Toward the Understanding of Jesus.* I am using his essay as the basis for our discussion of the problem, but the applications are mine. Simkhovitch says:

> In the year 6 Judea was annexed to Syria; in the year 70 Jerusalem and its temple were destroyed. Between these two dates Jesus preached and was crucified on Golgotha. During all that time the life of the little nation was a terrific drama; its patriotic emotions were aroused to the highest pitch and then still more inflamed by the identification of national politics with a national religion. Is it reasonable to assume that what was going on before Jesus' eyes was a closed book, that the agonizing problems of his people were a matter of indifference to him, that he had given them no consideration, that he was not taking a definite attitude towards the great and all-absorbing problem of the very people whom he taught?*

There is one overmastering problem that the socially and politically disinherited always face: Under what terms is survival possible? In the case of the Jewish people in the Greco-Roman world the problem was even more acute than under ordinary circumstances, because it had to do not only with physical survival in terms of life and limb but also with the actual survival of a culture and a faith. Judaism was a culture, a civilization, and a religion—a total world view in which there was no provision for any form of thoroughgoing dualism. The crucial problem of Judaism was to exist as an isolated, autonomous, cultural, religious, and political unit in the midst of the hostile Hellenic world. If there had been sharp lines distinguishing the culture from the religion, or the religion from political autonomy, a compromise could have been worked out. Because the Jews thought that a basic compromise was possible, they sought political annexation to Syria which would bring them under Roman rule directly and thereby guarantee them, within the framework of Roman policy, religious and cultural autonomy. But this merely aggravated the already tense nationalistic feeling and made a direct, all-out attack against Roman authority inevitable.

In the midst of this psychological climate Jesus began his teaching and his ministry. His words were directed to the House of Israel, a minority within the Greco-Roman world, smarting under the loss of status, freedom, and autonomy, haunted by the dream of the restoration of a lost glory and a former greatness. His message focused on the urgency of a radical change in the inner attitude of the people. He recognized fully that out of the heart are the issues of life and that no external force, however great and overwhelming, can at long last destroy a people if it does not first win the victory of the spirit against them. "To revile because one has been reviled—this is the real evil because it is the evil of the soul itself." Jesus saw this with almighty clarity. Again and again he came back to the inner life of the individual. With increasing insight and startling accuracy he placed his finger on the "inward center" as the crucial arena where the issues would determine the destiny of his people.

When I was a seminary student, I attended one of the great quadrennial conventions of the Student Volunteer Movement. One afternoon some seven hundred of us had a special group meeting, at which a Korean girl was asked to talk to us about her impression of American education. It was an occasion to be remembered. The Korean student was very personable and somewhat diminutive. She came to the edge of the platform and, with what seemed to be obvious emotional strain, she said, "You have asked me to talk with you about my impression of American education. But there is only one thing that a Korean has any right to talk about, and that is freedom from Japan." For about twenty minutes she made an impassioned plea for the freedom of her people, ending her speech with this sentence: "If you see a little American boy and you ask him what he wants, he says, 'I want a penny to put in my bank or to buy a whistle or a piece of candy.' But if you see a little Korean boy and you ask him what he wants, he says, 'I want freedom from Japan."

It was this kind of atmosphere that characterized the life of the Jewish community when Jesus was a youth in Palestine. The urgent question was what must be the attitude toward Rome. Was any attitude possible that would be morally tolerable and at the same time preserve a basic self-esteem—without which life could not possibly have any meaning? The question was not academic. It was the most crucial of questions. In essence, Rome was the enemy; Rome symbolized total frustration; Rome was the great barrier to peace of mind. And Rome was everywhere. No Jewish person of the period could deal with the question of his practical life, his vocation, his place in society, until first he had settled deep within himself this critical issue.

This is the position of the disinherited in every age. What must be the attitude toward the rulers, the controllers of political, social, and economic life? This is the question of the Negro in American life. Until he has faced and settled that question, he cannot inform his environment with reference to his own life, whatever may be his preparation or his pretensions.

In the main, there were two alternatives faced by the Jewish minority of which Jesus was a part. Simply stated, these were to resist or not to resist. But each of these alternatives has within it secondary alternatives.

Under the general plan of nonresistance one may take the position of imitation. The aim of such an attitude is to assimilate the culture and the social behavior-pattern of the dominant group. It is the profound capitulation to the powerful, because it means the yielding of oneself to that which, deep within, one recognizes as being unworthy. It makes for a strategic loss of self-respect. The aim is to reduce all outer or external signs of difference to zero, so that there shall be no ostensible cause for active violence or opposition. Under some circumstances it may involve a repudiation of one's heritage, one's customs, one's faith. Accurate imitation until the façade of complete assimilation is securely placed and the antagonism of difference dissolved—such is the function of this secondary alternative within the broader alternative of nonresistance. Herod was an excellent example of this solution.

To some extent this was also the attitude of the Sadducees. They represented the "upper" class. From their number came the high priests, and most of the economic security derived from contemporary worship in the temple was their monopoly. They did not represent the masses of the people. Any disturbance of the established order meant upsetting their position. They loved Israel, but they seem to have loved security more. They made their public peace with Rome and went on about the business of living. They were astute enough to see that their own position could be perpetuated if they stood firmly against all revolutionaries and radicals. Such persons would only stir the people to resist the inevitable, and in the end everything would be lost. Their tragedy was in the fact that they idealized the position of the Roman in the world and suffered the moral fate of the Romans by becoming like them. They saw only two roads open before them—become like the Romans or be destroyed by the Romans. They chose the former.

The other alternative in the nonresistance pattern is to reduce contact with the enemy to a minimum. It is the attitude of cultural isolation in the midst of a rejected culture. Cunning the mood may be—one of bitterness and hatred, but also one of deep, calculating fear. To take up active resistance would be foolhardy, for a thousand reasons. The only way out is to keep one's resentment under rigid control and censorship.

The issue raised by this attitude is always present. The opposition to those who work for social change does not come only from those who are the guarantors of the status quo. Again and again it has been demonstrated that the lines are held by those whose hold on security is sure only as long as the status quo remains intact. The reasons for this are not far to seek. If a man is convinced that he is safe only as long as he uses his power to give others a sense of insecurity, then the measure of their security is in his hands. If security or insecurity is at the mercy of a single individual or group, then control of behavior becomes routine. All imperialism functions in this way. Subject peoples are held under control by this device.

One of the most striking scenes in the movie *Ben Hur* was that in which a Roman legion marches by while hundreds of people stand silently on the roadside. As the last soldier passes, a very dignified, self-possessed Jewish gentleman, with folded arms and eyes smoldering with the utmost contempt, without the slightest shift of his facial muscles spits at the heel of the receding legionary—a consummate touch. Such—in part, at least—was the attitude of the Pharisee. No active resistance against Rome—only a terrible contempt. Obviously such an attitude is a powder keg. One nameless incident may cause to burst into flame the whole gamut of smoldering passion, leaving nothing in its wake but charred corpses, mute reminders of the tragedy of life. Jesus saw this and understood it clearly.

The other major alternative is resistance. It may be argued that even nonresistance is a form of resistance, for it may be regarded as an appositive dimension of resistance. Resistance may be overt action, or it may be merely mental and moral attitudes. For the purposes of our discussion resistance is defined as the physical, overt expression of an inner attitude. Resistance in this sense finds its most dramatic manifestation in force of arms.

Armed resistance is apt to be a tragic last resort in the life of the disinherited. Armed resistance has an appeal because it provides a form of expression, of activity, that releases tension and frees the oppressed from a disintegrating sense of complete impotency and helplessness. "Why can't we do something? Something must be done!" is the recurring cry. By "something" is meant action, direct action, as over against words, subtleties, threats, and innuendos. It is better to die fighting for freedom than to rot away in one's chains, the argument runs.

> Before I'd be a slave
> I'd be buried in my grave,
> And go home to my God
> And be free!

The longer the mood is contemplated, the more insistent the appeal. It is a form of fanaticism, to be sure, but that may not be a vote against it. In all action there is operative a fringe of irrationality. Once the mood is thoroughly established, any council of caution is interpreted as either compromise or cowardice. The fact that the ruler has available to him the power of the state and complete access to all arms is scarcely considered. Out of the depths of the heart there swells a great and awful assurance that because the cause is just, it cannot fail. Any failure is regarded as temporary and, to the devoted, as a testing of character.

This was the attitude of the Zealots of Jesus' day. There was added appeal in their position because it called forth from the enemy organized determination and power. It is never to be forgotten that one of the ways by which men measure their own significance is to be found in the amount of power and energy other men must use in order to crush them or hold them back. This is at least one explanation of the fact that even a weak and apparently inconsequential movement becomes formidable under the pressure of great persecution. The persecution becomes a vote of confidence, which becomes, in turn, a source of inspiration, power, and validation. The Zealots knew this. Jesus knew this. It is a matter of more than passing significance that he had a Zealot among his little band of followers, indeed among the twelve chosen ones.

In the face of these alternatives Jesus came forth with still another. On this point Simkhovitch makes a profound contribution to the understanding of the psychology of Jesus. He reminds us that Jesus expressed his alternative in a "brief formula—the Kingdom of Heaven is in us." He states further:

> Jesus had to resent deeply the loss of Jewish national independence and the aggression of Rome. . . . Natural humiliation was hurting and burning. The balm for that burning humiliation was humility. For humility cannot be humiliated. . . . Thus he asked his people to learn from him, "For I am meek and lowly in heart; and ye shall find rest unto your souls. For my yoke is easy, and my burden is light." *

It was but natural that such a position would be deeply resented by many of his fellows, who were suffering even as he was. To them it was a complete betrayal to the enemy. It was to them a counsel of acquiescence, if not of despair, full to overflowing with a kind of groveling and stark cowardice. Besides, it seemed like self-deception, like whistling in the dark. All of this would have been quite true if Jesus had stopped there. He did not. He recognized with authentic realism that anyone who permits another to determine the quality of his inner life gives into the hands of the other the keys to his destiny. If a man knows precisely what he can do to you or what epithet he can hurl against you in order to make you lose your temper, your equilibrium, then he can always keep you under subjection. It is a man's reaction to things that determines their ability to exercise power over him. It seems clear that Jesus understood the anatomy of the relationship between his people and the Romans, and he interpreted that relationship against the background of the profoundest ethical insight of his own religious faith as he had found it in the heart of the prophets of Israel.

The solution which Jesus found for himself and for Israel, as they faced the hostility of the Greco-Roman world, becomes the word and the work of redemption for all the cast-down people in every generation and in every age. I mean this quite literally. I do not ignore the theological and metaphysical interpretation of the Chris-

---

* *Toward the Understanding of Jesus,* pp. 60–61. Copyright 1921, 1937, 1947 by The Macmillan Co. and used with their permission.

tian doctrine of salvation. But the underprivileged everywhere have long since abandoned any hope that this type of salvation deals with the crucial issues by which their days are turned into despair without consolation. The basic fact is that Christianity as it was born in the mind of this Jewish teacher and thinker appears as a technique of survival for the oppressed. That it became, through the intervening years, a religion of the powerful and the dominant, used sometimes as an instrument of oppression, must not tempt us into believing that it was thus in the mind and life of Jesus. "In him was life; and the life was the light of men." Wherever his spirit appears, the oppressed gather fresh courage; for he announced the good news that fear, hypocrisy, and hatred, the three hounds of hell that track the trail of the disinherited, need have no dominion over them.

I belong to a generation that finds very little that is meaningful or intelligent in the teachings of the Church concerning Jesus Christ. It is a generation largely in revolt because of the general impression that Christianity is essentially an other-worldly religion, having as its motto: "Take all the world, but give me Jesus." The desperate opposition to Christianity rests in the fact that it seems, in the last analysis, to be a betrayal of the Negro into the hands of his enemies by focusing his attention upon heaven, forgiveness, love, and the like. It is true that this emphasis is germane to the religion of Jesus, but it has to be put into a context that will show its strength and vitality rather than its weakness and failure. For years it has been a part of my own quest so to understand the religion of Jesus that interest in his way of life could be developed and sustained by intelligent men and women who were at the same time deeply victimized by the Christian Church's betrayal of his faith.

During much of my boyhood I was cared for by my grandmother, who was born a slave and lived until the Civil War on a plantation near Madison, Florida. My regular chore was to do all of the reading for my grandmother—she could neither read nor write. Two or three times a week I read the Bible aloud to her. I was deeply impressed by the fact that she was most particular about the choice of scripture. For instance, I might read many of the more devotional Psalms, some Isaiah, the Gospels again and again. But the Pauline epistles, never—except, at long intervals, the thirteenth chapter of First Corinthians. My curiosity knew no bounds, but we did not question her about anything.

When I was older and was half through college, I chanced to be spending a few days at home near the end of summer vacation. With a feeling of great temerity I asked her one day why it was that she would not let me read any of the Pauline letters. What she told me I shall never forget. "During the days of slavery," she said, "the master's minister would occasionally hold services for the slaves. Old man McGhee was so mean that he would not let a Negro minister preach to his slaves. Always the white minister used as his text something from Paul. At least three or four times a year he used as a text: 'Slaves, be obedient to them that are your masters . . . , as unto Christ.' Then he would go on to show how it was God's will that we were slaves and how, if we were good and happy slaves, God would bless us. I promised my Maker that if I ever learned to read and if freedom ever came, I would not read that part of the Bible."

Since that fateful day on the front porch in Florida, I have been working on the problem her words presented. A part of the fruits of that search throw an important light upon the issues with which I am dealing. It cannot be denied that too often the weight of the Christian movement has been on the side of the strong and the powerful and against the weak and oppressed—this, despite the Gospel. A part of the responsibility seems to me to rest upon a peculiar twist in the psychology of Paul, whose wide and universal concern certainly included all men, bond and free.

Let us examine the facts. The apostle Paul was a Jew. He was the first great creative interpreter of Christianity. His letters are older than the Gospels themselves. It seems that because he was not one of the original disciples, he was never quite accepted by them as one able to speak with authority concerning the Master. This fact hung very heavily upon the soul of the apostle. He did not ever belong, quite. One of the disciples could always say, "But of course you do not quite understand, because, you see, you were not there when . . ."

But the fact remains: Paul was a Jew, even as Jesus was a Jew. By blood, training, background, and religion he belonged to the Jewish minority, about whom we have been speaking. But unlike them, for the most part, he was a free Jew; he was a citizen of Rome. A desert and a sea were placed between his status in the empire and that of his fellow Jews. A very searching dilemma was created by this fact. On the one hand, he belonged to the privileged class. He had the freedom of the empire at his disposal. There were certain citizenship rights which he could claim despite his heritage, faith, and religion. Should he deny himself merely because he was more fortunate than his fellows? To what extent could he accept his rights without feeling a deep sense of guilt and betrayal? He was of a minority but with majority privileges. If a Roman soldier in some prison in Asia Minor was taking advantage of him, he could make an appeal directly to Caesar. There was always available to him a protection guaranteed by the state and respected by the minions of the state. It was like a magic formula always available in emergencies. It is to the credit of the amazing power of Jesus Christ over the life of Paul that there is only one recorded instance in which he used his privilege.

It is quite understandable that his sense of security would influence certain aspects of his philosophy of history. Naturally he would have a regard for the state, for the civil magistrate, unlike that of his fellows, who regarded them as the formal expression of legitimatized intolerance. The stability of Paul's position in the state was guaranteed by the integrity of the state. One is not surprised, then, to hear him tell slaves to obey their masters like Christ, and say all government is ordained of God. (It is not to meet the argument to say that in a sense everything that is, is permitted of God, or that government and rulers are sustained by God as a concession to the frailty of man.) It would be grossly misleading and inaccurate to say that there are not to be found in the Pauline letters utterances of a deeply different quality—utterances which reveal how his conception transcended all barriers of race and class and condition. But this other side is there, always available to those who wish to use the weight of the Christian message to oppress and humiliate their fellows. The point is that this aspect of Paul's teaching is understandable against the background of his Roman citizenship. It influenced his philosophy of history and resulted in a major frustration that has borne bitter fruit in the history of the movement which he, Paul, did so much to project on the conscience of the human race.

Now Jesus was not a Roman citizen. He was not protected by the normal guarantees of citizenship—that quiet sense of security which comes from knowing that you belong and the general climate of confidence which it inspires. If a Roman soldier pushed Jesus into a ditch, he could not appeal to Caesar; he would be just another Jew in the ditch. Standing always beyond the reach of citizen security, he was perpetually exposed to all the "arrows of outrageous fortune," and there was only a gratuitous refuge—if any—within the state. What stark insecurity! What a breeder of complete civil and moral nihilism and psychic anarchy! Unless one actually lives day by day without a sense of security, he cannot understand what worlds separated Jesus from Paul at this point.

The striking similarity between the social position of Jesus in Palestine and that of the vast majority of American Negroes is obvious to anyone who tarries long over the facts. We are dealing here with conditions that produce essentially the same psychology. It is the similarity of a social climate at the point of a denial of full citizenship which creates the problem for creative survival. For the most part, Negroes assume that there are no basic citizenship rights, no fundamental protection, guaranteed to them by the state, because their status as citizens has never been clearly defined. There has been for them little protection from the dominant controllers of society and even less protection from the unrestrained elements within their own group.

The result has been a tendency to be their own protectors, to bulwark themselves against careless and deliberate aggression. The Negro has felt, with some justification, that the peace officer of the community provides no defense against the offending or offensive white man; and for an entirely different set of reasons the peace officer gives no protection against the offending Negro. Thus the Negro feels that he must be prepared, at a moment's notice, to protect his own life and take the consequence therefor. Such a predicament has made it natural for some of them to use weapons as a defense and to have recourse to premeditated or precipitate violence.

Living in a climate of deep insecurity, Jesus, faced with so narrow a margin of civil guarantees, had to find some other basis upon which to establish a sense of well-being. He knew that the goals of religion as he understood them could never be worked out within the then-established order. Deep from within that order he projected a dream, the logic of which would give to all the needful security. There would be room for all, and no man would be a threat to his brother. "The kingdom of God is within." "The Spirit of the Lord is upon me, because he hath anointed me to preach the gospel to the poor."

The basic principles of his way of life cut straight through to the despair of his fellows and found it groundless. By inference he says, "You must abandon your fear of each other and fear only God. You must not indulge in any deception and dishonesty, even to save your lives. Your words must be Yea—Nay; anything else is evil. Hatred is destructive to hated and hater alike. Love your enemy, that you may be children of your Father who is in heaven."

Fear

Fear is one of the persistent hounds of hell that dog the footsteps of the poor, the dispossessed, the disinherited. There is nothing new or recent about fear—it is doubtless as old as the life of man on the planet. Fears are of many kinds—fear of objects, fear of people, fear of the future, fear of nature, fear of the unknown, fear of old age, fear of disease, and fear of life itself. Then there is fear which has to do with aspects of experience and detailed states of mind. Our homes, institutions, prisons, churches are crowded with people who are hounded by day and harrowed by night because of some fear that lurks ready to spring into action as soon as one is alone, or as soon as the lights go out, or as soon as one's social defenses are temporarily removed.

The ever-present fear that besets the vast poor, the economically and socially insecure, is a fear of still a different breed. It is a climate closing in; it is like the fog in San Francisco or in London. It is nowhere in particular yet everywhere. It is a mood which one carries around with himself, distilled from the acrid conflict with which his days are surrounded. It has its roots deep in the heart of the relations between the weak and strong, between the controllers of environment and those who are controlled by it.

When the basis of such fear is analyzed, it is clear that it arises out of the sense of isolation and helplessness in the face of the varied dimensions of violence to which the underprivileged are exposed. Violence, precipitate and stark, is the sire of the fear of such people. It is spawned by the perpetual threat of violence everywhere. Of course, physical violence is the most obvious cause. But here, it is important to point out, a particular kind of physical violence or its counterpart is evidenced; it is violence that is devoid of the element of contest. It is what is feared by the rabbit that cannot ultimately escape the hounds. One can almost see the desperation creep into the quivering, pulsing body of the frightened animal. It is one-sided violence. If two men equally matched, or even relatively matched, are in deadly combat, the violence is clear-cut though terrible; there is gross equality of advantage. But when the power and tools of violence are on one side, the fact that there is no available and recognized protection from violence makes the resulting fear deeply terrifying.

In a society in which certain people or groups—by virtue of economic, social, or political power—have dead-weight advantages over others who are essentially without that kind of power, those who are thus disadvantaged know that they cannot fight back effectively, that they cannot protect themselves, and that they cannot demand protection from their persecutors. Any slight conflict, any alleged insult, any vague whim, any unrelated frustration, may bring down upon the head of the defenseless the full weight of naked physical violence. Even in such a circumstance it is not the fear of death that is most often at work; it is the deep humiliation arising from dying without benefit of cause or purpose. No high end is served. There is no trumpet blast to stir the blood and to anesthetize the agony. Here there is no going down to the grave with a shout; it is merely being killed or being beaten in utter wrath or indifferent sadism, without the dignity of being on the receiving end of a premeditated act hammered out in the white heat of a transcendent moral passion. The whole experience attacks the fundamental sense of self-respect and personal dignity, without which a man is no man.

In such physical violence the contemptuous disregard for personhood is the fact that is degrading. If a man knows that he is the object of deliberately organized violence, in which care has been exercised to secure the most powerful and deadly weapon in order to destroy him, there may be something great and stimulating about his end. Conceivably this is a lesson that may be learned from one interpretation of the slaying of the giant Goliath. The great Goliath, the symbol of the might and prowess of the Philistines, is equipped for battle, armor replete, sword and protectors in order. Then there is David, just a lad—perhaps in short shirt, possibly without even sandals. For him no armor, no sword, no helmet—just a boy with a slingshot in his hand. David's preparation for battle may be thought to reflect David's estimate of the might and prowess of the Philistines. When the great Goliath beheld David, and the full weight of the drama broke upon him with force, it well might be literally true that under the tension growing out of a sense of outraged dignity he burst a blood vessel and died of apoplexy.

Always back of the threat is the rumor or the fact that somewhere, under some similar circumstances, violence was used. That is all that is necessary. The threat becomes the effective instrument. There was a dog that lived at the end of my street in my hometown. Every afternoon he came down the street by the house. I could always hear him coming, giving a quick, sharp yelp in front of certain yards along the way. He was not hit by flying stones; each boy would catch the dog's eye and draw his arm back—the yelp followed immediately. The threat was sufficient to secure the reaction because, somewhere in the past, that particular motion had been identified with pain and injury. Such is the role of the threat of violence. It is rooted in a past experience, actual or reported, which tends to guarantee the present reaction of fear.

The disinherited experience the disintegrating effect of contempt in some such fashion as did Goliath. There are few things more devastating than to have it burned into you that you do not count and that no provisions are made for the literal protection of your person. The threat of violence is ever present, and there is no way to determine precisely when it may come crushing down upon you. In modern power politics this is called a war of nerves. The underprivileged in any society are the victims of a perpetual war of nerves. The logic of the state of affairs is physical violence, but it need not fulfill itself in order to work its perfect havoc in the souls of the poor.

Fear, then, becomes the safety device with which the oppressed surround themselves in order to give some measure of protection from complete nervous collapse. How do they achieve this?

In the first place, they make their bodies commit to memory ways of behaving that will tend to reduce their exposure to violence. Several years ago, when I was in India, I experienced precisely what is meant here. It was on our first evening in the country that a friend came to visit and to give advice about certain precautions to be observed. Just before he left, a final caution was given about snakes. He advised that we should not walk around at night without a light, not go into an unlighted room at night. We should sleep with a flashlight under the pillow, so that if it were necessary to get up during the night, a circle of light could be thrown on the floor before stepping out of bed, lest we disturb the nocturnal rambling of some unsuspecting cobra. I sat alone for some time after he left. During that period of concentration I was literally teaching my body how to behave, so that after that particular evening it would be extremely difficult for me to violate his expressed advice. My conditioning was so complete that, subsequently, my behavior was automatic.

This is precisely what the weak do everywhere. Through bitter experience they have learned how to exercise extreme care, how to behave so as to reduce the threat of immediate danger from their environment. Fear thus becomes a form of life assurance, making possible the continuation of physical existence with a minimum of active violence.

Children are taught how to behave in this same way. The children of the disinherited live a restricted childhood. From their earliest moments they are conditioned so as to reduce their exposure to violence. In Felix Salten's *Bambi,* the old stag counsels Bambi, giving to him in great detail a pattern of behavior that will reduce his chance of being shot without an opportunity for escape. He teaches him to distinguish human scent, the kinds of exposure that may be deadly, what precise kind of behavior is relatively safe. The stag is unwilling to leave Bambi until he is sure that the young deer has made his body commit to memory ways of behaving that will protect and safeguard his life.

The threat of violence within a framework of well-nigh limitless power is a weapon by which the weak are held in check. Artificial limitations are placed upon them, restricting freedom of movement, of employment, and of participation in the common life. These limitations are given formal or informal expression in general or specific policies of separateness or segregation. These policies tend to freeze the social status of the insecure. The threat of violence may be implemented not only by constituted authority but also by anyone acting in behalf of the established order. Every member of the controllers' group is in a sense a special deputy, authorized by the mores to enforce the pattern. This fact tends to create fear, which works on behalf of the proscriptions and guarantees them. The anticipation of possible violence makes it very difficult for any escape from the pattern to be effective.

It is important to analyze the functioning of segregation that we may better understand the nature of the fear it engenders. It is obvious that segregation can be established only between two groups that are unequal in power and control. Two groups that are relatively equal in power in a society may enter into a voluntary arrangement of separateness. Segregation can apply only to a relationship involving the weak and the strong. For it means that limitations are arbitrarily set up, which, in the course of time, tend to become fixed and to seem normal in governing the etiquette between the two groups. A peculiar characteristic of segregation is the ability of the stronger to shuttle back and forth between the prescribed areas with complete immunity and a kind of mutually tacit sanction; while the position of the weaker, on the other hand, is quite definitely fixed and frozen.

A very simple illustration is the operation of Jim Crow travel in trains in the southern part of the United States. On such a train the porter, when he is not in line of duty, may ride only in the Jim Crow coach—for the train porter is a Negro. But the members of the train crew who are not Negroes—the conductor, brakeman, baggageman—when they are not working, may ride either in the Jim Crow section or in any other section of the train. In the town in Florida in which I grew up as a boy it was a common occurrence for white persons to attend our church services and share in the worship. But it was quite impossible for any of us to do the same in the white churches of the community. All over the world, wherever ghettos are found, the same basic elements appear—a fact which dramatizes the position of weakness and gives the widest possible range to the policing effect of fear generated by the threat of violence.

Given segregation as a factor determining relations, the resources of the environment are made into instruments to enforce the artificial position. Most of the accepted social behavior-patterns assume segregation to be normal—if normal, then correct; if correct, then moral; if moral, then religious. Religion is thus made a defender and guarantor of the presumptions. God, for all practical purposes, is imaged as an elderly, benign white man, seated on a white throne, with bright, white light emanating from his countenance. Angels are blonds and brunets suspended in the air around his throne to be his messengers and execute his purposes. Satan is viewed as being red with the glow of fire. But the imps, the messengers of the devil, are black. The phrase "black as an imp" is a stereotype.

The implications of such a view are simply fantastic in the intensity of their tragedy. Doomed on earth to a fixed and unremitting status of inferiority, of which segregation is symbolic, and at the same time cut off from the hope that the Creator intended it otherwise, those who are thus victimized are stripped of all social protection. It is vicious and thoroughly despicable to rationalize this position, the product of a fear that is as sordid as it is unscrupulous, into acceptance. Under such circumstances there is but a step from being despised to despising oneself.

The fear that segregation inspires among the weak in turn breeds fear among the strong and the dominant. This fear insulates the conscience against a sense of wrongdoing in carrying out a policy of segregation. For it counsels that if there were no segregation, there would be no protection against invasion of the home, the church, the school. This fear perpetuates the Jewish ghettos in Western civilization, the restrictive covenants in California and other states, the Chinatowns, the Little Tokyos, and the Street of the Untouchables in Hindu lands.*

The Jewish community has long been acquainted with segregation and the persecution growing out of it. Jews have been all the more easily trapped by it because of the deep historical conviction that they are a chosen people. This conviction and its underscoring in the unique ethical insights of the prophets have tended to make all those who were not a part of Israel feel in some sense as if they

---

*Untouchability was outlawed by the Indian state. A Hindu government did what years of British rule failed to do. Perhaps this is as it should be.

were spiritual outcasts. The conscious and unconscious reaction inspired by this sense of being on the outside is a fertile seedbed for anti-Semitism. Anti-Semitism is a confession of a deep sense of inferiority and moral insecurity. It is the fear of the socially or politically strong in the presence of the threat of moral judgment implicit in the role of the Jewish community throughout human history. Jesus was intimately acquainted with this problem from the inside. Jesus knew all of this.

> His days were nurtured in great hostilities
> Focused upon his kind, the sons of Israel.
> There was no moment in all his years
> When he was free.*

It is instructive to inquire into the effects of fear on the disadvantaged. Fear becomes acute, in the form of panic or rage, only at the moment when what has been threat becomes actual violence; but the mere anticipation of such an encounter is overwhelming simply because the odds are basically uneven. This fact is important to hold in mind. The disadvantaged man knows that in any conflict he must deal not only with the particular individual involved but also with the entire group, then or later. Even recourse to the arbitration of law tends to be avoided because of the fear that the interpretations of law will be biased on the side of the dominant group. The result is the dodging of all encounters. The effect is nothing short of disaster in the organism; for, studies show, fear actually causes chemical changes in the body, affecting the bloodstream and the muscular reactions, preparing the body either for fight or for flight. If flight is resorted to, it merely serves as an incentive to one's opponent to track down and overpower. Furthermore, not to fight back at the moment of descending violence is to be a coward, and to be deeply and profoundly humiliated in one's own estimation and in that of one's friends and family. If he is a man, he stands in the presence of his woman as not a man. While it may be true that many have not had such experiences, yet each stands in candidacy for such an experience.

It is clear, then, that this fear, which served originally as a safety device, a kind of protective mechanism for the weak, finally be-

---

*From my privately published volume of poems *The Greatest of These*, p. 3.

comes death for the self. The power that saves turns executioner. Within the walls of separateness death keeps watch. There are some who defer this death by yielding all claim to personal significance beyond the little world in which they live. In the absence of all hope ambition dies, and the very self is weakened, corroded. There remains only the elemental will to live and to accept life on the terms that are available. There is a profound measure of resourcefulness in all life, a resourcefulness that is guaranteed by the underlying aliveness of life itself.

The crucial question, then, is this: Is there any help to be found in the religion of Jesus that can be of value here? It is utterly beside the point to examine here what the religion of Jesus suggests to those who would be helpful to the disinherited. That is ever in the nature of special pleading. No man wants to be the object of his fellow's pity. Obviously, if the strong put forth a great redemptive effort to change the social, political, and economic arrangements in which they seem to find their basic security, the whole picture would be altered. But this is apart from my thesis. Again the crucial question: Is there any help to be found for the disinherited in the religion of Jesus?

Did Jesus deal with this kind of fear? If so, how did he do it? It is not merely, What did he say? even though his words are the important clues available to us.

An analysis of the teaching of Jesus reveals that there is much that deals with the problems created by fear. After his temptation in the wilderness Jesus appeared in the synagogue and was asked to read the lesson. He chose to read from the prophet Isaiah the words which he declared as his fulfillment:

> The Spirit of the Lord is upon me,
> because he hath anointed me . . .
> to preach deliverance to the captives,
> and recovering of sight to the blind,
> to set at liberty them that are bruised,
> to preach the acceptable year of the Lord.

And he closed the book. . . . And he began to say unto them, This day is this Scripture fulfilled in your ears.

In the Song of Mary we find words which anticipate the same declaration of Jesus:

He hath scattered the proud in the imagination of their hearts.
He hath put down the mighty from their seats,
and exalted them of low degree.
He hath filled the hungry with good things;
and the rich he hath sent empty away.

The most specific statement which Jesus makes dealing with the crux of the problem is found in the tenth chapter of Matthew:

Fear them not therefore: for there is nothing covered, that shall not be revealed; and hid, that shall not be known. . . . And fear not them which kill the body, but are not able to kill the soul: but rather fear him which is able to destroy both soul and body in hell. Are not two sparrows sold for a farthing? and one of them shall not fall on the ground without your Father. But the very hairs of your head are all numbered. Fear ye not therefore, ye are of more value than many sparrows.

Again in Luke:

Fear not, little flock; for it is your Father's good pleasure to give you the kingdom.

In the great expression of affirmation and faith found in the Sermon on the Mount there appears in clearest outline the basis of his positive answer to the awful fact of fear and its twin sons of thunder—anxiety and despair:

Therefore I say unto you, Take no thought for your life, what ye shall eat, or what ye shall drink; nor yet for your body, what ye shall put on. Is not the life more than meat, and the body than raiment? Behold the fowls of the air: for they sow not, neither do they reap, nor gather into barns; yet your heavenly Father feedeth them. Are ye not much better than they? Which of you by taking thought can add one cubit unto his stature? And why take ye thought for raiment? Consider the lilies of the field, how they grow; they toil not, neither do they spin: And yet I say unto you, That even Solomon in all his glory was not arrayed like one of these. Wherefore, if God so clothe the grass of the field, which to day is, and to morrow is cast into the oven, shall he not much more clothe you, O ye of little faith? Therefore take no thought, saying, What shall we eat? or, What shall we drink? or, Wherewithal shall we be clothed? (For after all these things do the Gentiles seek:) for your heavenly Father knoweth that ye have need of all these things. But seek ye first the kingdom of God, and his righteousness; and all these things shall be added unto you. Take therefore no thought for the morrow: for the morrow shall take thought for the things of itself. Sufficient unto the day is the evil thereof.

The core of the analysis of Jesus is that man is a child of God, the God of life that sustains all of nature and guarantees all the intricacies of the life-process itself. Jesus suggests that it is quite unreasonable to assume that God, whose creative activity is expressed even in such details as the hairs of a man's head, would exclude from his concern the life, the vital spirit, of the man himself. This idea—that God is mindful of the individual—is of tremendous import in dealing with fear as a disease. In this world the socially disadvantaged man is constantly given a negative answer to the most important personal questions upon which mental health depends: "Who am I? What am I?"

The first question has to do with a basic self-estimate, a profound sense of belonging, of counting. If a man feels that he does not belong in the way in which it is perfectly normal for other people to belong, then he develops a deep sense of insecurity. When this happens to a person, it provides the basic material for what the psychologist calls an inferiority complex. It is quite possible for a man to have no sense of personal inferiority as such, but at the same time to be dogged by a sense of social inferiority. The awareness of being a child of God tends to stabilize the ego and results in a new courage, fearlessness, and power. I have seen it happen again and again.

When I was a youngster, this was drilled into me by my grandmother. The idea was given to her by a certain slave minister who, on occasion, held secret religious meetings with his fellow slaves. How everything in me quivered with the pulsing tremor of raw energy when, in her recital, she would come to the triumphant climax of the minister: "You—you are not niggers. You—you are not slaves. You are God's children." This established for them the ground of personal dignity, so that a profound sense of personal worth could absorb the fear reaction. This alone is not enough, but without it, nothing else is of value. The first task is to get the self immunized against the most radical results of the *threat* of violence. When this is accomplished, relaxation takes the place of the churning fear. The individual now feels that he counts, that he belongs. He senses the confirmation of his roots, and even death becomes a little thing.

All leaders of men have recognized the significance of this need for a sense of belonging among those who feel themselves disadvantaged. Several years ago I was talking with a young German woman who had escaped from the Nazis; first to Holland, then France, England, and finally to America. She described for me the powerful magnet that Hitler was to German youth. The youth had lost their sense of belonging. They did not count; there was no center of hope for their marginal egos. According to my friend, Hitler told them: "No one loves you—I love you; no one will give you work—I will give you work; no one wants you—I want you." And when they saw the sunlight in his eyes, they dropped their tools and followed him. He stabilized the ego of the German youth, and put it within their power to overcome their sense of inferiority. It is true that in the hands of a man like Hitler, power is exploited and turned to ends which make for havoc and misery; but this should not cause us to ignore the basic soundness of the theory upon which he operated.

A man's conviction that he is God's child automatically tends to shift the basis of his relationship with all his fellows. He recognizes at once that to fear a man, whatever may be that man's power over him, is a basic denial of the integrity of his very life. It lifts that mere man to a place of preeminence that belongs to God and to God alone. He who fears is literally delivered to destruction. To the child of God, a scale of values becomes available by which men are measured and their true significance determined. Even the threat of violence, with the possibility of death that it carries, is recognized for what it is—merely the threat of violence with a death potential. Such a man recognizes that death cannot possibly be the worst thing in the world. There *are* some things that are worse than death. To deny one's own integrity of personality in the presence of the human challenge is one of those things. "Be not afraid of them that kill the body, and after that have no more that they can do," says Jesus.

One of the practical results following this new orientation is the ability to make an objective, detached appraisal of other people, particularly one's antagonists. Such an appraisal protects one from inaccurate and exaggerated estimations of another person's significance. In a conversation with me Lincoln Steffens once said that he was sure he could rear a child who was a member of a minority group or who was a habitué of a ghetto so as to immunize him against the corroding effects of such limitations.

He said: "I would teach him that he must never call another man 'great'; but that he must always qualify the term with the limiting phrase 'as to,' of the Greek language. A man is never great in general, but he may be great as to something in particular.

"Let me give you an illustration. Once I was the house guest in Berlin of one of the world's greatest scientists. During the first few days of my sojourn, I was completely disorganized. I was nervous, tended to be inarticulate, generally confused, and ill at ease. I had either to get a hold on myself or bring my visit abruptly to an end. One morning while shaving it occurred to me that despite my profound limitations of knowledge in physics and mathematics, I knew infinitely more about politics than did my host. At breakfast I found my tongue and my dignity, and the basis of equality between us was at once restored. My host was a great man *as to* his particular field of natural science, while I was competent in the field of contemporary politics and affairs. This awareness gave me my perspective."

The illustration anticipates the second basic question that must be answered by the disinherited: "What am I?" This question has to do, not with a sense of innate belonging, but rather with personal achievement and ability. All of the inner conflicts and frustrations growing out of limitations of opportunity become dramatically focused here. Even though a man is convinced of his infinite worth as a child of God, this may not in itself give him the opportunity for self-realization and fulfillment that his spirit demands. Even though he may no longer feel himself threatened by violence, the fact remains that for him doors often are closed. There are vocational opportunities that are denied him. It is obvious that the individual must reckon with the external facts of his environment, especially those that constrict his freedom.

There is something more to be said about the inner equipment growing out of the great affirmation of Jesus that a man is a *child* of God. If a man's ego has been stabilized, resulting in a sure grounding of his sense of personal worth and dignity, then he is in a position to appraise his own intrinsic powers, gifts, talents, and abilities. He no longer views his equipment through the darkened lenses of those who are largely responsible for his social predicament. He can think of himself with some measure of detachment from the shackles of his immediate world. If he equips himself in terms of training in this mood, his real ability is brought into play. The fact that he is denied opportunity will not necessarily deter him. He will postpone defeat until defeat itself closes in upon him. The interesting fact is that defeat may not close in upon him. Curious indeed is the notion that plays hide-and-seek with human life: "I may be an exception." A large measure of illusion and self-deception is implicit in this notion, but again and again it has come to the rescue of desperate people forced to take desperate chances.

The psychological effect on the individual of the conviction that he is a child of God gives a note of integrity to whatever he does. It provides character in the sense of sure knowledge and effective performance. After all, this is what we mean by character when applied to ability in action. When a man is sick and calls a doctor, what he wants most to know about the doctor is not the make of his automobile, or whether he obeys traffic signals, or what church he attends, or how many children he has, or if he is married. What is most crucial about the doctor, so far as the sick man is concerned, is, Can he practice medicine?

Now, what we are discussing has profound bearing upon the kind of assurance and guidance that should be given to children who seem destined to develop a sense of defeat and frustration. The doom of the children is the greatest tragedy of the disinherited. They are robbed of much of the careless rapture and spontaneous joy of merely being alive. Through their environment they are plunged into the midst of overwhelming pressures for which there can be no possible preparation. So many tender, joyous things in them are nipped and killed without their even knowing the true nature of their loss. The normal for them is the abnormal. Youth is a time of soaring hopes, when dreams are given first wings and, as reconnoitering birds, explore unknown landscapes. Again and again a man full of years is merely the corroboration of the dreams of his youth. The sense of fancy growing out of the sense of fact—which makes all healthy personalities and gives a touch of romance and glory to all of life— first appears as the unrestrained imaginings of youth.

But the child of the disinherited is likely to live a heavy life. A ceiling is placed on his dreaming by the counsel of despair coming from his elders, whom experience has taught to expect little and to hope for less. If, on the other hand, the elders understand in their own experiences and lives the tremendous insight of Jesus, it is possible for them to share their enthusiasm with their children. This is the qualitative overtone springing from the depths of religious insight, and it is contagious. It will put into the hands of the child the key for unlocking the door of his hopes. It must never be forgotten that human beings can be conditioned in favor of the positive as well as the negative. A great and central assurance will cause parents to condition their children to high endeavor and great aspiring, and these in turn will put the child out of the immediate, clawing reaches of the tense or the sustained negations of his environment. I have seen it happen. In communities that were completely barren, with no apparent growing edge, without any point to provide light for the disadvantaged, I have seen children grow up without fear, with quiet dignity and such high purpose that the mark which they set for themselves has even been transcended.

The charge that such thinking is merely rationalizing cannot be made with easy or accepted grace by the man of basic advantage. It ill behooves the man who is not forced to live in a ghetto to tell those who must how to transcend its limitations. The awareness that a man is a child of the God of religion, who is at one and the same time the God of life, creates a profound faith in life that nothing can destroy.

Nothing less than a great daring in the face of overwhelming odds can achieve the inner security in which fear cannot possibly survive. It is true that a man cannot be serene unless he possesses something about which to be serene. Here we reach the high-water mark of prophetic religion, and it is of the essence of the religion of Jesus of Nazareth. Of course God cares for the grass of the field, which lives a day and is no more, or the sparrow that falls unnoticed by the wayside. He also holds the stars in their appointed places, leaves his mark in every living thing. And he cares for me! To be assured of this becomes the answer to the threat of violence—yea, to violence itself. To the degree to which a man knows *this,* he is unconquerable from within and without.

Deception

Deception is perhaps the oldest of all the techniques by which the weak have protected themselves against the strong. Through the ages, at all stages of sentient activity, the weak have survived by fooling the strong.

The techniques of deception seem to be a part of the nervous-reflex action of the organism. The cuttlefish, when attacked, will release some of the fluid from his sepia bag, making the water all around him murky; in the midst of the cloudy water he confuses his attacker and makes his escape. Almost any hunter of birds has seen the mother simulate a broken wing so as to attract attention to herself and thereby save the life of her young. As a boy I have seen the shadow of the hawk on the grassy meadow where I lay resting underneath a shade tree. Consider the behavior of the birds a few feet away as they see the shadow. I have seen them take little feet full of dried grass or leaves, turn an easy half somersault, and play dead. The hawk blinks his eyes, thinks he has had an optical illusion, and goes on to find birds that do not know enough to pretend to be dead. We often played a game of hide-and-seek in which the refrain was, "Lay low, slick duck, the hawk's around." Natural selection has finally resulted in giving to various animals neutral colors or blending colors so that they fade into the landscape and thus protect themselves from destruction by deceiving the enemy.

All little children well know this technique. They know that they cannot cope with the parental will on equal terms. Therefore, in order to carry on their own purposes, they work all kinds of simple—and not so simple—schemes for making the parents do the children's will as if it were their own. Until the teacher catches on, it is a favorite device of students. When a particular lesson has not been studied, or there is danger that the teacher will cover territory that extends beyond the day's preparation, some apparently innocent question is asked about the teacher's prejudice, pet interest, or particular concern. Once the teacher is discussing that particular point, there is nothing more to fear; for before he comes to the end of his talk, the bell will ring and all will be saved.

It is an ancient device that a man-dominated social order has forced upon women, even down to latest times. Olive Schreiner spent much of her energy attacking this form of deception by which the moral life of women was bound. Much of the constant agitation for an equal-rights amendment to the Constitution grows out of recognition of the morally degrading aspects of deception and dishonesty that enter into the relationship between men and women.

When the children of Israel were in captivity in Babylon, the prophet Ezekiel could not give words of comfort and guidance by direct and overt statement. If he had, he would not have lasted very long, and the result would have been a great loss to his people and a tightening of the bonds that held them. He would have been executed as a revolutionary in short order and all religious freedom would have been curtailed. What did the prophet do? He resorted to a form of deception. He put words in the mouth of an old king of Tyre that did not come from him at all, but from Nebuchadrezzar. It was Nebuchadrezzar who had said, "I am a God." He used what we would call now "double talk." But the Jews understood, even though the Babylonian "secret service" was helpess because he was not openly talking against the state.

In a certain southern city a blind Negro had been killed by a policeman. Feeling ran very high. The Negroes were not permitted to have any kind of eulogy or sermon at the funeral service. There was fear of rioting. Nevertheless, the funeral was held, with policemen very much in evidence. There was no sermon, but there was a central prayer. In the prayer the minister told God all that he would have said to the people had he not been under very rigid surveillance. The officers could do nothing, for the minister was not addressing the people; he was talking to his God. How tragically sordid! But it is the old, old method by which the weak have survived through the years.

One of the oldest of the Negro spirituals deals quite interestingly with this technique. The setting is very dramatic.

The slave had often heard his master's minister talk about heaven, the final abode of the righteous. Naturally the master regarded himself as fitting into the category. On the other hand, the slave knew that he too was going to heaven. He reasoned, "There must be two heavens—no, this cannot be true, because there is only one God. God cannot possibly be divided in this way. I have it! I am having my hell now. When I die, I shall have my heaven. The master's having his heaven now. When he dies, he will have his hell." The next day, chopping cotton beneath the torrid skies, the slave said to his mate:

> I got shoes,
> You got shoes,
> All God's children got shoes.
> When we get to heaven
> We're goin' to put on our shoes
> An' shout all over God's heaven,
> Heaven! Heaven!

Then, looking up to the big house where the master lived, he said:

> Everybody talkin' 'bout heaven
> Ain't goin' there!

Instances could be multiplied from all over the world, and from as far back in human history as records have been kept. It is an old, old defense of the weak against the strong. The question of deception is not academic, but profoundly ethical and spiritual, going to the very heart of all human relations. For it raises the issue of honesty, integrity, and the consequences thereof over against duplicity and deception and the attendant consequences. Does the fact that a particular course of action jeopardizes a man's life relieve him of the necessity for following that course of action? Are there circumstances under which the ethical question is irrelevant, beside the point? If so, where does one draw the line? Is there a fine distinction between literal honesty and honesty in spirit and intent? Or is truthtelling largely a matter of timing? Are there times when to tell the truth is to be false to the truth that is in you? These questions and many related ones will not be downed. For the disinherited they have to do with the very heart of survival.

It may be argued that a man who places so high a price upon physical existence and survival that he is willing to perjure his own soul has a false, or at least an inadequate, sense of values. "What shall a man give in exchange for his own soul?" Jesus asks. The physical existence of a man makes of him the custodian, the keeper, of the fragment of life which is his. He lives constantly under the necessity to have life fulfill itself. Should he take chances, even in behalf of the values of a kind other than those which have to do with his physical survival? With reference to the question of deception the disinherited are faced with three basic alternatives.

The first alternative is to accept the apparent fact that, one's situation being what it is, there is no sensible choice offered. The individual is disadvantaged because he is not a member of the "party in power," the dominant, controlling group. His word has no value anyway. In any contest he is defeated before he starts. He cannot meet his opponent on equal terms, because there is no basis of equality that exists between the weak and the strong. The only thing that counts is victory—or any level on which victory can be achieved. There can be no question of honesty in dealing with each other, for there is no sense of community. Such a mood takes for granted a facile insincerity.

The fact is, in any great struggle between groups in which the major control of the situation is on one side, the ethical question tends to become merely academic. The advantaged group assumes that they are going to be fooled, if it is possible; there is no expectation of honesty and sincerity. They know that every conceivable device will be used to render ineffective the advantage which they have inherited in their position as the strong. The pattern of deception by which the weak are deprived of their civic, economic, political, and social rights without its appearing that they are so deprived is a matter of continuous and tragic amazement. The pattern of deception by which the weak circumvent the strong and manage to secure some of their political, economic, and social rights is a matter of continuous degradation. A vast conspiracy of silence covers all these maneuvers as the groups come into contact with each other, and the question of morality is not permitted to invade it.

The tragic consequences of the alternative that there is *no* alternative are not far to seek. In the first place, it tends to destroy whatever sense of ethical values the individual possesses. It is a simple fact of psychology that if a man calls a lie the truth, he tampers dangerously with his value judgments. Jesus called attention to that fact in one of his most revealing utterances. His mother, in an attempt to excuse him from the harsh judgment of his enemies, said that he was a little out of his mind—not terribly crazy, but just a little off-balance. Those who did not like him said that he was all right with regard to his mind, but that he was full of the devil, and that it was by the power of the devil that he was casting out devils. Jesus, hearing the discussion, said that these men did not talk good sense: "A house . . . divided against itself . . . cannot stand." He suggested that if they continued saying that he was casting out devils by the power of the devil—and they knew that such was not the case—they would commit the unpardonable sin. That is to say, if a man continues to call a good thing bad, he will eventually lose his sense of moral distinctions.

Is this always the result? Is it not possible to quarantine a certain kind of deception so that it will not affect the rest of one's life? May not the underprivileged do with deception as it relates to his soul what the human body does with tubercle bacilli? The body seems unable to destroy the bacilli, so nature builds a prison for them, walls them in with a thick fibrosis so that their toxin cannot escape from the lungs into the bloodstream. As long as the victim exercises care in the matter of rest, work, and diet, normal activities may be pursued without harm. Is deception a comparable technique of survival, the fibrosis that protects the life from poison in its total outlook or in its other relations? Or, to change the figure, may not deception be regarded under some circumstances as a kind of blind spot that is functional in a limited area of experience? No! Such questions are merely attempts to rationalize one's way out of a critical difficulty.

The penalty of deception is to *become* a deception, with all sense of moral discrimination vitiated. A man who lies habitually becomes a lie, and it is increasingly impossible for him to know when he is lying and when he is not. In other words, the moral mercury of life is reduced to zero. Shakespeare has immortalized this aspect of character in his drama of Macbeth. Macbeth has a high sense of destiny, which is deeply underscored by the testimony of the witches. This is communicated to his wife, who takes it to head and to heart. By a series of liquidations their friends disappear and their enemies multiply, until Macbeth is king and his wife is queen. Together they swim across Scotland in seas of blood, tying laurels on their brows with other people's lives, heartstrings, and hopes. Then fatal things begin happening to them. Lady Macbeth walks in her sleep, trying in vain to wash blood from her hands. But the blood is not on her hands; it is on her soul. Macbeth becomes a victim of terrible visions and he cries:

> Methought I heard a voice cry "Sleep no more!
> Macbeth does murder sleep!" The innocent sleep.

One day, at the most crucial point in Macbeth's life, an attendant announces to him that Lady Macbeth is dead. His reply reveals, in one agonizing flash, the death of values that has taken place in him:

> She should have died hereafter;
> There would have been a time for such a word.
> To-morrow, and to-morrow, and to-morrow,
> Creeps in this petty pace from day to day
> To the last syllable of recorded time,
> And all of our yesterdays have lighted fools
> The way to dusty death. Out, out, brief candle!
> Life's but a walking shadow, a poor player
> That struts and frets his hour upon the stage
> And then is heard no more: it is a tale
> Told by an idiot, full of sound and fury,
> Signifying nothing.

Life is only a tale told by a fool, having no meaning because deception has wiped out all moral distinctions.

The second alternative is a possible derivation from the first one. The underprivileged may decide to juggle the various areas of compromise, on the assumption that the moral quality of compromise operates in an ascending-descending scale. According to this argument, not all issues are equal in significance nor in consequence; it may be that some compromises take on the aspect of inevitability because of circumstances over which the individual has no control. It is true that we are often bound by a network of social relations that operate upon us without being particularly affected by us. We are all affected by forces, social and natural, that in some measure determine our behavior without our being able to bring to bear upon them our private will, however great or righteous it may be.

All over the world there are millions of people who are condemned by the powerful in their society to live in ghettos. The choice seems to be the ghetto or suicide. But such a conclusion may be hasty and ill-advised; it may be the counsel of the kind of fear we discussed previously, or it may be the decision of cowardice. For all practical purposes there are great numbers of people who have decided to *live*, and to compromise on the matter of place and conditions. Further, we may say that those who have power know that the decision will be to live, and have counted on it. They are prepared to deal ruthlessly with any form of effective protest, because effective protest upsets the status quo. Life, then, becomes a grim game of wits, and the stakes are one's physical existence.

The term "compromise" then takes on a very special and highly differentiated meaning. It is less positive than ordinary deception, which may be regarded as deliberate strategy. If the assumption is that survival with some measure of freedom is at stake, then compromise is defined in terms of the actions which involve one's life continuation. It is a matter of behavior patterns. Many obvious interferences with freedom are ignored completely. Many insults are cast aside as of no consequence. One does battle only when not to do battle is to be vanquished without the recognition that comes from doing battle. To the morally sensitive person the whole business is sordid and degrading.

It is safe to say that the common attitude taken toward these deceptions that have to do with survival is that they are amoral. The moral question is never raised. To raise such a question is regarded as sheer stupidity. The behavior involved is in the same category as seeking and getting food or providing shelter for oneself. It belongs in the general classification of simple survival behavior. Obviously this is the reason why it is so difficult to make a moral appeal, either to the dominant group or to the disinherited, in order to bring about a change in the basic relations between them. For better or for worse, according to this aspect of our analysis, there is no point at which mere moral appeal makes sense. Whatever moral sensitiveness to the situation was present at some stage in the life of the individual has long since been atrophied, due to betrayal, suffering, or frustration.

The alternative, then, must be discussed from the point of view of the observer rather than from that of the victim. The rank and file of the oppressed do not formally raise the questions involved in their behavior. Specifically, the applicability of religion is restricted to those areas in which religious considerations commend themselves as being reasonable. A profound piece of surgery has to take place in the very psyche of the disinherited before the great claim of the religion of Jesus can be presented. The great stretches of barren places in the soul must be revitalized, brought to life, before they can be challenged. Tremendous skill and power must be exercised to show to the disinherited the awful results of the role of negative deception into which their lives have been cast. How to do this is perhaps the greatest challenge that the religion of Jesus faces in modern life.

Mere preaching is not enough. What are words, however sacred and powerful, in the presence of the grim facts of the daily struggle to survive? Any attempt to deal with this situation on a basis of values that disregard the struggle for survival appears to be in itself a compromise with life. It is only when people live in an environment in which they are not required to exert supreme effort into just keeping alive that they seem to be able to select ends besides those of mere physical survival. On the subsistence level, values are interpreted in terms of their bearing upon the one major concern of all activity—not being killed. This is really the form that the dilemma takes. It is not solely a question of keeping the body alive; it is rather how not to be killed. *Not to be killed* becomes the great end, and morality takes its meaning from that center. Until that center is shifted, nothing real can be accomplished. It is the uncanny and perhaps unwitting recognition of this fact that causes those in power to keep the disinherited from participation in meaningful social process. For if the disinherited get such a new center as patriotism, for instance—liberty within the framework of a sense of country or nation—then the aim of *not being killed* is swallowed up by a larger and more transcendent goal. Above all else the disinherited must not have any stake in the social order; they must be made to feel that they are alien, that it is a great boon to be allowed to remain alive, not be exterminated. This was the psychology of the Nazis; it grew out of their theory of the state and the place given the Hebrew people in their ideology. Such is also the attitude of the Ku Klux Klan toward Negroes.

Even within the disinherited group itself artificial and exaggerated emphasis upon not being killed tends to cheapen life. That is to say, the fact that the lives of the disinherited are lightly held by the dominant group tends to create the same attitude among them toward each other.

We come now to the third alternative—a complete and devastating sincerity. I have in my possession a copy of a letter from Mahatma Gandhi to Muriel Lester. The letter says in part: "Speak the truth, without fear and without exception, and see everyone whose work is related to your purpose. You are in God's work, so you need not fear man's scorn. If they listen to your requests and grant them, you will be satisfied. If they reject them, then you must make their rejection your strength." The acceptance of this alternative is to be simply, directly truthful, whatever may be the cost in life, limb, or security. For the individual who accepts this, there may be quick and speedy judgment with attendant loss. But if the number increases and the movement spreads, the vindication of the truth would follow in the wake. There must always be the confidence that the effect of truthfulness can be realized in the mind of the oppressor as well as the oppressed. There is no substitute for such a faith.

Emphasis upon an unwavering sincerity points up at once the major challenge of Jesus to the disinherited and the power of his most revolutionary appeal. "Let your communication be, Yea, yea; Nay, nay: for whatsoever is more than these cometh of evil." "Ye have heard that it hath been said, An eye for an eye, . . . but I say unto you, That ye resist not evil." What does he mean? Does he mean that factors having to do with physical survival are trivial or of no consequence? Is this emphasis merely the counsel of suicide? It seems inescapable that either Jesus was infinitely more realistic than we dare imagine or, taking his words at their face value, he is talking as one who has no understanding of the basic facts of life that touch this central problem. From our analysis of the life of Jesus it seems clear that it was from within the framework of great social pressures upon him and his group that he taught and lived to the very end. It is reasonable to assume, then, that he speaks out of understanding and that his words cannot be lightly disregarded, however devastating they may seem.

It may be argued that the insistence upon complete sincerity has to do only with man's relation to God, not with man's relation to man. To what does such a position lead? Unwavering sincerity says that man should always recognize the fact that he lives always in the presence of God, always under the divine scrutiny, and that there is no really significant living for a man, whatever may be his status, until he has turned and faced the divine scrutiny. Here all men stand stripped to the literal substance of themselves, without disguise, without pretension, without *seeming* whatsoever. No man can fool God. From him nothing is hidden.

> Thou compassest my path and my lying down,
> and art acquainted with all my ways.
> For there is not a word in my tongue,
> but, lo, O Lord, thou knowest it altogether. . . .
> Whither shall I go from thy spirit?
> or whither shall I flee from thy presence?
> If I ascend up into heaven, thou art there:
> if I make my bed in hell, behold, thou art there. . . .
> If I say, Surely the darkness shall cover me;
> even the night shall be light about me.
> Yea, the darkness hideth not from thee;
> but the night shineth as the day:
> the darkness and the light are both alike to thee.

Was it against the background of his heritage and his religious faith in the 139th Psalm that Jesus assumed his great ethical imperative? This seems to be conclusively brought out in his treatment of the climax of human history. The Judge is on his throne; the sheep are on the right, the goats on the left. The Judge speaks: "I was an hungred, and ye gave me no meat: . . . sick, and in prison, and ye visited me not." The climax of human history is interpreted as a time when the inner significance of men's deeds would be revealed to them. But here a new note is introduced. Sincerity in human relations is equal to, and the same as, sincerity to God. If we accept this explanation as a clue to Jesus' meaning, we come upon the stark fact that the insistence of Jesus upon genuineness is absolute; man's relation to man and man's relation to God are one relation.

A death blow is struck to hypocrisy. One of the major defense mechanisms of the disinherited is taken away from them. What does Jesus give them in its place? What does he substitute for hypocrisy? Sincerity. But is sincerity a mechanism of defense against the strong? The answer is No. Something more significant takes place. In the presence of an overwhelming sincerity on the part of the disinherited, the dominant themselves are caught with no defense, with the edge taken away from the sense of prerogative and from the status upon which the impregnability of their position rests. They are thrown back upon themselves for their rating. The experience of power has no meaning aside from the other-than-self reference which sustains it. If the position of ascendancy is not acknowledged tacitly and actively by those over whom the ascendancy is exercised, then it falls flat. Hypocrisy on the part of the disinherited in dealing with the dominant group is a tribute yielded by those who are weak. But if this attitude is lacking, or is supplanted by a simple sincerity and genuineness, then it follows that advantage due to the accident of birth or position is reduced to zero. Instead of relation between the weak and the strong there is merely a relationship between human beings. A man is a man, no more, no less. The awareness of this fact marks the supreme moment of human dignity.

Hate

Hate is another of the hounds of hell that dog the footsteps of the disinherited in season and out of season. During times of war hatred becomes quite respectable, even though it has to masquerade often under the guise of patriotism. To even the casual observer during the last war it was obvious that the Pearl Harbor attack by the Japanese gave many persons in our country an apparent justification for indulging all of their anticolored feelings. In a Chicago cab, en route to the University from Englewood, this fact was dramatized for me. The cab had stopped for a red light. Apropos of no conversation the driver turned to me, saying, "Who do they think they are? Those little yellow dogs think they can do that to white men and get away with it!"

During the early days of the war I noticed a definite rise in rudeness and over expressions of color prejudice, especially in trains and other public conveyances. It was very simple; hatred could be brought out into the open, given a formal dignity and a place of respectability. But for the most part we are not vocal about our hatred. Hating is something of which to be ashamed unless it provides for us a form of validation and prestige. If either is provided, then the immoral or amoral character of the hatred is transformed into positive violence.

Christianity has been almost sentimental in its effort to deal with hatred in human life. It has sought to get rid of hatred by preachments, by moralizing, by platitudinous judgments. It has hesitated to analyze the basis of hatred and to evaluate it in terms of its possible significance in the lives of the people possessed by it. This reluctance to examine hatred has taken on the character of a superstition. It is a subject that is taboo unless there is some extraordinary social crisis—such as war—involving the mobilization of all the national resources of the common life to meet it. There is a conspiracy of silence about hatred, its function and its meaning.

Hatred cannot be defined. It can only be described. If I were to project a simple diagram of hatred, revealing the anatomy of its development, the idea would break down as follows.

In the first place, hatred often begins in a situation in which there is contact without fellowship, contact that is devoid of any of the primary overtures of warmth and fellow-feeling and genuineness. Of course, it must be borne in mind that there can be an abundance of sentimentality masquerading under the cloak of fellowship. It is easy to have fellowship on your own terms and to repudiate it if your terms are not acceptable. It is this kind of fellowship that one finds often in the South between whites and Negroes. As long as the Negro is called John or Mary and accepts the profoundly humiliating position of an inferior status, fellowship is quite possible. Great sacrifices are even made for him, and all the weight of position and power are at the disposal of the weaker person. It is precisely because of this false basis of fellowship so often found that in the section of the country where there is the greatest contact between Negro and white there is the least real fellowship, and the first step along the road of bitterness and hatred is assured.

When we give to the concept a wider application, it is clear that much of modern life is so impersonal that there is always opportunity for the seeds of hatred to grow unmolested. Where there are contacts devoid of genuine fellowship, such contacts stand in immediate candidacy for hatred.

In the second place, contacts without fellowship tend to express themselves in the kind of understanding that is strikingly unsympathetic. There is understanding of a kind, but it is without the healing and reinforcement of personality. Rather, it is like the experience of going into a man's office and, in that moment before being seated, when the full gaze of the other is focused upon you, suddenly wondering whether the top button of your vest is in place, but not daring to look. In a penetrating, incisive, cold understanding there is no cushion to absorb limitations or to provide extenuating circumstances for protection.

It is a grievous blunder to assume that understanding is always sympathetic. Very often we use the phrase "I understand" to mean something kindly, warm, and gracious. But there is an understanding that is hard, cold, minute, and deadly. It is the kind of understanding that one gives to the enemy, or that is derived from an accurate knowledge of another's power to injure. There is an understanding of another's weakness, which may be used as a weapon of offense or defense. Understanding that is not the outgrowth of an essential fellow-feeling is likely to be unsympathetic. Of course, there may be pity in it—even compassion, sometimes—but sympathy, almost never. I can sympathize only when I see myself in another's place.

In the third place, an unsympathetic understanding tends to express itself in the active functioning of ill will. A few years ago I was going from Chicago to Memphis, Tennessee. I found a seat across from an elderly lady, who took immediate cognizance of my presence. When the conductor came along for the tickets, she said to him, pointing in my direction, "What is *that* doing in this car?"

The conductor answered, with a touch of creative humor, *"That* has a ticket."

For the next fifty miles this lady talked for five or ten or fifteen minutes with each person who was seated alone in that coach, setting forth her philosophy of human relationships and the basis of her objection to my presence in the car. I was able to see the atmosphere in the entire car shift from common indifference to active recognition of and, to some extent, positive resentment of my presence; an ill will spreading its virus by contagion.

In the fourth place, ill will, when dramatized in a human being, becomes hatred walking on the earth. The outline is now complete and simple—contacts without fellowship developing hatred and expressing themselves in unsympathetic understanding; an unsympathetic understanding tending to express itself in the exercise of ill will; and ill will, dramatized in a man or woman, becoming hatred walking on the earth.

In many analyses of hatred it is customary to apply it only to the attitude of the strong towards the weak. The general impression is that many white people hate Negroes and that Negroes are merely the victims. Such an assumption is quite ridiculous. I was once seated in a Jim Crow car which extended across the highway at a railway station in Texas. Two Negro girls of about fourteen or fifteen sat behind me. One of them looked out of the window and said, "Look at those kids." She referred to two little white girls, who were skating towards the train. "Wouldn't it be funny if they fell and spattered their brains all over the pavement!" I looked at them. Through what torture chambers had they come—torture chambers that had so attacked the grounds of humaneness in them that there was nothing capable of calling forth any appreciation of understanding of white persons? There was something that made me shiver.

Hatred, in the mind and spirit of the disinherited, is born out of great bitterness—a bitterness that is made possible by sustained resentment which is bottled up until it distills an essence of vitality, giving to the individual in whom this is happening a radical and fundamental basis for self-realization.

Let me illustrate this. Suppose you are one of five children in a family and it happened, again and again, that if there was just enough for four children in any given circumstance, you were the child who had to do without. If there was money for four pairs of shoes and five pairs were needed, it was you who did without shoes. If there were five pieces of cake on the plate, four healthy slices and one small piece, you were given the small slice. At first, when this happened, you overlooked it, because you thought that your sisters and brothers, each in his turn, would have the same experience; but they did not. Then you complained quietly to the brother who was closest to you in understanding, and he thought that you were being disloyal to your mother and father to say such a thing. In a moment of self-righteousness you spoke to your father about it. Your father put you on the carpet so severely that you decided not to mention it again, but you kept on watching. The discrimination continued.

At night, when the lights were out and you were safely tucked away in bed, you reached down into the quiet places of your little heart and lifted out your bundle of hates and resentments growing out of the family situation, and you fingered them gently, one by one. In the darkness you muttered to yourself, "They can keep me from talking about it to them, but they can't keep me from resenting it. I hate them for what they are doing to me. No one can prevent me there." Hatred becomes for you a source of validation for your personality. As you consider the family and their attitude toward you, hatred gives you a sense of significance which you fling defiantly into the teeth of their estimate of you.

In Herman Melville's *Moby Dick* there is an expression of this attitude. You will doubtless recall the story. Ahab had his leg bitten off in an encounter with the white whale. He collects a motley crew, and they sail into the northern seas to find and conquer the whale. A storm comes up at sea, and Ahab stands on deck with his ivory leg fastened to the floor. He leans against the railing in utter defiance of the storm. His hair is disheveled, his face is furrowed, and there is a fever in his blood that only the conquest of the white whale can cure. In effect, he says to the lightning, "You may destroy this vessel, you may dry up the bowels of the sea, you may consume me; *but I can still be ashes."*

It is this kind of attitude that is developed in the mind and soul of the weak and the disinherited. As they look out upon their world, they recognize at once that they are the victims of a systematic denial of the rights and privileges that are theirs, by virtue both of their being human and of their citizenship. Their acute problem is to deal with the estimate that their environment places upon them; for the environment, through its power-controlling and prestige-bearing representatives, has announced to them that they do not rate anything other than that which is being visited upon them. If they accept this judgment, then the grounds of their self-estimate is destroyed, and their acquiescence becomes an endorsement of the judgment of the environment. Because they are despised, they despise themselves. If they reject the judgment, hatred may serve as a device for rebuilding, step by perilous step, the foundation for individual significance; so that from within the intensity of their necessity they declare their right to exist, despite the judgment of the environment.

I remember that once, when moving from one home to another, I came upon a quiet family of mice in a box in the basement. Their presence created a moral problem for me, for I did not feel that I had the right to take their lives. Then I remembered my responsibility to the family that was moving in, and, with heaviness of heart,

I took my daughter's little broom and descended upon them with a mighty stroke. Sensing the impending tragedy, one of them raised himself on his haunches to meet the stroke of the broom with a squeal of defiance, affirming the core of his mouse integrity in the face of descending destruction. Hatred makes this sort of profound contribution to the life of the disinherited, because it establishes a dimension of self-realization hammered out of the raw materials of injustice.

A distinct derivative from hatred's contribution to self-realization, when self-realization is established as a rallying point for the personality, is the tremendous source of dynamic energy provided. Surplus energy is created and placed at the disposal of the individual's needs and ends. In a sense the whole personality is alerted. All kinds of supports for implementing one's affirmed position are seized upon. A strange, new cunning possesses the mind, and every opportunity for taking advantage, for defeating the enemy, is revealed in clear perspective. One of the salient ways by which this expresses itself is the quality of endurance that appears. It is the sort of thing that causes a little boy, when he is being overpowered by a big boy, to refrain from tears or from giving any expression that will reveal the depths of his pain and hurt. He says to himself grimly, "I'll die before I cry."

I have already pointed out that the relationship between the strong and the weak is characterized often by its amoral aspect. When hatred serves as a dimension of self-realization, the illusion of righteousness is easy to create. Often there are but thin lines between bitterness, hatred, self-realization, defiance, and righteous indignation. The logic of the strong-weak relationship is to place all moral judgment of behavior out of bounds. A type of behavior that, under normal circumstances, would call for self-condemnation can very easily, under these special circumstances, be regarded as necessary and therefore defensible. To take advantage of the strong is regarded merely as settling an account. It is open season all the time, without the operation of normal moral inhibitions. It is a form of the old *lex talionis*—eye for an eye, tooth for a tooth.

Thus hatred becomes a device by which an individual seeks to protect himself against moral disintegration. He does to other human beings what he could not ordinarily do to them without losing his self-respect. This is an aspect of hatred that has almost universal application during a time of war and national crisis. Doubtless you will recall that during the last war a very interesting defense of hatred appeared in America. The reasoning ran something like this: American boys have grown up in a culture and a civilization in which they have absorbed certain broad attitudes of respect for human personality, and other traits characteristic of gentlemen of refinement and dignity. Therefore they are not prepared psychologically or emotionally to become human war machines, to make themselves conscious instruments of death. Something radical has to happen to their personality and their overall outlook to render them more effective tools of destruction. The most effective way by which this transformation can be brought about is through discipline in hatred; for if they hate the enemy, then that hatred will immunize them from a loss of moral self-respect as they do to the enemy what is demanded of them in the successful prosecution of the war. To use a figure, a curtain was dropped in front of their moral values and their ethical integrity as human beings and Americans, and they moved around in front of that curtain to do their death-dealing work on other human beings. The curtain of protection was the disciplined hatred. A simple illustration of what I mean is this: There are some people who cannot tell you face to face precisely what they think of you unless they get angry first. Anger serves as a protection of their finer sense of values as they look you in the eye and say things which, under ordinary circumstances, they would not be able to say.

When I was a boy, my mother occasionally found it necessary to punish me and my sister. My sister, when whipped, would look my mother in the face, showing no visible signs of emotional reaction. This attitude caused the burden of proof to shift from her shoulders to my mother's shoulders, with the result that my mother did not whip my sister with such intensity growing out of self-righteous indignation as if the reaction had been otherwise. When my turn came, all the neighbors knew what was happening in the Thurman family. Therefore my mother whipped me with an attention to detail that was radically different from the experience she had with my sister. My attitude fed her indignation to the point of giving her complete immunity from self-condemnation. This is precisely what hatred does in human beings faced with hard and brutal choices in dealing with each other.

It is not difficult to see how hatred, operating in this fashion, provides for the weak a basis for moral justification. Every expression of intolerance, every attitude of meanness, every statute that limits and degrades, gives further justification for life-negation on the part of the weak toward the strong. It makes possible for an individual to be life-affirming and life-negating at one and the same time. If a man's attitude is life-negating in his relationships with those to whom he recognizes no moral responsibility, his conduct is without condemnation in his own mind. In his relations with his fellows to whom he recognizes moral responsibility, his attitude is life-affirming. There must be within him some guarantee against contagion by the life-negating attitude, lest he lose a sense of moral integrity in all of his relationships. Hatred seems to function as such a guarantee. The oppressed can give themselves over with utter enthusiasm to life-affirming attitudes toward their fellow sufferers, and this becomes compensation for their life-negating attitude toward the strong.

Of course, back of this whole claim of logic is the idea that there is a fundamental justice in life, upon which the human spirit in its desperation may rely. In its more beatific definition it is the basis of the composure of the martyr who is being burned at the stake; he seems to be caught up in the swirl of elemental energy and power that transforms the weakness and limitation of his personality into that which makes of him a superhuman being.

It is clear, then, that for the weak, hatred seems to serve a creative purpose. It may be judged harshly by impersonal ethical standards, but as long as the weak see it as being inextricably involved in the complicated technique of survival with dignity, it cannot easily be dislodged. Jesus understood this. What must have passed through his mind when he observed the contemptuous disregard for the Jews by the Romans, whose power had closed in on Israel? What thoughts raced through his mind when Judas of Galilee raised his rallying banner of defiance, sucking into the tempest of his embittered spirit many of the sons of Judah? Is it reasonable to assume that Jesus did not understand the anatomy of hatred? In the face of the obvious facts of his environment he counseled against hatred, and his word is, "Love your enemies, . . . that ye may be the children of your Father which is in heaven: for he maketh his sun to rise on the evil and on the good, and sendeth rain on the just and the unjust." Why?

Despite all the positive psychological attributes of hatred we have outlined, hatred destroys finally the core of the life of the hater. While it lasts, burning in white heat, its effect seems positive and dynamic. But at last it turns to ash, for it guarantees a final isolation from one's fellows. It blinds the individual to all values of worth, even as they apply to himself and to his fellows. Hatred bears deadly and bitter fruit. It is blind and nondiscriminating. True, it begins by exercising specific discrimination. This it does by centering upon the persons responsible for the situations which create the reaction of resentment, bitterness, and hatred. But once hatred is released, it cannot be confined to the offenders alone. It is difficult for hatred to be informed as to objects when it gets under way. I remember that when I was an undergraduate in Atlanta, Georgia, a man came into the president's office, in which I was the errand boy. The president was busy, so the man engaged me in conversation. Eventually he began talking about his two little boys. He said, among other things, "I am rearing my boys so that they will not hate Negroes. Do not misunderstand me. I do not love them, but I am wise enough to know that if I teach my boys to hate Negroes, they will end up hating white people as well." Hatred cannot be controlled once it is set in motion.

Some years ago a medical friend of mine gave me a physical examination. After weighing me he said, "You'd better watch your weight. You are getting up in years now, and your weight will have a bad effect on your vital organs." He explained this in graphic detail. While he was talking, I chuckled; for, as I looked at him, I saw a man about 5 feet 4 inches in height who weighed 215 pounds. My friend, the doctor, thought his body knew that he was a doctor. But his body did not know he was a doctor; the only thing it knew was that he was accumulating more energy through his food than his body was able to consume. Hence his body did precisely what mine was doing. It stored energy in the form of fat.

Hatred is like that. It does not know anything about the pressures exerted upon the weak by the strong. It knows nothing about the extenuating circumstances growing out of a period of national crisis, making it seemingly necessary to discipline men in hatred of other human beings. The terrible truth remains. The logic of the development of hatred is death to the spirit and disintegration of ethical and moral values.

Above and beyond all else it must be borne in mind that hatred tends to dry up the springs of creative thought in the life of the hater, so that his resourcefulness becomes completely focused on the negative aspects of his environment. The urgent needs of the personality for creative expression are starved to death. A man's horizon may become so completely dominated by the intense character of his hatred that there remains no creative residue in his mind and spirit to give to great ideas, to great concepts. He becomes lopsided. To use the phrase of Zarathustra, he becomes "a cripple in reverse."

Jesus rejected hatred. It was not because he lacked the vitality or the strength. It was not because he lacked the incentive. Jesus rejected hatred because he saw that hatred meant death to the mind, death to the spirit, death to communion with his Father. He affirmed life; and hatred was the great denial. To him it was clear,

> Thou must not make division.
> Thy mind, heart, soul, and strength must ever search
> To find the way by which the road
> To all men's need of thee must go.
> This is the Highway of the Lord.*

* From my privately published volume of poems *The Greatest of These*, p. 9.

Epilogue

For every man there is a necessity to establish as securely as possible the lines along which he proposes to live his life. In developing his life's working paper he must take into account many factors, in his reaction to which he may seem to throw them out of line with their true significance. As a man he did not happen. He was born; he has a name; he has forebears; he is the product of a particular culture; he has a mother tongue; he belongs to a nation; he is born into some kind of faith. In addition to all of these he exists in some curious way as a person independent of all other facts. There is an intensely private world, all his own; it is intimate, exclusive, sealed.

The life working paper of the individual is made up of a creative synthesis of what the man is in all his parts and how he reacts to the living process. It is wide of the mark to say that a man's working paper is ever wrong; it may not be fruitful, it may be negative, but it is never wrong. For such a judgment would imply that the synthesis is guaranteed to be of a certain kind, of a specific character, resulting in a foreordained end.

It can never be determined just what a man will fashion. Two men may be born of the same parents, grow up in the same environment, be steeped in the same culture and inspired by the same faith. Close or even cursory observation may reveal that each has fashioned a life working paper so unique that they take to different roads, each day bringing them farther and farther apart. Or it may be that they move along precisely parallel lines that never meet.

Always, then, there is the miracle of the working paper. Wherever there appears in human history a personality whose story is available and whose reach extends far, in all directions, the question of his working paper is as crucial as is the significance of his life. We want to know what were the lines along which he decided to live his life. How did he relate himself to the central issues of his time? What were the questions which he had to answer? Was he under some necessity to give a universal character to his most private experience?

Our attention is called to such a figure because of the impact which his life makes upon human history. For what is human history but man's working paper as he rides high to life, caught often in the swirling eddies of tremendous impersonal forces set in motion by vast impulses out of the womb of the Eternal. When a solitary individual is able to mingle his strength with the forces of history and emerge with a name, a character, a personality, it is no ordinary achievement. It is more than the fact that there is a record of his life—as singular as that fact may be. It means that against the background of anonymity he has emerged articulate, and particular.

Such a figure was Jesus of Nazareth. To some he is the grand prototype of all the distilled longing of mankind for fulfillment, for wholeness, for perfection. To some he is the Eternal Presence hovering over all the myriad needs of humanity, yielding healing for the sick of body and soul, giving a lift to those whom weariness has overtaken in the long march, and calling out hidden purposes of destiny which are the common heritage. To some he is more than a Presence; he is the God fact, the Divine Moment in human sin and human misery. To still others he is a man who found the answer to life's riddle, and out of a profound gratitude he becomes the Man most worthy of honor and praise. For such his answer becomes humanity's answer and his life the common claim. In him the miracle of the working paper is writ large, for what he did all men may do. Thus interpreted, he belongs to no age, no race, no creed. When men look into his face, they see etched the glory of their own possibilities, and their hearts whisper, "Thank you and thank God!"

CONCERNING
LOVE

THE GREATEST OF THESE

"Now abideth faith, hope, love, these three; but the greatest of these is love."

> While there is a lower class
> I am in it.
> While there is a criminal element
> I am of it.
> While there is a man in jail
> I am not free.

Thus spoke a man whose life, whose deeds
These words fulfilled.
Contacts across all barriers abound
Where the world is narrowed in fact and dream.
If there is found no will to love
To make an act of grace toward fellow men,
Contacts degrade, outrage, destroy
The tender shoots of simple trust.
Love abides where all else dies
From sheer revulsion and disgust.

The fruit it bears sustains the nerve,
Strengthens the weak, the insecure,
Breaks the chains of fear that
Hold the minds of men in hate's embrace,
Condemns the things that shrink the soul.
It is the "precious bane" for those who seek
To know the Way of God among the sons of men.
It meets men where they are, cruel,
Lustful, greedy, callous, of low design—
It treats them there, as if they were full grown
And crowned with all that God would have them be.
For love's own sake and that alone,
Men do with joyous hope and quiet calm
What no command of Life or Death could force of them
If love were not.
To be God's child, to love with steady mind,
With fervent heart, this is to know
The Truth that makes man free.

MORE LOVING IN MY HEART

I want to be more loving in my heart!

I want to be more loving. Often there are good and sufficient reasons for exercising what seems a clean direct resentment. Again and again, I find it hard to hold in check the sharp retort, the biting comeback when it seems that someone has done violence to my self-respect and decent regard. How natural it seems to "give as good as I get," to "take nothing lying down," to announce to all and sundry in a thousand ways that "no one can run over me and get away with it!" All this is a part of the thicket in which my heart gets caught again and again. Deep within me, I want to be more loving—to glow with a warmth that will take the chill off the room which I share with those whose lives touch mine in the traffic of my goings and comings. I want to be more loving!

I want to be more loving in my heart! It is often easy to have the idea in mind, the plan to be more loving. To see it with my mind and give assent to the thought of being loving—this is crystal clear. But I want to be more loving in my heart! I must feel like loving; I must ease the tension in my heart that ejects the sharp barb, the stinging word. I want to be more loving in my heart that, with unconscious awareness and deliberate intent, I shall be a kind, a gracious human being. Thus, those who walk the way with me may find it easier to love, to be gracious because of the Love of God which is increasingly expressed in my living.

I want to be more loving in my heart!

CONTRADICTIONS NOT FINAL

Two men faced each other in a prison cell. They belonged to different countries, their roots watered by streams from different cultures. One was under sentence of death, scheduled to be executed within a few short hours. The other was a visitor and friend—this, even though months before they had been enemies in a great war. They bade each other farewell for the last time. The visitor was deeply troubled, but he could not find his way through the emotional maze in which he was caught to give voice to what cried out for utterance. This is what he wanted to say but could not:

"We may not be able to stop and undo the hard old wrongs of the great world outside, but through you and me no evil shall come either in the unknown where you are going, or in this imperfect and haunted dimension of awareness through which I move. Thus between us we shall cancel out all private and personal evil, thus arrest private and personal consequences to blind action and reaction, thus prevent specifically the general incomprehension and misunderstanding, hatred and revenge of our time from spreading further!"

The forces at work in the world which seem to determine the future and the fate of mankind seem so vast, impersonal, and unresponsive to the will and desire of any individual that it is easy to abandon all hope for a sane and peaceful order of life for mankind. Nevertheless, it is urgent to hold steadily in mind the utter responsibility of the solitary individual to do everything with all his heart and mind to arrest the development of the consequence of private and personal evil resulting from the interaction of the impersonal forces that surround us. To cancel out between you and another all personal and private evil, to put your life squarely on the side of the good thing because it is good, and for no other reason, is to anticipate the Kingdom of God at the level of your functioning.

At long last a man must be deeply convinced that the contradictions of life which he encounters are not final, that the radical tension between good and evil, as he sees it and feels it, does not have the last word about the meaning of life and the nature of existence, that there is a spirit in man and in the world working always against the thing that destroys and cuts down. Thus he will live wisely and courageously his little life, and those who see the sunlight in his face will drop their tools and follow him. There is no ultimate negation for the man for whom it is categorical that the ultimate destiny of man on this planet is a good destiny.

THE BINDING UNITY

There is a unity that binds all living things into a single whole. This unity is sensed in many ways. Sometimes, when walking alone in the woods far from all the traffic which makes up the daily experience, the stillness settles in the mind. Nothing stirs. The imprisoned self seems to slip outside its boundaries and the ebb and flow of life is keenly felt. One becomes an indistinguishable part of a single rhythm, a single pulse.

Sometimes there is a moment of complete and utter identity with the pain of a loved one; all the intensity and anguish are *felt*. One enters through a single door of suffering into the misery of the whole human race with no margin left to mark the place which was one's own. What is felt belongs nowhere but is everywhere binding and holding in a tight circle of agony until all of life is gathered into a single timeless gasp!

There are other moments when one becomes aware of the thrust of a tingling joy that rises deep within until it bursts forth in radiating happiness that bathes all of life in its glory and its warmth. Pain, sorrow, grief are seen as joy "becoming" and life gives a vote of confidence to itself, defining its meaning with a sureness that shatters every doubt concerning the broad free purpose of its goodness.

There are the times of personal encounter when a knowledge of caring binds two together and what is felt is good! There is nothing new nor old, only the knowledge that what comes as the flooding insight of love binds all living things into a single whole. The felt reverence spreads and deepens until to live and to love are to do *one* thing. To hate is to desire the nonexistent of the object of hate. To love is the act of adoration and praise shared with the Creator of life as the Be-all and the End-all of everything that is.

And yet there always remains the hard core of the self, blending and withdrawing, giving and pulling back, accepting and rejoicing, yielding and unyielding—what may this be but the pulsing of the unity that binds all living things in a single whole—the God of life extending Himself in the manifold glories of His creation?

KEEP OPEN THE DOOR OF THY HEART

Keep open the door of thy heart.
It matters not how many doors are closed against thee.

It is a wondrous discovery when there is disclosed to the mind the fact that there may be no direct and responsible relation between two human beings that can determine their attitude toward each other. We are accustomed to thinking that one man's attitude toward another is a response to an attitude. The formula is very neat: love begets love, hate begets hate, indifference begets indifference. Often this is true. Again and again we try to mete out to others what we experience at their hands. There is much to be said for the contagion of attitudes. There are moments in every man's life when he tries to give as good or as bad as he gets. But this presupposes that the relation between human beings is somehow mechanical, as if each person is utterly and completely separated. This is far from the truth, even though it may seem to square with *some* of the facts of our experienced behavior.

There is a profound ground of unity that is more pertinent and authentic than all the unilateral dimensions of our lives. This a man discovers when he is able to keep open the door of his heart. This is one's ultimate responsibility, and it is not dependent upon whether the heart of another is kept open for him. Here is a mystery: If sweeping through the door of my heart there moves continually a genuine love for you, it bypasses all your hate and all your indifference and gets through to you at your center. You are powerless to do anything about it. You may keep alive in devious ways the fires of your bitter heart, but they cannot get through to me. Underneath the surface of all the tension, something else is at work. It is utterly impossible for you to keep another from loving you. True, you may scorn his love, you may reject it in all ways within your power, you may try to close every opening in your own heart—it will not matter. This is no easy sentimentality, but it is the very essence of the vitality of all being. The word that love is stronger than hate and goes beyond death is the great disclosure to one who has found that when he keeps open the door of his heart, it matters not how many doors are closed against him.

SURROUNDED BY THE LOVE OF GOD

I am surrounded by the love of God.

The earth beneath my feet is the great womb out of which the life upon which my body depends comes in utter abundance. There is at work in the soil a mystery by which the death of one seed is transformed a thousandfold in newness of life. The magic of wind, sun and rain creates a climate that nourishes every living thing. It is law, and more than law; it is order, and more than order—there is a brooding tenderness out of which it all comes. In the contemplation of the earth, I know that I am surrounded by the love of God.

The events of my days strike a full balance of what seems both good and bad. Whatever may be the tensions and the stresses of a particular day, there is always lurking close at hand the trailing beauty of forgotten joy or unremembered peace. The weakness that engulfs me in its writhing toils reveals hidden strengths that could not show their face until my own desperation called them forth. In contemplation of the events of my days, I know that I am surrounded by the love of God.

The edge of hope that constantly invades the seasoned grounds of despair, the faith that keeps watch at the doors through which pass all the labors of my life and heart for what is right and true, the impulse to forgive and to seek forgiveness even when the injury is sharp and clear—these and countless other things make me know that by day and by night my life is surrounded by the love of God.

I am surrounded by the love of God.

Reconciliation

What a man knows as his birthright in his experience before God he must accept and confirm as his necessity in his relations with his fellows. It is in the presence of God that he feels he is being *totally* dealt with, that the words of the Psalmist find a resting place in his own heart: Thou hast "not dealt with us according to our sins, nor rewarded us according to our iniquities" (Ps. 103:10). The sins, bitterness, weakness, virtues, loves, and strengths are all gathered and transmuted by His love and His grace, and we become whole in His Presence. This is the miracle of religious experience—the sense of being totally dealt with, completely understood, and utterly cared for. This is what a man seeks with his fellows. This is why the way of reconciliation and the way of love finally are one way.

The building blocks for the society of man and for the well-being of the individual are the fundamental desire to understand others and to be understood. The crucial sentence is, "Every man wants to be cared for, to be sustained by the assurance of the watchful and thoughtful attention of others." Such is the meaning of love.

Sometimes the radiance of love is so soft and gentle that the individual sees himself with all harsh lines wiped away and all limitations blended with his strengths in so happy a combination that strength seems to be everywhere and weakness is nowhere to be found. This is a part of the magic, the spell of love. Sometimes its radiance kindles old fires that have long since grown cold from the neglect of despair, or new fires are kindled by a hope born full-blown without beginning and without end. Sometimes the same radiance blesses a life with a vision of its possibilities never before dreamed of or sought, stimulating new endeavor and summoning all latent powers to energize the life at its inmost core.

But there are other ways by which love works its perfect work. There is a steady anxiety that surrounds man's experience of love. It may stab the spirit by calling forth a bitter, scathing self-judgment. The heights to which it calls may seem so high that all incentive is lost and the individual is stricken with utter hopelessness and despair. It may throw in relief old and forgotten weaknesses to which one has made the adjustment of acceptance—but which now stir in their place to offer themselves as testimony of one's unworthiness and to challenge the love with their embarrassing reality. At such times one expects love to be dimmed, in the mistaken notion that it is ultimately based upon merit and worth.

Behold the miracle! Love has no awareness of merit or demerit; it has no scale by which its portion may be weighed or measured. It does not seek to balance giving and receiving. Love loves; this is its nature. This does not mean that it is blind, naïve, or pretentious, but rather that love holds its object securely in its grasp, calling all that it sees by its true name but surrounding all with a wisdom born both of its passion and its understanding. Here is no traffic in sentimentality, no catering either to weakness or to strength. Instead, there is robust vitality that quickens the roots of personality, creating an unfolding of the self that redefines, reshapes, and makes all things new. Such an experience is so fundamental that an individual knows that what is happening to him can outlast all things without itself being dissipated or lost.

Whence comes this power which seems to be the point of referral for all experience and the essence of all meaning? No created thing, no single unit of life, can be the source of such fullness and completeness. For in the experience itself a man is caught and held by something so much more than he can ever think or be that there is but one word by which its meaning can be encompassed—God. Hence the Psalmist says that as long as the love of God shines on us undimmed, not only may no darkness obscure, but we may find our way to a point in other hearts beyond all weakness and all strength, beyond all that is good or evil. There is nothing outside ourselves—no circumstance, no condition, no vicissitude—that can ultimately separate us from the love of God or of one another. And we pour out our gratitude to God that this is so!

The appearance of love may be used as a technique of social control or for the manipulation of other people while the manipulator himself has no sense of personal involvement. The ethic may become divorced from the spiritual and/or religious commitment out of which it comes, by which it is inspired. In other words, instead of being a moral imperative it can become a moral pretension. The love ethic may become a love dogma or doctrine, to which the mind may make an intellectual adjustment and to which mere mental assent may be given. This may be one of the real perils when the ethic becomes incorporated in a system or in the organizational structure of an institution.

The reason for this is not far to seek. Neither a man nor an institution can embrace an ethical imperative without either becoming more and more expressive of it in the common life or developing a kind of increasing enmity to it. Here is the essential challenge of the modern world to the Christian Church.

What then is the nature of the kind of discipline that love provides? In the first place, it is something that I must quite deliberately *want* to do. For many of us this is the first great roadblock. In our relations with each other there is often so much that alienates, that is distasteful, there seems to be every ground for refraining from the kind of concern that love demands. It is curious how we feel the other person must demonstrate a worthiness that commends itself to us before we are willing to *want* to move in outflow, in the self-giving that love demands. We want to be accepted just as we are, but at the same time we want the other person to *win* the right to our acceptance of him. This is an important part of the sin of pride. There must be genuine repentance for such an attitude. Forgiveness for this sin is the work of the grace of God in the human heart. A man seeks it before God and becomes aware of forgiveness only when, in his attitude toward his fellows, he comes to want to make available to them the consciousness of what God shares with him. God enables him to *want* to love. This is one of the reasons why I cannot separate the discipline of love from the discipline of religious experience.

In the second place, I must find the opening or openings through which my love can flow into the life of the other, and at the same time locate in myself openings through which his love can flow into me. Most often this involves an increased understanding of the other person. This is arrived at by a disciplined use of the imagination. We are accustomed to thinking of imagination as a useful tool in the hands of the artist as he reproduces in varied forms what he sees beyond the rim of fact that circles him round. There are times when it is regarded merely as a delightful, whimsical trait of the "childish mind." Our judgment trembles on the edge of condescension, pity, or even ridicule when imagination is confused with fancy in reports of the inner workings of the mind of the "simpleton" or "fool." But we recognize and applaud the bold, audacious leap of the mind of the scientist when it soars far out beyond what is known to fix a beachhead on distant, unexplored shores. But the imagination shows its greatest powers as the *angelos* of God in the miracle it creates when one man, standing on his own ground, is able while there to put himself in another man's place. To send his imagination forth to establish a point of focus in another man's spirit, and from that vantage point so to blend with the other's landscape that what he sees and feels is authentic—this is the great adventure in human relations. Yet this is not enough. The imagination must report its findings accurately, without regard for all previous prejudgments and private or collective fears. And even this is not enough. There must be both a spontaneous and a deliberate response to such knowledge which will result in the sharing of resources at their deepest level.

Very glibly we are apt to use such words as "sympathy," "compassion," "sitting where they sit," but in experience it is genuinely to be rocked to one's foundations. We resist making room for considerations that will bend us out of the path of preoccupation with ourselves, our needs, our problems. We corrupt our imagination when we give it range over only our own affairs. Here we experience the magnification of our own wills, the distortion of our own problems, and the enlargement of the areas of our misery. The activity of which we deprive our imagination in the work of understanding others turns in upon ourselves with disaster and sometimes terror.

In the third place, there must be a sense of leisure out of which we relate to others. The sense of it is far more important than the fact of leisure itself. Somehow it must be conveyed to the other person that our effort to respond to his need to be cared for is one with our concern to be cared for ourselves. Despite the pressures under which we live, it is entirely possible to develop a sense of leisure as the climate in which we function. We cannot be in a hurry in matters of the heart. The human spirit has to be explored gently and with unhurried tenderness. Very often this demands a reconditioning of our nervous responses to life, a profound alteration in the tempo of our behavior pattern. Whatever we learn of leisure in the discipline of silence, in meditation and prayer, bears rich, ripe fruit in preparing the way for love. Failure at this point can be one of unrelieved frustration. At first, for most of us, skill in tarrying with another has to be cultivated and worked at by dint of much self-discipline. At first it may seem mechanical, artificial, or studied, but this kind of clumsiness will not remain if we persist. How indescribably wonderful and healing it is to encounter another human being who listens not only to our words, but manages, somehow, to listen to *us*. Everyone needs this and everyone needs to give it, as well—thus we come full circle in love.

If all this is true, then it is clear that any structure of society, any arrangement under which human beings live, that does not provide maximum opportunities for free-flowing circulation among one another, works against social and individual health. Any attitudes, private or group, which prohibit people from coming into "across-the-board" contact with each other work against the implementation of the love ethic. So considered, segregation, prescriptions of separation, are a disease of the human spirit and the body politic. It does not matter how meaningful the tight circle of isolated security may be in which individuals or groups move. The very existence of such circles, whether regarded as a necessity of religious faith, political ideology, or social purity, precludes the possibility of the experience of love as a part of the necessity of man's life.

The experience of love is either a necessity or a luxury. If it be a luxury, it is expendable; if it be a necessity, then to deny it is to perish. So simple is the reality, and so terrifying. Ultimately there is only one place of refuge on this planet for any man—that is in another man's heart. To love is to make of one's heart a swinging door.

Mysticism and the Experience of Love

Because mysticism deals with the inner personal response to God, it may seem at first glance to be life denying as over against life affirming; life denying because the intent of the person is to retreat within, to disentangle his life from those things that make for fragmentation, divisiveness, and attachment. It cannot be denied that this element is very pronounced. The evidence is abundant in all the literature of mysticism. One of the great words in this literature is detachment, and by detachment is meant the relaxation of one's hold upon the testimony and the experience of the senses. It speaks intimately of self-denial, even of self-annihilation, or of utter and complete absorption in the experience of union with God.

Much of the emphasis upon spiritual exercises is focused upon what such exercises will enable the individual to achieve when he is able to rise above and transcend the fierce demands of the senses. These exercises are meant to "ready" the spirit for an awareness of the Presence of God dwelling in the core of the individual's being.

It is for this reason that great emphasis is placed upon silence, on becoming still within. The insistence is not so much that something invade the life of man from without but rather that, through quietness and inner solitariness, the individual becomes conscious of what is there all the time. "Be still and know that I am God," is the way the Psalmist puts it.

1 8 9

When I was a theological student in Rochester, New York, very late one night I was returning to the Seminary by way of Main Street, the central artery of traffic for the city. The hour was so late that streetcars ran only infrequently and there was almost no traffic. As I walked along, I became aware of what seemed to be the sound of rushing water. I realized that I had been hearing this rumbling for quite some time, but had only suddenly become aware of it. The next day I was talking about this with one of my professors who told me that for a certain distance under Main Street there was a part of the old Erie Canal. This was the sound of water that I had heard. The sound itself was continuous, but when there was the normal traffic in the daytime, the sound could not be heard. It was only when the surface noises had stopped that the sound came through. This is analogous to the mystic's witness of God within, whose Presence may not become manifest until the traffic of the surface life is somehow stilled. This is what is meant by the experience of centering down.

The mystic cannot escape the necessity for giving some kind of "data content" to his experience. How he speaks of this content reflects the religious, cultural, and social heritage in which he finds meaning and in which he is rooted. For instance, if central to his experience is the recognition of God as being the Creator of life and existence, then God must, in a very definite manner, stand over against creation. God is the subject and all existences of whatever form are predicates. What then is the relation between God and his creatures? He cannot be wholly transcendent because this would not satisfy the demands of the mystic's experience, which is a personal response to God. Here we are face to face with what is claimed to be a form of personal communion between two principals, man and God. This means that either the soul of man must be regarded as a very part of God or else some other means must be devised to make authentic communication in the mystic sense between man and God possible. The mystic claims that some connection does take place, man and God do communicate.

For me the importance of the mystic's claim does not rest on the degree to which he is able to establish empirical verification of his experience, if by empirical verification we mean a body of separate evidence—evidence that is of the nature of proof of the integrity of his experience. And here is the interesting dilemma and the fascinating paradox. The mind insists that all experiences fall into order in a system of meaning. What the mystic experiences within must somehow belong to that which is without. It is reasonable then for the individual to expect to validate his claim of truth by his experience of life in the world. What he experiences in the world must not seem radically different from the quality and the kind that takes place within. And yet at the same time the validity of his inner experience cannot finally rest upon any kind of manifestation. The integrity of the personal response does not rise or fall by the degree to which the response is checked by data from the outside. And yet the necessity for trying to find external validation and vindication can never be relaxed.

To love means to have an intrinsic interest in another person. It is not of necessity contingent upon any kind of group or family closeness. True, such closeness may provide a normal setting for the achieving of intrinsic interest, but the fact that two men are brothers having the same parents provides no mandatory love relationship between them. In his letter to the Philippians, the Apostle Paul writes, "My prayer to God is that your love may grow more and more rich in knowledge and in all manner of insight that you may have a sense of what is vital, that you may be transparent and of no harm to anyone, your life covered with that harvest of righteousness that Jesus Christ produces to the praise and to the glory of God." Men do not love in general, but they do love in particular. To love means dealing with persons in the concrete rather than in the abstract. In the presence of love, there are no types or stereotypes, no classes and no masses.

An intrinsic interest is therefore not possible apart from a sense of fact where other persons are concerned. This sense of fact means that the other person is dealt with as he is and in the light of the details of his life. It does not mean becoming so involved in the bill of particulars of other human beings that we cannot get through to them. But it does mean defining the other person in his context and establishing a perspective with regard to that context and where he is located in it. To state it conventionally and categorically, it means meeting a person where he is and dealing with him there as if he were where he should be.

One day a woman was brought to Jesus because she had been taken in adultery and her accusers wanted Jesus to pass judgment upon her. It was his claim that he was not opposed to the law and it was the insistence of the law, said her accusers, that a person caught in adultery should be stoned to death. Did Jesus agree with the law and thus condone the stoning of the woman or did he not? His reply to the question seemed at once to be an evasion. He said, "Let the man among you who is without sin cast the first stone." The implication being that after that any man may throw. Then he did a curious thing. He was such a gentleman that he did not look at the woman in the face and add his gaze to the stares of the hostile accusers. No, he looked on the ground. After a time, he lifted his face, looked the woman in the eyes and said, "Woman, where are your accusers? Does no man condemn you? Neither do I. Go in peace and don't do it any more." He met her where she was, admittedly an adulteress, but he dealt with her at that point of fact as if she were where, at her best, she saw herself as being. Thus he took her total fact into account and encountered her at a point in herself that was beyond all her faults.

A person's *fact* includes more than his plight, predicament, or need at a particular moment in time. It is something total which must include awareness of the person's potential. This, too, is a part of the person's fact. This is why love always sees more than is in evidence at any moment of viewing.

The sense of fact with reference to an increasingly large area of the other person's fact is most crucial. The area of the other person's fact is an expanding thing if such a person lives into life and deepens the quality and breadth of his experience. This makes love between persons dynamic rather than static. It means further that the intrinsic interest must be informed. And constantly. There is no substitute for hard understanding of more and more and more of another's fact. This serves as a corrective against doing violence to those for whom we have a sense of caring because of great gaps in our knowledge of their fact. This is generally the weakness in so much lateral good will in the world. It is uninformed, ignorant, sincere good will. It does not seek to feed its emotion with a healthy diet of facts, data, information from which insights opening the door to the other person's meaning are derived. I think that this is why it is impossible to have intrinsic interest in people with whom we are out of living or vicarious contact.

Often we are enjoined by the interpreters of the Christian faith that we must love humanity "for Christ's sake." The reasoning is that inasmuch as Christ died for humanity, then as his followers we should love humanity in the way that he loved humanity, to the extent of giving our lives if necessary. We manage to stop short of this. As a parenthetical statement which goes to the heart of the theological position about Jesus Christ giving his life in the crucifixion for humanity—it was a voluntary giving of self, devoid of all aspects of obligation or response to external demands. To speak of the love for humanity is meaningless. There is no such thing as humanity. What we call humanity has a name, was born, lives on a street, gets hungry, needs all the particular things we need. As an abstract, it has no reality whatsoever. Now this is not to say that love does not require us to develop a climate of acceptance which may surround any person who comes within our ken, but we should be clear what is at work here.

One who has no sense of being an object of love is seriously handicapped in making someone else an object of his love. There is much to be said for the Christian doctrine which insists that we are able to love others because He first loved us. A person who has grown up feeling always outside of the reach of other people's caring has a dual handicap which may be paradoxical in character. On the one hand, because he sees himself as being beyond the pale of love and affection, he is apt to pass a judgment upon himself which insists on his own unworthiness. Because he feels despised, at long last he begins to despise himself. On the other hand, there may be a kind of inner compensation for this lack. This inner compensation may very easily result in an exaggeration of self-love, a preoccupation with one's own needs, interests, concerns. In short, it may make such a person thoroughly self-centered. The result of the self-centeredness may be the building of a wall that shuts everybody out.

There are some people who have the quality of "built in awareness" of others as a special talent or special gift. It is not far off the mark to say that there are some individuals who by constitution are born lovers, who have what a friend of mine calls "the gift of intimacy." To be near them is to find yourself warmed by their fire. Their presence in the midst seems to activate in others a contagion of good feeling towards the world in general. But for most of us, it is a thing that has to be worked at, cultivated as a kind of inner development. We have all experienced this warmth in some degree.

You know what a difference it makes when you feel that another person is truly aware of you, of your presence, or even of your existence. I know a nurse, for instance, who can walk into a sick room, take a quick all-pervading look at the patient in bed, then walk over to the bed, touch a pillow here or make some shift in the covers there, do some little thing that adds enormously to the immediate comfort of the patient.

To be to another human being what is needed at the time that the need is most urgent and most acutely felt, this is to participate in the precise act of redemption. The imagination acting under the most stringent orders can develop a technique all its own in locating and reporting to us its findings. We are not the other persons, we are ourselves. All that they are experiencing we can never know— but we can make accurate soundings which when properly read, will enable us to be to them what we could never be without such awareness. The degree to which our imagination becomes the *angelos* of God, we ourselves may become His *instruments.*

The other person's fact includes the good and the bad, the beautiful and the ugly. It may be a fact, for instance, that here is a person who is mean, greedy, even vicious and ungracious. Here is a person who by his action declares himself on every hand to all and sundry or to you in particular that he has no active membership in the human family. This is a fact and it is his fact. It must be taken into account. To ignore it is to be utterly sentimental and false. Always there is the insistence at the very center of the Christian faith, for instance, that even the enemy must be loved. The injunction is, "But I say unto you, love your enemies that you may be children of your Father who sends His rain on the just and the unjust." It is clear and needs no underscoring that what seems to be the natural thing is to hate one's enemy. The insistence here is that the individual is enjoined to move from the natural impulse to the level of deliberate intent. One has to bring to the center of his focus a desire to love even one's enemy.

In the last analysis, every judgment of the other person is importantly a self-judgment. There remains the real question: If I could see this man in his own context and get behind the thing that he is doing to the real center of his life, then I would be able to deal with him there in a manner that is total, wholesome, and redemptive rather than to deal with him at the point of his deed which is always partial. In so doing, I establish psychological distance not only between him and his deed but between me and his deed. I must help him to come to an understanding of his deed both in terms of what it is doing to him as well as what it is doing to me, or to others.

This may be impossible because I may not be able to get close enough to him to give a personal face-to-face communication. Thus we come to our second consideration, what I must do if I would love him, if I would deal with him at a point beyond all his faults and virtues. I must find a way to bring home to him the meaning of his deed, the meaning that transcends the intent of the deed itself. This may be done by binding him with limitations and penalties, by laws and conventions that will cause him to raise crucial questions about his deed and its meaning. Once these questions are raised in his mind, there is a chance now that he may measure his deed by his true intent as a human being. At such a moment, he is apt to stand in self-judgment.

Meanwhile, what is happening to my love? It must keep on loving. I must not ever give him up, no more than I am willing to give myself up. The responsibility of love is to love. Where love persists, it awakens the mind and the imagination to a wide variety of insights and techniques that will run interference for the clear-flowing affection.

It is for this reason that there can be no love apart from suffering. Love demands that we expose ourselves at our most vulnerable point by keeping the heart open. Why? Because this is our own deepest need. When I love, even though I may in the act identify with the other person in his predicament,, what I can never enter into are the experiences which resulted in his deed. I do not want other men to deal with me on the basis of what I may do under some particular circumstance, but rather I wish to be dealt with in an inclusive, total, integrated manner. This is what it means to be understood. This is to have the experience of freedom, to be one's self, and to be rid of the awful burden of pretensions.

DEEP RIVER

On Viewing the Coast of Africa

From my cabin window I look out on the full moon, and the ghosts of my forefathers rise and fall with the undulating waves. Across these same waters how many years ago they came! What were the inchoate mutterings locked tight within the circle of their hearts? In the deep, heavy darkness of the foul-smelling hold of the ship, where they could not see the sky, nor hear the night noises, nor feel the warm compassion of the tribe, they held their breath against the agony.

How does the human spirit accommodate itself to desolation? How did they? What tools of the spirit were in their hands with which to cut a path through the wilderness of their despair? If only Death of the body would come to deliver the soul from dying! If some sacred taboo had been defiled and this extended terror was the consequence—there would be no panic in the paying. If some creature of the vast and pulsing jungle had snatched the life away—this would even in its wildest fear be floated by the familiarity of the daily hazard. If Death had come being ushered into life by a terrible paroxysm of pain, all the assurance of the Way of the Tribe would have carried the spirit home on the wings of precious ceremony and holy ritual. But this! Nothing anywhere in all the myths, in all the stories, in all the ancient memory of the race had given hint of this tortuous convulsion. There were no gods to hear, no magic spell of witch doctor to summon; even one's companion in chains muttered his quivering misery in a tongue unknown and a sound unfamiliar.

O my Fathers, what was it like to be stripped of all supports of life save the beating of the heart and the ebb and flow of fetid air in the lungs? In a strange moment, when you suddenly caught your breath, did some intimation from the future give to your spirits a hint of promise? In the darkness did you hear the silent feet of your children beating a melody of freedom to words which you would never know, in a land in which your bones would be warmed again in the depths of the cold earth in which you will sleep unknown, unrealized and alone?

Sorrow Songs— The Ground of Hope (I)

The mystery of life and death persists despite the exhaustless and exhaustive treatment it has been given in song and story, philosophy and science, art and religion. The human spirit is so involved in the endless cycle of birth, of living and dying, that in some sense each man is an authority, a key interpreter of the meaning of the totality of the experience. The testimony of the individual, then, is always fresh if he is able to make himself articulate to his fellows. Even when he is not, there is the persistent conviction that in some profound sense he himself knows and understands. When the external circumstances of life are dramatic or unusual, causing the human spirit to make demands upon all the reaches of its resourcefulness in order to keep from being engulfed, then the value of its findings made articulate, has more than passing significance.

I have chosen, coincidentally with the suggestion of Dean Sperry, to examine the Negro spirituals as a source of rich testimony concerning life and death, because in many ways they are the voice, sometimes strident, sometimes muted and weary, of a people for whom the cup of suffering overflowed in haunting overtones of majesty, beauty, and power! For many years it has been a growing conviction with me that the clue to the meaning of the spirituals is to be found in religious experience and spiritual discernment. To be sure, the amazing rhythm and the peculiar, often weird 1-2-3-5-6-8 of the musical scale are always intriguing and challenging to the modern mind. The real significance of the songs, however, is revealed at a deeper level of experience, in the ebb and flow of the tides that feed the rivers of man's thinking and aspiring. Here, where the elemental and the formless struggle to a vast consciousness in the mind and spirit of the individual, shall we seek the needful understanding of the songs of these slave singers. The insights disclosed are not original in any personal or private sense. The unique factor of the inspiring revelation is that, in the presence of their naked demand upon the primary sources of meanings, even without highly specialized tools or skills, the universe responded to them with overwhelming power.

In one of the essays which make up the little book of meditations *Deep River*, I located three major sources of raw materials over which the slave placed the alchemy of his desiring and aspiring: the world of nature, the stuff of experience, and the Bible, the sacred book of the Christians who had enslaved him. It was from the latter two that the songs of life and death originate. An examination of some of the insights to be found here is at once the purpose and proposal of my lecture.

Death was a fact, inescapable, persistent. For the slave, it was extremely compelling because of the cheapness with which his life was regarded. The slave was a tool, a thing, a utility, a commodity, but he was not a *person*. He was faced constantly with the imminent threat of death, of which the terrible overseer was the symbol, and the awareness that he (the slave) was only chattel property, the dramatization. It is difficult for us, so far removed in time and mood from those agony-ridden days, to comprehend the subtle psychological factors that were at work in the relationship between slave and master. If a slave were killed, it was merely a property loss, a matter of bookkeeping. The notion of personality, of human beings as ends so basic to the genius of the Christian faith, had no authentic application in the relationship between slave and master. The social and religious climate were uncongenial to such an ethic. Of course, there were significant exceptions to the general rule—which exceptions, by the light they cast, revealed the great moral darkness by which the period was engulfed. The situation itself stripped death of dignity, making it stark and nasty, like the difference between tragedy and melodrama. Death by violence at the hand of nature may

stun the mind and shock the spirit, but death at the hands of another human being makes for panic in the mind and outrages the
spirit. To live constantly in such a climate makes the struggle for
essential human dignity unbearably desperate. The human spirit is
stripped to the literal substance of itself. The attitude toward death
is profoundly influenced by the experience of life.

It is important then to examine this literature to see what is
revealed here concerning the attitude toward death. How significant
is death? Is it the worst of all possible things that can happen to an
individual:

> Oh Freedom! Oh Freedom!
> Oh Freedom, I love thee!
> And before I'll be a slave,
> I'll be buried in my grave,
> And go home to my Lord and be free.

Obvious indeed is it here that death is not regarded as life's
worst offering. There are some things in life that are worse than
death. A man is not compelled to accept life without reference to
the conditions upon which the offering is made. Here is something
more than a mere counsel of suicide. It is a primary disclosure of an
elemental affirmation having to do directly, not only with the ultimate dignity of the human spirit, but also with the ultimate basis of
self-respect. We are face to face with a gross conception of the immortality of man, gross because it is completely exhaustive in its
desperation. A radical conception of the immortality of man is apparent because the human spirit has a final word over the effect of
circumstances. It is the guarantee of the sense of alternative in human experience, upon which, in the last analysis, all notions of
freedom finally rest. Here is a recognition of death as the one fixed
option which can never be taken from man by any power, however
great, or by any circumstance, however fateful. If death were not
implicit in the fact of life in a time-space dimension, then in no true
sense would there be any authentic options in human experience.
This concept regards death merely as a private option, private because it involves the single individual as if he and he alone existed
in all the universe; option, because, while it assumes the inevitability of death as a factor in life, it recognizes the element of time which
brings the inevitable factor under some measure of control.

The fact that death can be reduced to a manageable unit in any sense, whatsoever, reveals something that is profoundly significant concerning its character. The significant revelation is in the fact that death, as an event, is spatial, time encompassed, if not actually time bound, and therefore partakes of the character of the episodic. Death not only affects man by involving him concretely in its fulfillment, but man seems to be aware that he is being affected by death in the experience itself. There is, therefore, an element of detachment for the human spirit, even in so crucial an experience. Death is an experience in life and a man, under some circumstances, may be regarded as a spectator *of*, as well as a participant *in*, the moment of his own death. The logic here is that man is both a space binder and a time binder.

The second attitude toward death that comes to our attention is one of resignation mixed with elements of fear and a manifestation of muted dread—this, despite the fact that there seems to have been a careful note of familiarity with the experiences of death. It is more difficult for us to imagine what life was like under a less complex order of living than is our lot. We are all of us participants in the modern conspiracy to reduce immediate contact with death to zero except under the most extraordinary circumstances. We know that death is a commonplace in the experience of life and yet we keep it behind a curtain or locked in a closet, as it were. To us death is gruesome and aesthetically distasteful as a primary contact for ourselves and our children. For most of us, when members of our immediate families die, the death itself takes place in a hospital. Particularly is this true of urban dwellers. From the hospital, the deceased is carried to a place of preparation for burial, the mortuary. When we see the beloved one again, the body has been washed, embalmed, and dressed for burial. Our exposure to the facts involved, the silent intimacies in preparation for burial, are almost entirely secondary, to say the least. The hospital and the mortuary have entered profoundly into the life of modern man, at this point. The result is that death has been largely alienated from the normal compass of daily experience. Our sense of personal loss may be great but our primary relationship with death under normal circumstances tends to be impersonal and detached. We shrink from direct personal contact with death. It is very difficult for us to handle the emotional upsets growing out of our experience with death when we are de-

nied the natural moments of exhaustive reaction which are deriva-
tives of the performance of last personal services for the dead.
Therapeutic effects are missed. Tremendous emotional blocks are
set up without release, making for devious forms of inner chaos, which
cause us to limp through the years with our griefs unassuaged.

This was not the situation with the creators of the Spirituals.
Their contact with the dead was immediate, inescapable, dramatic.
The family or friends washed the body of the dead, the grave clothes
were carefully and personally selected or especially made. The cof-
fin itself was built by a familiar hand. It may have been a loving
though crude device, or an expression of genuine, first-class crafts-
manship. During all these processes, the body remained in the home—
first wrapped in cooling sheets and then "laid out" for the time interval before burial. In the case of death from illness all of the final
aspects of the experience were shared by those who had taken their
turn "keeping watch." Every detail was etched in the mind and
emotions against the background of the approaching end. The "death
rattle" in the throat, the spasm of tense vibration in the body as the
struggle for air increased in intensity, the sheer physical panic
sometimes manifest—all these were a familiar part of the commonplace pattern of daily experience. Out of a full, rich knowledge of
fact such a song as this was born:

> I want to die easy when I die.
> I want to die easy when I die.
>   Shout salvation as I fly,
> I want to die easy when I die.

A quiet death without the seizure of panic, the silent closing of the
door of earthly life, this is the simple human aspiration here.

As if to provide some measure of contrast, the age-old symbolism of the river of death appears in a song like this:

> Chilly water, chilly water,
> Hallelujah to that lamb,
> I know that water is chilly and cold,
> Hallelujah to that lamb.
> But I have Jesus in my soul,
> Hallelujah to that lamb.
> Satan's just like a snake in the grass

Hallelujah to that lamb.
He's watching for to bite you as you pass
Hallelujah to that lamb.

In a bold and audacious introduction of still another type of symbolism which has all the graphic quality of the essentially original, revealing the intimate personal contact with death and the dying, this old, old song announces:

Same train carry my mother;
Same train be back tomorrer;
Same train, same train.
Same train blowin' at the station,
Same train be back tomorrer;
Same train, same train.

There is a sense of the meaning of death as a form of frustration (for those who remain) with a dimension of realism rare and moving in this song:

You needn't mind my dying,
You needn't mind my dying,
You needn't mind my dying,
Jesus goin' to make up my dying bed.

In my dying room I know,
Somebody is going to cry.
All I ask you to do for me,
Just close my dying eyes.

In my dying room I know,
Somebody is going to mourn.
All I ask you to do for me,
Just give that bell a tone.

In the third place, death is regarded as release, as complete surcease from anxiety and care. This is to be distinguished from that which may come after death. We are thinking here of the significance of death regarded somewhat as a good in itself. The meaning of death in such a view is measured strictly against the background of immediate life experience. It is not a renunciation of life because its terms have been refused, but an exulting sigh of sheer release from a very wearying burden:

> I know moon-rise, I know star-rise,
>   I lay this body down.
> I walk in the moon-light, I walk in the star-light,
>   To lay this body down.
>
> I walk in the graveyard, I walk through the graveyard
>   To lay this body down.
> I lie in the grave and stretch out my arms,
>   To lay this body down.

Man, the time binder, one with the shimmering glory of moonlight and starlight and yet housed in a simple space-binding body, is heir to all the buffetings of the fixed and immovable, yet he can lay the body down and stretch out his arms and be at one with moonrise and starlight.

The note of the transcendence of death is never lacking— whether it is viewed merely as release or as the door to a heaven of endless joys. We shall examine the place and significance of the concepts dealing with that which is beyond death at a later point in our discussion. But the great idea about death itself is that it is not *the master of life*. It may be inevitable, yes; gruesome, perhaps; releasing, yes; but triumphant, *never*. With such an affirmation ringing in their ears, it became possible for them, slaves though they were, to stand anything that life could bring against them.

It is next in order to examine the attitude taken toward life, because the attitude toward death cannot be separated from the attitude toward life. Was life merely a "veil of soul-making"? Was it merely a vast anteroom to the great beyond? Was it regarded as an end in itself? Or was it a series of progressions, a pilgrimage, a meaningful sojourn?

There seem to be no songs dealing with the origin of life as such or the origin of the individual life in particular. Life was regarded essentially as the given—it was accepted as a fact without reflection as to cause or reason. They were content to let the mystery remain intact.

Given the fact of life, there is much which has to do with interpretations of its meanings, its point and even its validity. In the first place, life is regarded as an experience of evil, of frustration, of despair. There are at least two moods in evidence here—one mood has to do with an impersonal characteristic of life itself. Loneliness and discouragement—such is the way of life. One cannot escape— such experiences are inherent in the process itself. Hence:

> Let us cheer the weary traveler,
> Let us cheer the weary traveler,
> Along the heavenly way.

This has some elements similar to the philosophy of unyielding despair developed by Bertrand Russell in his essay on a Free Man's Worship.

> Sometimes I feel like a motherless child,
> A long way from home.

Here again is another song which reflects the same temper. There is also the familiar note in:

> Nobody knows the trouble I've seen,
> Nobody knows my sorrow.
> Nobody knows the trouble I've seen,
> Glory, Hallelujah!

All the reaches of despair are caught up and held in a trembling wail in:

> I couldn't hear nobody pray,
> Oh, I couldn't hear nobody pray.
> Oh, way down yonder by myself,
> And I couldn't hear nobody pray.

A climactic chord in the mood of the seventh chapter of Paul's letter to the Romans is to be found in:

> O wretched man that I am!
> O wretched man that I am!
> Who will deliver poor me?

> My heart is filled with sadness and pain,
> Who will deliver poor me?

The solitariness of the human spirit, the intensely personal characteristic of all experience as distinguished from mere frustration or despair, is evident in such a song as:

> I've got to walk my lonesome valley,
> I've got to walk it for myself.
> Nobody else can walk it for me,
> I've got to walk it for myself!

Here we are in the presence of an essential insight into all human experience. It seems, sometimes, that it is the solitariness of life that causes it to move with such intensity and power. In the last analysis all the great moments of profoundest meaning are solitary. We walk the ways of life together with our associates, our friends, our loved ones. How precious it is to lean upon another, to have a staggered sense of the everlasting arms felt in communion with a friend. But there are thresholds before which all must stop and no one may enter save God, and even He in disguise. I am alone but even in my aloneness I seem sometimes to be all that there is in life, and all that there is in life seems to be synthesized in me.

It is a matter of more than passing interest that this element of overwhelming poignancy is relieved somewhat by a clear note of triumph. Out of the fullness of a tremendous vitality the lowering clouds are highlighted by an overflowing of utter exuberance:

> I feel like a motherless child;
> I feel like a motherless child;
> Glory hallelujah!
> Sometimes my way is sad and lone,
> When far away and lost from home;
> Glory hallelujah!

The same note appears in a softer key, expressive of a quiet but sure confidence:

> Soon-a-will be done with troubles of the world;
> Soon-a-will be done with troubles of the world;
> Going home to live with God.

Or again the quality of triumph is to be found in the total accent of the song:

> All-a-my troubles will soon be over with,
> All-a-my troubles will soon be over with,
> All over this world.

The second mood suggested in the interpretation of life as an experience of evil, of frustration, of despair, has to do with a personal reaction to the vindictiveness and cruelty of one's fellows. The mood is set in a definite moral and ethical frame of reference which becomes a screening device for evaluating one's day-by-day human relations. It would be expected that these songs would point indirectly to be sure, but definitely, to the slave owner. But for the most part, the songs are strangely silent here. Many indeed have been the speculations as to the reason for this unnatural omission. There are those who say we are dealing with children so limited in mentality that there is no margin of selfhood remaining for striking out, directly or indirectly, in a frenzy of studied fury against the slave owner. This is arrant nonsense, as the vast number of slave insurrections all through this terrible period will certify. There are those who say that the religion was so simple, so naive, so completely otherworldly that no impression was made by the supra-immoral aspects of the environment; only a simple acceptance of one's fate. Any person who has talked with an ex-slave could hardly hold such a position.

There seems to be a more comprehensive answer than any of these. The fact was that the slave owner was regarded as one outside the pale of moral and ethical responsibility. The level of high expectation of moral excellence for the master was practically *nihil*. Nothing could be expected from him but gross evil—he was in terms of morality—amoral. The truth seems to be that the slave owner as a class did not warrant a high estimate of ethical judgment. There is no more tragic result from this total experience than the fact that even at the present time such injunctions as "love your enemies" are often taken for granted to mean the enemy within the group itself. The relationship between slave and master, as far as both the slave and the master were concerned, was "out of bounds" in terms of moral responsibility. It seems clear, then, that the second mood has to do with those "we group" relationships of the slave and his fellow bondsmen.

Such is the meaning of:

> Down on me, down on me,
> Looks like everybody in the whole round world is
>   down on me.
> Talk about me as much as you please,
> I'll talk about you when I get on my knees.
> Looks like everybody in the whole round world is
>   down on me.
>
> Sometimes I'm up, sometimes I am down
> Sometimes I'm almost on the ground
> Looks like everybody in the whole round world is
>   down on me.

To refer to the refrain of one other such song:

> Oh, this is a sin-trying world,
> This is a sin-trying world.

In the second place, life is regarded as a pilgrimage, a sojourn, while the true home of the spirit is beyond the vicissitudes of life with God! This is a familiar theme of the human spirit. We are dealing with a striking theory of time. Time is measured in terms of events, actions, therefore intentions and desires. All experience, then, is made up of a series of more or less intense meaning—units that may fall in such rapid succession that the interval between is less than any quantitative value. Within the scope of an event-series all of human life is bound. Freedom can only mean, in this sense, the possibility of release from the tyranny of succeeding intervals of events. The totality of life, then, in its existential aspects, is thus completely exhausted in time. Death in such a view means complete cessation of any sense of interval and therefore of any sense of events. In short, here death means either finality or complete absorption from time-space awareness. Whatever transpires beyond death, while it can be thought of only in terms of time-space intervals, is of another universe of discourse, another quality of being.

It is in order now to raise a question as to the relation between *before* and *after* in terms of death and life. There seems to be no real break between before and after. Any notion of the continuity of life that transcends the fact of death is significant because of the advantage that is given to the meaning of life. Even though it be true that death is a process moving toward fulfillment in a single climactic event, as contrasted with life, death seems ever to be a solitary event; while life does not seem to be a single event but a process. Even at birth, the process of life seems to be well under way, well advanced. In the light of man's conscious experience with life, death seems to be a moment for the release of potentials of which the individual is in some sense already aware. Life then becomes illustrative of a theory of time that is latitudinal or flowing. On the other hand, death is suggestive of a theory of time that is circular or wheel-like.

Life always includes movement, process, inner activity, and some form of irritation. Something more is implicit than what is apparent in any cycle or series of cycles that sustain all manifestations. In such a view, life takes on a definite character of timelessness. There are no isolated, unrelated and, therefore, inconsequential events or moments. Every day is fraught with antecedents and consequences the logic of which is *inner relatedness* rather than *outer seeming*. Every day is a day of judgment and all life is lived under a continuous and inner scrutiny.

To think of life, then, as a pilgrimage means that not only is life characterized by an undertow of continuity but also that the individual has no alternative but to participate responsibly in that continuity. It is this concept rooted in the New Testament interpretation of the meaning of life that is to be found in many of the Spirituals. A few of such songs have been mentioned in other connections. One of the great utterances of this character is:

> Done made my vow to the Lord,
> And I never will turn back,
> I will go, I shall go,
> To see what the end will be.
>
> My strength, Good Lord, is almost gone,
> I will go, I will go,
> To see what the end will be.
> But you have told me to press on,
> I will go, I shall go,
> To see what the end will be.

The goal of the pilgrimage looms large by inference in some of the songs. The goal is not defined as such in many of them—but

the fact of the goal pervades the temper with which the journey is
undertaken or endured. There is something filled with breathless
anticipation and great strength in these lines:

> Wait a little while,
> Then we'll sing a new song,
> Wait a little while,
> Then we'll sing a new song.
>
> Sometimes I get a heavenly view,
> Then we'll sing a new song.
> And then my trials are so few,
> Then we'll sing a new song.

There is no attempt to cast a false glow over the stark rugged-
ness of the journey. The facts of experience are seen for what they
are—difficult, often even unyielding:

> It is a mighty rocky road,
> Most done travelling.
> Mighty rocky road,
> Most done travelling.
> Mighty rocky road,
> Bound to carry my soul to the Lord.
>
> Hold out your light you heaven-bound soldier,
> Let your light shine around the world.

Of the sheer will to carry on under the compelling aegis of a
great commitment, what could be more accurately expressive than:

> Stay in the field,
> Stay in the field,
> Until the war is ended.
> Mine eyes are turned to the heavenly gate,
> Till the war is ended.
> I'll keep my way, or I'll be too late,
> Till the war is ended.

Here is still another variation of the same basic theme:

> Oh, my good Lord, show me the way.
> Enter the chariot, travel along.

Noah sent out a morning dove,
Enter the chariot, travel along,
Which brought back a token of heavenly love,
Enter the chariot, travel along.

What, then, is the fundamental significance of all these interpretations of life and death? What are these songs trying to say? They
express the profound conviction that God was not done with them,
that God was not done with life. The consciousness that God had
not exhausted His resources, or better still that the vicissitudes of
life could not exhaust God's resources, did not ever leave them. This
is the secret of their ascendancy over circumstances and the basis
of their assurances concerning life and death. The awareness of the
presence of a God who was personal, intimate, and active was the
central fact of life and around it all the details of life and destiny
were integrated.

It must be borne in mind that there seems to be little place in
their reckoning for the distinction between God and Jesus. In some
of the songs the terms God and Jesus are used interchangeably—to
illustrate:

Did you ever see such a man as God?
A little more faith in Jesus,
A preaching the Gospel to the poor,
A little more faith in Jesus.

For the most part, a very simple theory of the incarnation is
ever present. The simpler assumptions of Christian orthodoxy are
utilized. There was no elaborate scheme of separate office and function between God and Jesus and only a very rare reference to the
Holy Spirit. Whether the song uses the term, Jesus, or the oft repeated Lord, or Saviour, or God, the same insistence is present—
God is in them, in their souls, as they put it, and what is just as
important, He is in the facts of their world. In short, God is active
in history in a personal and primary manner. People who live under
great pressures, grappling with tremendous imponderables which left
to themselves they could not manage, have no surplus energy for
metaphysical distinctions. Such distinctions apart from the necessity of circumstances or urgency of spirit, belong to those upon whom
the hold of the environment is relatively relaxed. Urgency forces a

reach for the ultimate, which ultimate in the intensity of demand is incorporated in the warp and woof of immediacy.

It is next in order to examine the large place given to the other-worldly emphasis in these songs. What is the meaning of Heaven, of the final Judgment? In such considerations we come to grips with the conception of immortality implicit and explicit in the songs, and the basis for it.

Again and again I have heard many people (including descendants of these singers) speak disparagingly of the otherworldly emphasis as purely a mechanism of escape and sheer retreat. The argument is that such an emphasis served as a kind of soporific, making for docility and submission. It is further charged that here we are dealing with a clever device by which these people were manipulated into a position which rendered them more completely defenseless than they would have been without it.

Such an argument must be examined. In the first place, the facts make clear that religion did serve to deepen the capacity of endurance and the absorption of suffering. It was a precious bane! What greater tribute could be paid to religious faith in general and to their religious faith in particular than this: It taught a people how to ride high to life, to look squarely in the face those facts that argue most dramatically against all hope and to use those facts as raw material out of which they fashioned a hope that the environment, with all of its cruelty, could not crush. With untutored hands—with a sure artistry and genius created out of a vast vitality, a concept of God was wrenched from the Sacred Book, the Bible, the chronicle of a people who had learned through great necessity the secret meaning of suffering. This total experience enabled them to reject annihilation and affirm a terrible right to live. The *center of focus* was beyond themselves in a God who was a companion to them in their miseries even as He enabled them to transcend their miseries. And this is good news! Under God the human spirit can triumph over the most radical frustrations! This is no ordinary achievement. In the presence of an infinite desperation held at white heat in the consciousness of a people, out of the very depth of life, an infinite energy took shape on their behalf.

> Oh rise, shine, for thy light is a coming.
> Oh rise, shine, for thy light is a coming.
> My Lord says he's coming by and by.

Do we wonder then that they sang:

> Oh religion is a fortune.
> I really do believe.
> Oh religion is a fortune,
> I really do believe!

In the second place, this religious emphasis did not paralyze action, it did not make for mere resignation. On the contrary, it gave the mind a new dimension of resourcefulness. I had a college classmate who cleared his throat just before responding to the question of his teacher. The clearing of the throat broke the impasse between his mind and his immediate environment so that he could have a sense of ascendancy in his situation. It was in some such fashion as this that these religious songs functioned. (Of course, they did much more than this.) Once the impasse was broken, many things became possible to them. They could make their religion vehicular in terms of the particular urgencies of the moment. "Steal away to Jesus" became an important call to those who had ears to hear. In other words, far from paralyzing action, religion made for detachment from the environment so that they could live in the midst of the traffic of their situation with the independence of solitude. The pragmatic result for them was an awareness that against the darkness of their days, something warred, "a strange new courage." To them it was the work of God and who could say to them *nay*?

We turn now to an examination of the place and significance of the notion of judgment. Taking their clue from the word picture given by Jesus in the Gospels, the Judgment was the climax of human history. This made a tremendous appeal to the imagination. The figure of Gabriel was added to the imagery of Jesus. There are many references to Gabriel:

> O get your trumpet Gabriel
> And come down on the sea.
> Now don't you sound your trumpet
> Till you get orders from me—
> I got a key to that Kingdom
> I got a key to that Kingdom
> And the world can't do me no harm.

To mention the refrain of one other song:

> Gabriel, Gabriel, blow your trumpet!
> My Lord says he's going to rain down fire.

Some of these songs are almost pure drama. Consider this very old hymn, no record of which is to be found in any of the available collections:

> Oh, He's going to wake up the dead,
> Going to wake up the dead,
> God's going to wake up the dead.
> One of these mornings bright and fair,
> God's going to wake up the dead.

The judgment is personal *and* cosmic so that even the rocks and mountains, the stars, the sea, are all involved in so profound a process:

> My Lord what a morning!
> My Lord what a morning!
> When the stars begin to fall.
>
> You will hear the trumpet sound
> To wake the nations underground,
> Standing at my God's right hand,
> When the stars begin to fall.

The matter of most crucial importance is this—a man is brought face to face with his own life—personal accountability is the keynote:

> When the master calls me to Him
> I'll be somewhere sleeping in my grave.
> In that great day when he calls us to him
> I'll be somewhere sleeping in my grave.

The deep intimacy between the soul and God is constantly suggested. Even the true name of the individual is known only to God. There are references to the fact that the designation, Child of God, is the only name that is necessary. This gnosis of the individual is an amazing example of the mystical element present in the slave's religious experience. The slave's answer to the use of terms of personal designation that are degrading is to be found in his private knowledge that his name is known only to the God of the entire universe. In the Judgment everybody will at last know who he is, a fact which he has known all along.

> O' nobody knows who I am, who I am,
> Till the Judgment morning.

Judgment takes place in time. It is a moment when the inner significance of a man's deeds is revealed. God shall deal with each according to his history. It was with reference to the Judgment that life took on a subdued character. Everybody is judged. The Judge is impartial. There is distinct continuity between the life on earth and the Judgment. Excuses are of no avail. God, the Judge, knows the entire story.

> O', He sees all you do,
> He hears all you say,
> My Lord's-a-writing all the time.

Judgment was not thought of as being immediately after death. There is a time element between death and final judgment. Life, death, judgment, this was the thought sequence. When the final judgment takes place there will be no more time. What takes place after judgment has a necessitous, mandatory character ascribed to it. Man can influence his judgment before death—after death everything is unalterable. This notion of the ultimate significance of life on earth is another aspect of the theory of time to which we have made reference. Here is a faithful following of the thought of the Gospels.

And yet there is more to be said concerning the idea of the Judgment. What does the concept say? Are we dealing with a matter of fact and of literal truth? If we are, then the symbolism of the Judgment is necessarily an essential symbolism. What is the literal truth seeking expression in this symbolism? It is this: The life of man is significantly capable of rising to the demands of maximum moral responsibility. That which is capable of a maximum moral responsibility functioning in the tiny compass of single events takes on the aspects of the beyond-event, hence beyond time, therefore eternal. The conclusion seems inescapable that man is interpreted as having only mortal manifestations, but even these mortal manifestations have immortal overtones. If this were not true then there would be no significance in the symbolic fact of judgment. The literal truth requires a symbolism that is completely vehicular or revelatory.

Finally, we turn to an examination of the place and significance of the fact of Heaven in the thinking of these early singers. Heaven was a place—it was not merely an idea in the mind. This must be held in mind, constantly. The thinking about it is spatial. It is the thinking of Jesus in the Fourth Gospel. "I go to prepare a place for you. If I go and prepare a place for you I shall come again, and take you unto myself that where I am there ye may be also." "In my father's house are many mansions." These word pictures supplied a concreteness to the fulfillment of all earth's aspirations and longings. The songs are many, expressing highly descriptive language of this character:

> I haven't been to heaven
> But I've been told,
> The streets are pearl
> And the gates are gold;
> Not made with hands.

What a plaintive wistfulness is found here:

> In bright mansions above,
> In bright mansions above,
> Lord, I want to live up yonder;
> In bright mansions above.

Such an aspiration was in sharp contrast to dimly lighted cabins with which they were familiar. Perfection, truth, beauty, even goodness are again and again symbolized by light. This is universal.

Heaven was as intensely personal as the facts of their experience or as the fact of the Judgment. Here at last was a place where the slave *was counted in.* He had the dignity of personal registration.

> O write my name, O write my name,
> The angels in heaven are going to write my name.
> Yes, write my name with a golden pen,
> The angels in heaven are going to write my name.

Heaven is regarded as a dimension of self-extension in the sense of private possession:

> I want God's heaven to be mine, to be mine,
> Yes, I want God's heaven to be mine.

Who is there that can escape the irony and the triumph in:

> I got a robe,
> You got a robe,
> All God's children got robes.
> When we get to heaven
> We're going to put on our robes,
> We're going to shout all over God's heaven.

There will be no proscription, no segregation, no separateness, no slave row, but complete freedom of movement—the most psychologically dramatic of all manifestations of freedom.

All of these songs and many others like them argue for an authentic belief in personal immortality. In large part it is a belief growing out of the necessities of life as they experienced it. Family ties are restored, friends and particularly loved ones are reunited. The most precious thing of all was the fact that personal identity was not lost but heightened. Heaven would not be heaven, it would have no meaning, if the fact of contrasting experiences was not always possible and evident. There was a great compulsion to know then a new and different life, which knowledge could only be real if the individual were able to recall how it once was with him. We are not surprised to find a great emphasis on reunion. There was nothing more heart-tearing in that far-off time of madness than the separation of families at the auction block. Wives were sold from their husbands to become breeders for profit, children were separated from their parents and from each other—in fact, from the beginning, the slave population was a company of displaced and dispossessed people. The possibility of ever seeing one's loved ones again was very remote. The conviction grew that this is the kind of universe that cannot deny ultimately the demands of love and longing. The issue of reuniting with loved ones turned finally on the hope of immortality and the issue of immortality turned on the fact of God. Therefore God would make it right and once again God became the answer.

This personal immortality carried with it also the idea of rest from labor, of being able to take a long sigh cushioned by a deep sense of peace. If time is regarded as having certain characteristics that are event transcending and the human spirit is not essentially time bound but a time binder, then the concept of personal survival of death follows automatically. For man is never completely involved in, nor absorbed by, experience. He is an experiencer with recollection and memory—so these songs insist. The logic of such a position is that man was not born *in* time, that he was not created by a time-space experience, but rather that man was born *into* time. Something of him enters all time-space relationships, even birth, completely and fully intact, and is not created by the time-space relationship. In short, the most significant thing about man is what Eckhart calls the "uncreated element" in his soul. This was an assumed fact profoundly at work in the life and thought of the early slaves.

This much was certainly clear to them—the soul of man was immortal. It could go to heaven or hell, but it could not *die*. Most of the references to hell are by inference. Not to be with God was to be in hell but it did not mean not to *be*.

It is in order to raise the same question about heaven that was raised previously about the Judgment. Are we dealing here with a matter of literal truth? Or are we once again dealing with necessary symbolism growing out of literal truth? In other words, what is the intrinsic meaning attached to or to be drawn out of the concept of heaven? Is this mere drama or some crude art form? Certain facts are quite evident in the picture given. Heaven was specific! An orderly series of events was thought to take place. The human spirit rests—the fulfillment of the exhausted. A crown, a personal crown is given—a fulfillment for those who strive without the realization of their strivings. There is a room of one's own—the fulfillment of life in terms of the healing balm of privacy. There are mansions— the fulfillment of life in terms of living with a high quality of dig-

nity. There are robes, slippers—the fulfillment of life in terms of
the restoration of self-respect. The idea at the core of the literal truth
in the concept of heaven is this—life is totally right, structurally
dependable, good essentially as contrasted with the moral concepts
of good and evil. It affirms that the contradictions of human experience are not ultimate. The profoundest desires of man are of God,
and therefore they cannot be denied ultimately.

> Our ship is on the ocean but
> We'll anchor by and by.

To use the oft-repeated phrase of Augustine, "Thou hast made us
for Thyself, and our souls are restless till they find their rest in thee."
There is an order, a moral order in which men participate, that
gathers up into itself, dimensional fulfillment, limitless in its creativity and design. Whatever may be the pressures to which one is
subjected, the snares, the buffetings, one must not for a moment
think that there is not an ultimate value always at stake. It is this
ultimate value at stake in all experience that is the final incentive
to decency, to courage and hope. Human life, even the life of a slave,
must be lived worthily of so grand an undertaking. At every moment
a crown was placed over his head that he must constantly grow tall
enough to wear. Only of that which is possessed of infinite potentials can an infinite demand be required. The unfulfilled, the un-
developed only has a future; the fulfilled, the rounded out, the finished
can only have a past. The human spirit participates in both past and
future in what it regards as the *present* but it is independent of both.

We may dismiss, then, the symbolism of these songs as touch-
ing life and death if we understand the literal truth with which they
have to do. The moment we accept the literal truth, we are once
again faced with the urgency of a vehicular symbolism. The cycle is
indeed vicious. To be led astray by the crassness, the materialistic
character of the symbolism so that in the end we reject the literal
truth, is to deny life itself of its dignity and man the right or necessity of dimensional fulfillment. In such a view the present moment
is all there is—man is no longer a time binder but becomes a prisoner in a tight world of momentary events—no more and no less.
His tragedy would be that nothing beyond the moment could happen
to him and all of his life could be encompassed within the boundary

of a time-space fragment. For these slave singers such a view was completely unsatisfactory and it was therefore thoroughly and decisively rejected. And this is the miracle of their achievement causing them to take their place alongside the great creative religious thinkers of the human race. They made a worthless life, the life of chattel property, a mere thing, a body, *worth living!* They yielded with abiding enthusiasm to a view of life which included all the events of their experience without exhausting themselves in those experiences. To them this quality of life was insistent fact because of that which deep within them, they discovered of God, and his far-flung purposes. God was not through with them. And He was not, nor could He be exhausted by, any single experience or any series of experiences. To know Him was to live a life worthy of the loftiest meaning of life. Men in all ages and climes, slave or free, trained or untutored, who have sensed the same values, are their fellow-pilgrims who journey together with them in increasing self-realization in the quest for the city that hath foundations, whose Builder and Maker is God.

Sorrow Songs— The Ground of Hope (II)

A BALM IN GILEAD

There is a balm in Gilead,
To make the spirit whole.
There is a balm in Gilead,
To heal the sin-sick soul.

The peculiar genius of the Negro slave is revealed here in much of its structural splendor. The setting is the Book of Jeremiah. The prophet has come to a "Dead Sea" place in his life. Not only is he discouraged over the external events in the life of Israel, but he is also spiritually depressed and tortured. As a wounded animal he cried out, "Is there no balm in Gilead? Is no physician there?" It is not a question of fact that he is raising—it is not a question directed to any particular person for an answer. It is not addressed either to God or to Israel, but rather it is a question raised by Jeremiah's entire life. He is searching his own soul. He is stripped to the literal substance of himself, and is turned back on himself for an answer. Jeremiah is saying actually, "There must be a balm in Gilead; it cannot be that there is no balm in Gilead." The relentless winnowing of his own bitter experience has laid bare his soul to the end that he is brought face to face with the very ground and core of his own faith.

The slave caught the mood of this spiritual dilemma, and with it did an amazing thing. He straightened the question mark in Jeremiah's sentence into an exclamation point: "There *is* a balm in Gilead!" Here is a note of creative triumph.

The melody itself is most suggestive. It hovers around the basic scale without any straying far afield. Only in one place is there a sharp lifting of a tonal eyebrow—a suggestion of escape; and then the melody swings back to work out its destiny within the zones of melodic agreement.

The basic insight here is one of optimism—an optimism that grows out of the pessimism of life and transcends it. It is an optimism that uses the pessimism of life as raw material out of which it creates its own strength. Many observers of Negroes have remarked that they are a happy-go-lucky people. They are quick to laugh. They are stereotyped as buffoons and clowns. What is overlooked is the fact that the basic laughter of the Negro is vital and dynamic, leaping out of an elemental faith in life itself, which makes a sense of ultimate defeat not only unrealistic but impossible. This humor arises out of the creative unfolding of two very profound insights.

In the first place, there is the insight that life is its own restraint. The logic of this notion is that there is a moral order by which the life of the individual is bound. It is inescapable, and applies to all men alike. If this is true, men do reap what they sow; not only because it is so written in the Book, but also because it is a part of the nature of life. In the last analysis life cannot be fooled, however powerful and clever the individual may be. This notion is a dynamic weapon in the hands of the disadvantaged. It makes it possible for them to ride high to life, and particularly to keep their spirits from being eaten away by gloom and hopelessness. The slave made this discovery long ago; this insight came to him crystal clear, and was a boon and a saviour.

Let us see how the slave's mind worked on this. The master is just a man after all, bound by the same moral laws and physical laws that bind the slave. The fact that he is in power simply increases his temptation to think that he is not bound by the same things that bind the slave. In his sense of security, made possible by the illusion

of omnipotence, he forgets to be mindful of the things that ultimately bind him. The coming of the Civil War with all its tragic
consequences—the laying waste of plantations, the complete destruction and disintegration of wealth, the withering of well-nigh
limitless powers—the stark and gaping emptiness of the big house
which once rang with laughter and joy: all these were climactic vin-
dications to the slaves that life is its own restraint, that no man can
beat the game.

How easy it is to forget this—to think that life will make an
exception in one's own case. This is a timely lesson for our nation
as a whole. At the moment we stand as the graphic masters of much
of the earth by virtue of our vast resourcefulness, our material resources, and the techniques by which we have reduced great con-
glomerates of nature to simple units of control and utility. It is a
terrifying truth that life is its own restraint, and that the moral law
that binds in judgment the life of the individual binds the nation
and the race. Unless there is a great rebirth of high and holy moral
courage, which will place at the center of our vast power an abiding
sense of moral responsibility, both because of our treatment of mi-
norities at home and our arrogance abroad, we may very easily become the most hated nation on earth. No amount of power, wealth,
or prestige can stay this judgment. If we would be beloved we must
share that kind of spirit as the expression of the true genius of our
democratic government.

It is the fundamental realization of the notion that life is its
own restraint that sustained the slave in his darkest days, and gave
him an elemental vigor that expressed itself in a deep optimism arising out of the pessimism of life. He picks up the searching words of
Jeremiah and sings his affirmation, "There is a balm in Gilead!" Of
course there are those who may say that this is merely a defense
mechanism, likened unto the mood of a man in prison who thanks
God that he is there; for if he were not, he might be hit by a stray
bullet. Such reflections regard this mood as a defense mechanism,
which becomes a substitute for action that would relieve the pressure. The only answer to this is that there would have been no survival in this philosophy for the Negro if it were merely a mechanism
of sheer defense.

The second insight here is that the contradictions of life are
not in themselves either final or ultimate. This points up the basic

difference between pessimism and optimism. The pessimist appraises the facts of experience, and on their face value is constrained to pass a final judgment on them. If there are contradictions between good and evil—between that which makes for peace and that which makes for turbulence—then these contradictions are regarded from this point of view as being in themselves ultimate and final; and because they are ultimate, inescapable, and therefore binding. Back of such a view is the conception that life in essence is fixed, finished, unchanging. Man is caught in the agonizing grip of inevitables; and whatever may be his chance or circumstantial assignment, all his alternatives are reduced to zero. For the man in power this is a happy philosophy. All notions of social superiority based on the elevation of a principle of racial inequality lifted to the dimension of a law of life, find their nourishment here. They state in bold terms that the God òf the universe is basically partial, immoral, or amoral; or, from the point of view of the underprivileged by birth or election, God is demoniacal. This undermines all hope for the oppressed, and if it is embraced gives them no sense of the future that is different from the experience of the past. The structure of the universe is stacked against them, and they may die in ultimate defiance of it, but their death will be but a futile gesture, bringing havoc to all who survive the relentless logic of such abiding fatalism.

But if perchance the contradictions of life are not ultimate, then there is always the growing edge of hope in the midst of the most barren and most tragic circumstances. It is a complete renunciation of the thoroughgoing dualism of the point of view just discussed. It is a matter of supreme significance that men are never quite robbed of all hope. There is something present in the spirit of man, sometimes even taking the form of great arrogance, sometimes quietly nourishing the springs of resistance to a great tyranny—there is something in the spirit of man that knows that the dualism, however apparently binding, runs out, exhausts itself, and leaves a core of assurance that the ultimate destiny of man is good. This becomes the raw material of all hope, and is one of the taproots of religious faith for the human spirit. When it applies to the individual and becomes the norm of human relationships, a new sense of the ethical significance of life becomes manifest. Just as no man is ever quite willing—protestations to the contrary notwithstanding—to give himself up, so we are under judgment not to give each other up. The root of this judgment is found in the fact that deep within us is the conviction that man's destiny is a good destiny. To illustrate. For a period—how long we do not know but certainly ever since the memory of man became self-conscious—there has been war among men. Yet in times of even temporary cessation from struggle, or in times of greatest conflict, the dream of peace continues to nourish the hope of the race. This dream persists, even though we do not know what peace on earth would be like because it has never been experienced. We continue to hope against all evidence to the contrary, because that hope is fed by a conviction deeper than the processes of thought that the destiny of man is good. It is this spirit that has been captured by the spiritual. Yes, *"There is a balm in Gilead to heal the sin-sick soul."* The day that this conviction leaves the spirit of man, his moment on the earth is over, and the last fond hope of the race perishes from the earth forever, and a lonely God languishes while before Him His dreams go silently to dust.

THE BLIND MAN

The Blind Man stood on the road and cried;
Crying that he might receive his sight.

Since early morning the blind man had been waiting by the roadside. Word had come to his village the night before that the Healer would pass that way in the morning. The persistent hope for sight had never quite left him. True, he had been blind all his life, and yet, through all the corridors of his spirit, the simple trust persisted that he would some day gain his sight. At last, with his head slightly tilted the better to reassure himself of the quiet thud of walking feet, he *knows*. All his life he had waited for that precise moment. There is no greater tragedy than for the individual to be brought face to face with one's great moment only to find that one is unprepared. Years ago I read a poem by Sara Teasdale that pictured a woman climbing a hill; all the way up she thought how grand it would be when she reached the crest, lungs full of air, a wide, almost limitless view as far as eyes could see; but "the briars were always pulling" at her gown. Then she crossed the crest; when, she did not know, for the briars were always pulling at her gown, and now all the rest of the way would "be only going down. . . ." But the blind man was ready. As Jesus approached he began crying, "Jesus, thou son of David, have mercy on me." Over and over he said it, until the words became one with the walking rhythm of the approaching feet of Jesus and his disciples. The rest of the story depicts the healing of the blind man, who goes on his way rejoicing.

The slave singers did a strange thing with this story. They identified themselves completely with the blind man at every point but the most crucial one. In the song, the blind man does not receive his sight. The song opens with the cry; it goes through many nuances of yearning, but always it ends with the same cry with which it began. The explanation for this is not far to seek; for the people who sang this song had not received their "sight." They had longed for freedom with all their passionate endeavors, but it had not come. This brings us face to face with a primary discovery of the human spirit. Very often the pain of life is not relieved—there is the cry of great desire, but the answer does not come—only the fading echo of one's lonely cry. Jesus, in the garden of Gethsemane, prayed that the cup might pass, but he had to drink it to the last bitter dregs. The Apostle Paul prayed for the "thorn" to be taken from his flesh, but he had to carry the thorn to his grave. These are but two illustrations from the early history of the church that etch in clear outline the same basic insight. For the slave, freedom was not on the horizon; there stretched ahead the long road down which there marched in interminable lines only the rows of cotton, the sizzling heat, the riding overseer with his rawhide whip, the auction block where families were torn asunder, the barking of the bloodhounds— all this, but not freedom.

Human slavery has been greatly romanticized by the illusion of distance, the mint julep, the long Southern twilight, and the lazy sweetness of blooming magnolias. But it must be intimately remembered that slavery was a dirty, sordid, inhuman business. When the slaves were taken from their homeland, the primary social unit was destroyed, and all immediate tribal and family ties were ruthlessly broken. This meant the severing of the link that gave the individual African a sense of *persona*. There is no more hapless victim than one who is cut off from family, from language, from one's roots. He is completely at the mercy of his environment, to be cowed, shaped, and molded by it at will. When the Negro Mission of Friendship was in India several years ago, one of the things that puzzled the students and friends there was the fact that we spoke no African language and wore no distinctively African dress. Again and again they asked, "Why do you speak only the language of the conqueror? Why do you wear only Western clothes?"

Again, the slave was cut off from his religion, whatever kind it was. When the master gave the slave his (the master's) God, for a long time it meant that it was difficult to disentangle religious experience from slavery sanction. The existence of these songs is in itself a monument to one of the most striking instances on record in which a people forged a weapon of offense and defense out of a psychological shackle. By some amazing but vastly creative spiritual insight the slave undertook the redemption of a religion that the master had profaned in his midst.

In instance after instance, husbands were sold from wives, children were separated from parents; a complete and withering attack was made on the sanctity of the home and the family. Added to all this, the slave women were constantly at the mercy of the lust and rapacity of the master himself, while the slave husband or father was powerless to intervene. Indeed, the whole sorry picture is a revelation of a depth of moral degradation that even in retrospect makes forgiveness one of the greatest fruits of the spirit.

Frustration with no answer in the environment! Under such circumstances, what does one do? This is the fundamental issue raised by this song. It is quite possible to become obsessed with the idea of making everything and everybody atone for one's predicament. All one's frustrations may be distilled into a core of bitterness and disillusionment that expresses itself in a hardness of attitude and a total mercilessness—in short, one may become mean. You have seen people like that. They seem to have a fierce grudge against life; because they are unable to corner it and wreak their churning vengeance against it, they penalize everything else they touch. They show no favors, demand none. They trust no one and have no interest in doing so, but on the slightest provocation lash out in an almost maniacal fury. Sometimes they are less obvious and show no emotion, but are deliberate and calculating in their attack and conquest. For them life is essentially evil, and they are essentially vengeful. "Cruel" is the word that may describe them. They are out to settle a score with life. They have nothing to lose, because they have lost everything. This is one alternative for those who face a complete and overwhelming frustration.

Or such persons may withdraw completely into themselves. Very carefully they build a wall around themselves and let no one penetrate it. They carry the technique of detachment to a highly developed art. Such people are not happy, nor are they unhappy, they are completely indifferent. They look out on life through eyes that have burned out, and nothing is left but a dead, cold stare. Life has been reduced to routine, long ago learned by heart, and for them laid aside. There comes to mind the statue over the grave of the wife of Henry Adams in the old Rock Creek Cemetery in Washington—perhaps you have seen it. There is the seated figure of a woman whose chin is resting on her supporting right hand. The whole figure is draped in a large, inclusive fold of greenish bronze. She is looking steadily ahead, with eyes open but unseeing. The total effect is of something that is burned out—no spark is left; and yet there is a certain sense of being alive. This is the mood and tense of the person who embraces the second alternative. A great silence envelops the life, like the stillness of absolute motion suddenly stopped. A proud people irretrievably beaten in battle, who must give quarter to the occupying enemy, sometimes react this way. It is what may be called "the silence of a great hatred." Sometimes the attitude expresses itself in terms of aggressive cynicism and a pose of bold, audacious, belligerent defiance.

The final alternative is creative—thought of in terms of a second wind. It involves the exercise of a great and dynamic will. An accurate appraisal of all circumstances is clearly seen, understood, challenged; and despite the facts revealed, hope continues even against odds and evidence. Stephen Benet depicts this very dramatically in *John Brown's Body*. There is a scene in which Lincoln is probing the universe to find the right way . . . the sure answer to his urgent problem. He thinks of himself as an old hunting dog, whose energies are spent, "tail down, belly flattened to the ground"—he can't go a step further. There is complete exhaustion; but the will remains, and becomes the rallying point for a new persistency that finally unlocks the door through which he moves to release and fulfillment. He goes on because he must go on.

This is the discovery made by the slave that finds its expression in the song—a complete and final refusal to be stopped. The spirit broods over all the stubborn and recalcitrant aspects of experience, until they begin slowly but inevitably to take the shape of one's deep desiring. There is a bottomless resourcefulness in man that ultimately enables him to transform "the spear of frustration into a shaft of light." Under such a circumstance even one's deepest distress becomes so sanctified that a vast illumination points the way to the land one seeks. This is the God in man; because of it, man stands in immediate candidacy for the power to absorb all the pain of life without destroying his joy. He who has made that discovery knows at last that he can stand anything that can happen to him. "The Blind Man stood on the road and cried"—the answer came in the cry itself. What a panorama of the ultimate dignity of the human spirit!

DEEP RIVER

I've known rivers ancient as the
  world and older than the flow of
  human blood in human veins.
My soul has grown deep like the rivers.
I bathed in the Euphrates when
  dawns were young,
I built my hut near the Congo and
  it lulled me to sleep,
I looked upon the Nile and raised
  the Pyramids above it,
I heard the singing of the Mississippi
  when Abe Lincoln went down to
  New Orleans,
And I've seen its muddy bosom turn
  all golden in the sunset.
I've known rivers;
Ancient, dusky rivers;
My soul has grown deep like
  the rivers.*

The fascination of the flowing stream is a constant source of wonder and beauty to the sensitive mind. It was ever thus. The restless

*Langston Hughes, "The Negro Speaks of Rivers." Copyright 1926 by Alfred A. Knopf, Inc., renewed 1954 by Langston Hughes. Reprinted from *Selected Poems of Langston Hughes* by permission of the publisher.

movement, the hurrying, ever-changing stream has ever been the bearer of the longings and yearnings of mankind for land beyond the horizon where dreams are fulfilled and deepest desires satisfied. It is not to be wondered at that in this spiritual there is a happy blending of majestic rhythm and poignant yearning:

> Deep River, my home is over Jordan;
> Deep River, my home is over Jordan.
> O don't you want to go to that Gospel Feast
> That Promised Land where all is Peace?
> Deep River, I want to cross over into camp ground.

This is perhaps the most universal insight, and certainly the most intellectual of all the spirituals. In a bold stroke it thinks of life in terms of a river. Of course it must be added that to these early singers—slaves as they were—quite practically the river may have been for many the last and most formidable barrier to freedom. To slip over the river from one of the border states would mean a chance for freedom in the North—or, to cross the river into Canada would mean freedom in a new country, a foreign land. But let us reflect on a deeper meaning here. To think of life as being like a river is a full and creative analogy.

The analogy is complete in the first place because a river has a very simple beginning. The Mississippi River, for instance, rises in the northern part of the United States, fed by perpetual snows; at its source it is unpretentious, simple. It increases in momentum, in depth, in breadth, in turbulence as it makes its journey down the broad expanse of America, until at last it empties itself into the Gulf of Mexico, which, in a sense, is the triumph of its own achievement!

It is the nature of the river to flow; it is always moving, always in process, always on its way. Long ago Heraclitus reminded us that "no man bathes twice in the same stream." There seems ever to be an infinite urgency that keeps the waters on business bent. They may be caught here and there in swirling pools, or temporarily stilled behind a sudden dam, but not for long. Once again they take up their march to fulfill their destiny, to keep their tryst with the sea.

Life is like that! Life on this planet—so the scientists tell us—began its long trek across the aeons, in a simple gelatinous form in far-off ages in some primeval ocean bed. It increased in complexity, in breadth, in turbulence, through myriad forms and combinations down to the latest times. Your life and my life began as a simple form, moving through varying stages of prenatal fulfillment, until by a great climactic spasm you and I were born. Then, once again, in simple beginning, increasing in anxiety, in turbulence, sometimes in depth, often in breadth, we make our way across the broad expanse of the years.

Our life represents essential process. It is small wonder that classic Buddhism makes so much of the experience of flux in human life. We seem always to be on our way. When I was ten years old I said that the thing I sought would come to pass when I was fifteen. When I became fifteen, it would come to pass when I was eighteen; and so on and on through the years; it is around the next turning. Life is like that. Growth is made possible in human life because of this essential characteristic.

> I shall arrive! What time, what circuit first
> I ask not; but unless God send His hail,
> Or blinding fireballs, sleet, or stifling snow,
> In some time, His good time, I shall arrive!
> He guides me and the bird. In His good time.

We are never able to do anything in quite the way we want to do it. No single experience, however great, is quite able to represent us adequately. Life is essentially dynamic and alive. It's this aliveness that guarantees and sustains all the particular manifestations of life by which we are surrounded and of which we are a part. With reference to no experience are we able to write "Q.E.D."; life is essentially unfinished. All judgments concerning experience are limited and partial. It is for this reason that in the last analysis judgment belongs with God. Even our self-judgments are limited, because we can never quite get our hands on all the materials, all the facts in each case. In any total sense we must act on the basis of evidence that is never quite conclusive.

The analogy is complete again, because of the striking relationship that the river maintains with all the banks it touches. Every bank that is touched by a river gives of itself to the water. It has no option: it is the nature of the relationship that the bank yield of itself to the river that drains it. No exceptions are allowed—there can be no substitutes. To be a bank is to give itself to the river. If I want to know the story of the Mississippi River, I need not follow it through all its meanderings across the continent; all I need do is to take a shovelful of delta sand where it empties into the Gulf, analyze it carefully, and there would stand revealed the essence of its story. Life is like that! If we think for a moment of the individual as the bank of the river and of life as the river, the analogy becomes fascinating. All our experiences leave their marks.

Or as Tennyson puts it on the lips of Ulysses:

> I am a part of all that I have met.
> Yet all experience is an arch wherethrough
> Gleams that untravelled land whose margin
> Fades forever and forever when I move.

I cannot escape. All experience is raw material that goes into the making of me. Though my experiences shape me ultimately, yet I am not my experiences. I am an experiencer—but without my particular experiences I should not be what I am. I am what I am at any particular moment by standing on the shoulders of an infinite series of yesterdays. A man cannot be quite separated from his yesterdays. Modern psychology, mental healing, modern education all take into account this basic fact. The amazing transformation of the material ideas, concepts, and ideologies of a whole nation in one generation is a case in point. It is the nature of life that we are kneaded and molded by our experience of life.

One of the profound insights of Jesus of Nazareth is that the history of a man's life is his judgment. This illustrates the point in an amazing dimension. He gives us a picture of the climax of human history in what is generally called the Great Judgment. It is a dramatic picture. The Judge, like some Oriental despot, sits enthroned. Before him come all the nations of the earth. Yet the Judge is merely a timekeeper, a recorder. He does not arbitrarily send a man to the right or left; it is the man's deeds that do it. The Judge is almost a figurehead—the point is made so sharply. In bold, awful outline the principle is etched in unforgettable austerity—the history of a man's life is his judgment. It is the lesson of the river! "It was always a serious thing to live."

The analogy persists, because a river has times of drought and times of flood. Due to a lack of rainfall, principally, the channel narrows. Rocks, the formation of certain bank contours that had been covered by the river, stand revealed without the pretense made possible by the sheltering stream. In some instances the channel becomes but a faint trickle of its former self.

Through melting snows and heavy rainfall the channel sometimes becomes swollen. The river that at one time was full of peace and quiet balance, bearing on its bosom much to sustain and make glad the life of man, becomes a wild, unrestrained monster. Reckless of consequences, impersonal to good and ill, the turbulent waters roll on their relentless way. The rising of the water is a fear-inspiring experience. Have you ever been in a flood? If you have, you've seen the waters creep slowly up the banks to the very top and beyond. There is perfect indifference to the plight of the victims—prayers, cries, cursings make no difference—the water continues to rise. It is the floodtime of the river.

Life is like that. There comes a time of dryness in life; everything seems to be at low tide. There is no sharp, tragic moment; no great or sudden draining of one's powers—only the silent loss of enthusiasm for living. Nothing seems to matter—just a great dryness of the spirit. No great demands are made on life—there are no particular hopes on the horizon—no great anticipation or expectation lures one on. It is the time of drought. I do not mean here the reaction to tragedy or frustration. For some people it comes as a reaction to some phenomenal spurt of energy expended in achieving a special goal. Of course there are some who are dry by temperament, and who find it most necessary to keep in direct touch with some person or even some object that keeps the waters of life flowing at full channel. The time of drought may be seasonal, or it may be specially circumstanced. It is therefore of greatest importance to understand its cause, and to discover early in life what special reserves must be tapped so as to bring flowing fully and freshly the refreshing, life-giving currents. There is perhaps no greater revelation of character than what is revealed by the things to which one appeals for regeneration, for restoration!

Life is like the river in floodtimes as well. There is something uncanny about the way in which disaster sometimes befalls the individual. One is often reminded of the words of Jesus—"For he that hath, to him shall be given: and he that hath not, from him shall be taken even that which he hath." Here is a person whose life is moving along smoothly without deep disturbance. One is surrounded by friends and loved ones; one has reasonable comforts, good health, emotional security, and all the other things that go to make for tranquility of mind and body. Then it comes! Death to loved ones, incurable illness, loss of job, some greater deception—these and things like them converge on life, and strip one bare of all external props and securities. Out of the depths of one's frustration or alarm one may cry out that life is not good but evil; there is some basic demoniacal monster in control of the life of man—there can be no God, no future life, nothing but the survival of the fittest and every man for himself. It is the floodtime of the river. The answer to the floodtime of the river is a greater opening *to* the sea. The answer to the drought of the river is a larger opening *from* the sea. The sea is the answer both to the drought and the floodtime of the river. The meaning of all this becomes clearer as we examine the final aspect of the analogy.

The analogy is complete in the last analysis because the river has a goal. The goal of the river is the sea. The river is ever on its way to the sea, whose far-off call "all waters hear." All the waters, in all the earth, are en route to the sea. Nothing can keep them from getting there. Men may build huge dams, there may be profound disturbances of the earth's surface that throw the river out of its course and force it to cut a new channel across a bed of granite, but at last the river will get to the sea. It may twist and turn, fall back on itself and start again, stumble over an infinite series of hindering rocks, but at last the river must answer the call of the sea. It is restless till it finds its rest in the sea.

All the waters of all the earth come from the sea. Paradox of paradoxes: that out of which the river comes is that into which the river goes. The goal and the source of the river are the same! From gurgling spring to giant waterfall; from morning dew to torrential downpour; from simple creek to mighty river—the source and the goal are the same: the sea.

Life is like that! The goal of life is God! The source of life is God! That out of which life comes is that into which life goes. He out of whom life comes is He into whom life goes. God is the goal of man's life, the end of all his seeking, the meaning of all his striv-

ing. God is the guarantor of all his values, the ultimate meaning—
the timeless frame of reference. That which sustains the flower of
the field, the circling series of stars in the heavens, the structure of
dependability in the world of nature everywhere, the stirring of the
will of man to action, the dream of humanity, developed and free,
for which myriad men, sometimes in solitariness in lonely places or
in great throngs milling in crowded squares—all this and infinitely
more in richness and variety and value is God. Men may be thrown
from their courses—they may wander for a million years in desert
and waste land, through sin and degradation, war and pestilence,
hate and love—at last they must find their rest in Him. If there is
that which at any time, anywhere in the universe, can ultimately
withstand the divine urgency—then whatever it is that shows such
strength is co-equal with God. Such a position to me is not only un-
tenable, but is also a denial of the basic ethical monotheism that for
me is the most satisfactory explanation of the meaning of life.

The source of life is God. The mystic applies this to human life
when he says that there is in man an uncreated element; or in the
Book of Job where it is written that his mark is in their foreheads.
In the last analysis the mood of reverence that should characterize
all men's dealings with each other finds its basis here. The demand
to treat all human beings as ends in themselves, or the moral imperative that issues in respect for personality, finds its profound inspiration here. To deal with men on any other basis, to treat them
as if there were not vibrant and vital in each one the very life of the
very God, is the great blasphemy; it is the judgment that is leveled
with such relentless severity on modern man. "Thou hast made us
for thyself and our souls are restless till they find their rest in thee,"
says Augustine. Life is like a river.

> Deep River, my home is over Jordan—
> Deep River, I want to cross over into camp ground.

MOMENTS
OF CELEBRATION

Fall

THE FALL OF THE YEAR

For many of us the fall of the year is a time of sadness and the long memory. All around us there are the evidences of fading, of withdrawal, of things coming to an end. What was alive and growing only a few short days or weeks ago seems now to have fulfilled itself and fallen back into the shadows. Vegetation withers but there is no agony of departure; there seems to be only death and stillness in the fall.

Those who have been ill all summer seem to get a deepening sense of foreboding in the fall. It is the time of the changing of the guard. It is the season of the retreat of energy. It is a time of letting go. It is the period of the first exhaustion. It is the period of the storms, as if the wind itself becomes the Avenging Angel too impatient to wait for the coming of death and the quiet fading of bud and flower and leaf. The rain is not gentle in the fall, it is feverish, truculent, and vicious. All the fury of wind and rain are undertoned by a vast lull in tempo and the running down of all things. There is a chill in the air in the fall. It is not cold; it is chilly, as if the temperature cannot quite make up its mind. The chill is ominous, the forerunner of the vital coldness of winter.

But the fall of the year is more than all this; much, much more. It marks an important change in the cycle of the year. This change means that summer is past. One season ends by blending into another. Here is a change of pace accenting a rhythm in the passing of time. How important this is! The particular mood inspires recollection and reflection. There is something very steadying and secure in the awareness that there is an underlying dependability in life— that change is a part of the experience of living. It is a reminder of the meaning of pause and plateau.

But fall provides something more. There is a harvest, a time of ingathering, of storing up in nature; there is a harvest, a time of ingathering, of storing up in the heart. There is the time when there must be a separation of that which has said its say and passes—that which ripens and finds its meaning in sustaining life in other forms. Nothing is lost, nothing disappears; all things belong, each in its way, to a harmony and an order which envelops all, which infuses all.

Fall accentuates the goodness of life and finds its truest meaning in the strength of winter and the breath of spring. Thank God for the fall.

Thanksgiving

A LITANY OF THANKSGIVING

Today, I make my Sacrament of Thanksgiving.
I begin with the simple things of my days:
    Fresh air to breathe,
    Cool water to drink,
    The taste of food,
    The protection of houses and clothes,
    The comforts of home.
For these, I make an act of Thanksgiving this day!

I bring to mind all the warmth of humankind that I have
        known:
    My mother's arms,
    The strength of my father,

    The playmates of my childhood,
    The wonderful stories brought to me from the lives of
        many who talked of days gone by when fairies and
        giants and all kinds of magic held sway:

The tears I have shed, the tears I have seen;
The excitement of laughter and the twinkle in the eye
   with its reminder that life is good.
For all these I make an act of Thanksgiving this day.

I finger one by one the messages of hope that awaited me
   at the crossroads:
The smile of approval from those who held in their hands
   the reins of my security;
The tightening of the grip in a single handshake when I
   feared the step before me in the darkness;
The whisper in my heart when the temptation was fiercest
   and the claims of appetite were not to be denied;
The crucial word said, the simple sentence from an open
   page when my decision hung in the balance.
For all these I make an act of Thanksgiving this day.

I pass before me the mainsprings of my heritage:
The fruits of the labors of countless generations who lived
   before me, without whom my own life would have no
   meaning;
The seers who saw visions and dreamed dreams;
The prophets who sensed a truth greater than the mind
   could grasp and whose words could only find fulfillment
   in the years which they would never see;
The workers whose sweat has watered the trees, the leaves
   of which are for the healing of the nations;
The pilgrims who set their sails for lands beyond all horizons, whose courage made paths into new worlds and
   far-off places;
The saviors whose blood was shed with a recklessness that
   only a dream could inspire and God could command.
For all this I make an act of Thanksgiving this day.

I linger over the meaning of my own life and the commitment to which I give the loyalty of my heart and mind:
The little purposes in which I have shared with my loves,
   my desires, my gifts;
The restlessness which bottoms all I do with its stark in-

sistence that I have never done my best, I have never
dared to reach for the highest;
The big hope that never quite deserts me, that I and my
kind will study war no more, that love and tenderness
and all the inner graces of Almighty affection will cover
the life of the children of God as the waters cover the
sea.

All these and more than mind can think and heart can feel,
I make as my sacrament of Thanksgiving to Thee,
Our Father, in humbleness of mind and simplicity of heart.

THE HARVEST
OF THE HEART

This is the season of gathering in, the season of the harvest in nature. Many things that were started in the spring and early summer
have grown to fruition and are now ready for reaping. Great and
significant as is the harvest in nature, the most pertinent kind of ingathering for the human spirit is what I call "the harvest of the heart."
Long ago, Jesus said that men should not lay up for themselves treasures on earth, where moths corrupt and thieves break in and steal,
but that men should lay up for themselves treasures in heaven. This
insight suggests that life consists of planting and harvesting, of sowing and reaping. We are always in the midst of the harvest and always in the midst of the planting. The words that we use in
communication, the profound stirrings of the mind out of which
thoughts and ideas arise, the ebb and flow of desires out of which
the simple or complex deed develops, are all caught in the process
of reaping and sowing, of planting and harvesting. There are no
anonymous deeds, no casual processes. Living is a shared process.
Even as I am conscious of things growing in me planted by others,
which things are always ripening, so others are conscious of things
growing in them planted by me, which are always ripening. Inasmuch as I do not live or die unto myself, it is of the essence of wisdom for me conscientiously to live and die in the profound awareness
of other people. The statement, "Know thyself," has been taken
mystically from the statement, "Thou hast seen thy brother, thou
hast seen thy God."

Christmas

THE BIRTH OF JESUS

Oscar Wilde says in *De Profundis,* "There is always room in an ignorant man's mind for a great idea." It is profoundly significant to me that the Gospel story in Luke reveals that the announcement of the birth of Jesus came first to simple shepherds, who were about their appointed tasks. After theology has done its work, after the reflective judgment of men from the heights or lonely retreats of privilege and security has wrought its most perfect pattern, the birth of Jesus remains the symbol of the dignity and inherent worthfulness of the common man. Stripped bare of art forms and liturgy, the literal substance of the story remains: Jesus Christ was born in a stable! He was born of humble parentage in surroundings that are the common lot of those who earn their living by the sweat of their brow. Nothing can rob the common man of this heritage. When he beholds Jesus, he sees in him the possibilities of life for even the humblest and a dramatic revelation of the meaning of God.

THE SINGING OF ANGELS

There must be always remaining in every man's life some place for the singing of angels, some place for that which in itself is breathlessly beautiful and, by an inherent prerogative, throws all the rest of life into a new and creative relatedness, something that gathers up in itself all the freshets of experience from drab and commonplace areas of living and glows in one bright white light of penetrating beauty and meaning—then passes. The commonplace is shot through with new glory; old burdens become lighter; deep and ancient wounds lose much of their old, old hurting. A crown is placed over our heads that for the rest of our lives we are trying to grow tall enough to wear. Despite all the crassness of life, despite all the hardness of life, despite all the harsh discords of life, life is saved by the singing of angels.

THE CHRISTMAS CANDLES

I will light the candle of fellowship this Christmas. I know that the experiences of unity in human relations are more compelling than the concepts, the fears, the prejudices which divide. Despite the tendency to feel my race superior, my nation the greatest nation, my faith the true faith, I must beat down the boundaries of my exclusiveness until my sense of separateness is completely enveloped in a sense of fellowship. There must be free and easy access by all, to all the rich resources accumulated by groups and individuals in years of living and experiencing. This Christmas, I will light the candle of fellowship, a candle that must burn all the year long.

I will light the candle of hope this Christmas. There is strange irony in the fact that there seemed to have existed a more secure basis for hope in the world during the grimmest days of the war than in the vast uncertainties of the postwar and cold war world. Now millions of people are thrown back upon themselves for food which they do not possess, for resources that have long since been exhausted, for vitality which has already run its course. The miracle of fulfillment dreamed of by the uprooted and persecuted masses of men, women, and children takes now the form of a hideous nightmare, as peace is so long deferred. But hope is the mood of Christmas; the raw materials are a newborn babe, a family, and work. Even in the grimness of the postwar world, babies are being born—an endless procession that is life's answer to death. Life keeps coming on, keeps seeking to fulfill itself, keeps affirming the possibility of hope.

Hope is the growing edge! I shall look well to that growing edge this Christmas. All around worlds are dying out, new worlds are being born; all around life is dying but life is being born. The fruit ripens on the trees, while the roots are silently at work in the darkness of the earth against a time when there shall be new leaves, fresh blossoms, green fruit. Such is the growing edge! It is the one more thing to try when all else has failed, the upward reach of life. It is the incentive to carry on. Therefore, this Christmas I will light the candle of hope that must burn all the year long.

WHAT IS CHRISTMAS?

Christmas is a mood, a quality, a symbol. It is never merely a fact. As a fact it is a date on the calendar; to the believer it is the anniversary of the Event in human history. An individual may relate himself meaningfully to the fact or to the Event, but that would not make Christmas.

The mood of Christmas—what is it? It is a quickening of the presence of other human beings into whose lives a precious part of one's own has been released. It is a memory of other days when in one's path an angel appeared spreading a halo over an ordinary moment or a commonplace event. It is an iridescence of sheer delight that once bathed one's whole being with something more wonderful than words can ever tell. Of such is the mood of Christmas.

The quality of Christmas—what is it? It is the fullness with which fruit ripens, blossoms unfold into flowers, and live coals glow in the darkness. It is the richness of vibrant colors—the calm purple of grapes, the exciting redness of tomatoes, the shimmering light of the noiseless stirring of a lake at sunset. It is the sense of plateau behind a large rock where one may take temporary respite from winds that chill. Of such is the quality of Christmas.

The symbol of Christmas—what is it? It is the rainbow arched over the roof of the sky when the clouds are heavy with foreboding. It is the cry of life in the newborn babe when, forced from its mother's nest, it claims its right to live. It is the brooding Presence of the Eternal Spirit making crooked paths straight, rough places smooth, tired hearts refreshed, dead hopes stirred with the newness of life. It is the promise of tomorrow at the close of every day, the movement of life in defiance of death, and the assurance that love is sturdier than hate, that right is more confident than wrong, that good is more permanent than evil.

AGAINST THE BACKGROUND OF THE YEAR

Our Father, another Christmas has moved within our
ken and our minds linger over many moments that
stand stark against the background of the year—
Moments that filled our cup of fear to the brim, spilling
over into the byways of our mind until there was no
longer room even to know that we were afraid—
Moments of decision, when all that we were seemed to
hang in the balance, waiting for a gentle nudging of
Thy spirit to break the tie and send us on with a new
direction, a new desire and new way of life—
Moments of sadness, brought on by the violent collapse
or quiet sagging of a lifetime of dream-building upon
which our hopes and aspirations rested in sure integrity—
Moments of awareness, when our whole landscape was
invaded by the glow of Thy spirit, making dead things
come to newness of life and old accepted ways turn
into radiant shafts of beauteous light—
Moments of joy mingled with the deadly round of daily
living, when all our inward parts clapped their hands
and a new song was born in our heart—
Moments of peace amid the noisy clang of many conflicts within and without—

Moments of reassurance, when we discovered that our searching anxieties were groundless, without foundation—

Moments of reconciliation, made possible by a deeper understanding and a greater wisdom—

Moments of renewal, without which life would have been utterly impossible and for us this day there would be no Christmas and no day—

Moments of praise and thanksgiving when, in one grand sweep, the sheer wonder and beauty of living overwhelmed us—

Our Father, another Christmas has moved within our ken and our minds linger over many moments that stand stark against the background of the year—

CHRISTMAS RETURNS

Christmas returns, as it always does, with its assurance that life is good.

It is the time of lift to the spirit,
When the mind feels its way into the commonplace,
And senses the wonder of simple things: an evergreen tree,
Familiar carols, merry laughter.

It is the time of illumination,
When candles burn, and old dreams
Find their youth again.

It is the time of pause,
When forgotten joys come back to mind, and past dedications renew their claim.

It is the time of harvest for the heart,
When faith reaches out to mantle all high endeavor,
And love whispers its magic word to everything that breathes.

Christmas returns, as it always does, with its assurance that life is good.

G I F T S   O N   M Y   A L T A R

I place these gifts on my altar this Christmas;
    Gifts that are mine, as the years are mine.
    The quiet hopes that flood the earnest cargo of my
        dreams;
    The best of all good things for those I love.
    A fresh new trust for all whose faith is dim.
    The love of life, God's precious gift in reach of all:
    Seeing in each day the seeds of the morrow,
    Finding in each struggle the strength of renewal,
    Seeking in each person the face of my brother.
I place these gifts on my altar this Christmas;
    Gifts that are mine, as the years are mine.

J O Y   I S   O F   M A N Y   K I N D S

Joy is of many kinds. Sometimes it comes silently, opening all closed doors and making itself at home in the desolate heart. It has no fore-runner save itself; it brings its own welcome and salutation.

Sometimes joy is compounded of many elements: a touch of sadness, a whimper of pain, a harsh word tenderly held until all its arrogance dies, the casting of the eye into the face that understands, the clasp of a hand that holds, then releases, a murmur of tender-ness where no word is spoken, the distilled moment of remembrance of a day, a night, an hour, lived beyond the sweep of the daily round— joy is often compounded of many things.

There is earned joy: an impossible job tackled and conquered, leaving no energy for assessing the price or measuring the cost, only an all-inclusive sense of well-being in the mind, and slowly creeping through all the crevices of the spirit—or it may be some dread has reared its head, gathering into itself all hope that is unassigned, un-til it becomes the master of the house, then relief comes through fresh knowledge, new insight, clearer vision. What was dread now proves groundless and the heart takes to wings like an eagle in its flight.

There is the joy that is given. There are those who have in themselves the gift of Joy. It has no relation to merit or demerit. It is not a quality they have wrested from the vicissitudes of life. Such people have not fought and won a hard battle, they have made no conquest. To them Joy is given as a precious ingredient in life. Whenerever they go, they give birth to Joy in others—they are the heavenly troubadours, earthbound, who spread their music all around and who sing their song without words and without sounds. To be touched by them is to be blessed of God. They give even as they have been given. Their presence is a benediction and a grace. In them we hear the music in the score and in their faces we sense a glory which is the very light of Heaven.

Chanukah

CHANUKAH AND CHRISTMAS

There must always remain in every people's life some space for the celebration of those events of the past that bear their fruit in the present—those events in which the race seems to catch its breath and to give the long look forward and backward. Such events are surrounded by a quality all their own, and yet they seem to gather into themselves the essence of all striving and the meaning of all hope.

Chanukah is such an event. Here was a moment in the life of Israel in which a people was faced with an ultimate choice. On the one hand, to renounce the very heart of a faith in One God with whom they were covenanted and to give a false value to a profound communal commitment. On the other hand, to say "yes" to a truth by which the steps of the past had been guided when there was no light, and no guide save one. One man in his vision became, first, a whole nation and then the whole race of mankind, as he affirmed in his deed: the Lord God is one and alone is worthy to be worshiped and to be praised. From him has come a way that, for generations of men, has become The Way.

Christmas is such an event. Here was a moment in the life of Israel in which a baby was born in surroundings as commonplace as the leaves and branches of the olive tree. In him was seen, by many, that for which their hearts had hungered and of which their dreams had foretold. He grew into manhood exhibiting in word and deed a fresh new quality of the age-old response of the spirit of man to the call of God. God was everything to him. His was the vision of a great creative ideal that all men are children of God, that the normal relation of one man to another is love, and that there is a personal Power, God, equally available to rich and poor, to Jew and Gentile, to men and women, to the wise and the foolish, to the just and the unjust. For millions his birth marks the turning point in human history. Christmas is an event, above all events, for it marks the moment when a new meaning is given to ancient words: The eyes of the blind are opened, the captive are set free, and the acceptable year of the Lord is become literal truth!

Chanukah and Christmas spring from the same womb and are mothered by the same brooding spirit: one marks freedom from tyranny and the preservation of the Eternal Light for all the generations of men; the other announces that there is a Presence in the common life, a Light that lighteth every man that cometh into the world.

Yom Kippur

THE DAY OF ATONEMENT

We join our brothers of the House of Israel as they assess, even as we ourselves do likewise, the stewardship of the common life, the private undertaking, and the individual enterprise. We are aware of the vast responsibility which is ours for the common life. In so many ways we have been silent when we should have spoken out. We have withheld the hand when we should have extended it in grace and in companionship. We have been blind to so much because we would not see. There are doors of truth into which we have not entered because of our preoccupation with lesser things and minor goals. In our private lives we have failed to meet the inner demands of our own conscience. We have done violence to the truth that is within us.

On the other side, there have been so many moments of wholeness in which we have participated, when we have felt purified, cleansed, and somehow redeemed. We have been surrounded by so much of grace and goodness in which we have shared consciously and deliberately. We have been cognizant of needs that extend beyond our household and our friends.

We acknowledge, then, before Thee, O God, our Father, the

mixture of Life which is ours—so much that is unworthy, so much that is good. So many times, our Father, we have mounted upon wings as eagles because of the upward sweep of Thy spirit within us. So often we have groveled in the mud, unworthy of the good that we see.

We spread our lives out before Thee, complete and utter, seeking only that Thou wilt scrutinize them with the great wisdom that Thou hast accumulated. Pour out upon us in abiding measure Thy spirit, O living God, without which we stumble in the darkness and perish.

The Season of Remembrance

THE TIME OF
RECOLLECTION

Again and again, it comes:
The Time of Recollection,
The Season of Remembrance.
Empty vessels of hope fill up again;
Forgotten treasures of dreams reclaim
   their place;
Long-lost memories come trooping back to me.
This is my season of remembrance,
My time of recollection.

Into the challenge of my anguish
I throw the strength of all my hope:
I match the darts of my despair
   with the treasures of my dreams;
Upon the current of my heart
I float the burdens of the years;
I challenge the mind of death
   with my love of life.
Such to me is the Time of Recollection,
The Season of Remembrance.

The New Year

THIS IS A NEW YEAR

This is a New Year. The calendar says so. I note the fact by marking it so when I wish to designate the day and the year as distinguished from some other day and year. It may be that my contract says so. It is indicated clearly in the lease I signed or the agreement I attested. It is curious how much difference can be marked between two dates—December 31 and January 1.

Yet there are many things that move unchanged, paying no attention to a device like the calendar or arrangements such as contracts or leases. There is the habit pattern of an individual life. Changes in that are not noted by the calendar, even though they may be noted *on* the calendar. Such changes are noted by events that make for radical shifts in values or the basic rearrangement of purposes. There are desires of the heart or moods of the spirit that may flow continuously for me whatever year the calendar indicates. The lonely heart, the joyful spirit, the churning anxiety may remain unrelieved, though the days come and go without end.

But, for many, this will be a New Year. It may mark the end of relationships of many years' accumulation. It may mean the first encounter with stark tragedy or radical illness or the first quaffing of the cup of bitterness. It may mean the great discovery of the riches of another human heart and the revelation of the secret beauty of one's own. It may mean the beginning of a new kind of living because of marriage, of graduation, of one's first job. It may mean an encounter with God on the lonely road or the hearing of one's name called by Him, high above the noise and din of the surrounding traffic. And when the call is answered, the life becomes invaded by smiling energies never before released, felt or experienced. In whatever sense this year is a New Year for you, may the moment find you eager and unafraid, ready to take it by the hand with joy and with gratitude.

FACING THE PROBLEM

A friend of mine was given an assignment in a class in dramatics. Each time she tried to read her selection aloud before the class, tears came and her strong emotional reaction made it impossible to go through with it. One day the teacher asked her to remain after class for a conference. The essence of the teacher's words to her was this: "You must read the selection before the class tomorrow. I understand what is happening to you and that is why I insist that you do this tomorrow. It is important that you realize that you must read this selection through, crying every step of the way, perhaps, if you expect to read it through without crying."

A very wise teacher. There are experiences through which we must go, crying all the way, perhaps, if we are ever to go through them without crying, and to go through them without crying must be done.

St. Francis of Assisi, in his youth, found it impossible to control his deep physical and emotional revulsion against leprosy. So acute was his reaction that he could not ever run the risk of looking at a leper. Shortly after he had made his first commitment to his Lord, he was riding down the road, when suddenly there appeared a leper. Instinctively, he turned his horse around and went galloping off in the opposite direction, his whole body bathed in nervous sweat. Then he realized what he was doing. Leprosy was one of the things he could not stand—as long as that was true, leprosy would be his jailer, his master. He turned around as abruptly as before, found the leper and, according to the story, remained with him, living intimately with him until every trace of his previous reaction had been mastered. Thus freed, he could be of tremendous service to the victims of the disease.

You must go through some things, crying all the way, perhaps, if you are ever to live with them without crying. This is an important law of living. There are many experiences which we face that are completely overwhelming. As we see them, they are too terrible even to contemplate. And yet we must face them and deal with them directly. We chide ourselves because at first we tend to go to pieces. Go to pieces, then. Weep all the way through the first terrible impact, if need be. This may be the only way that you will ever be able to deal with the problem without emotional upheaval. To deal with it without emotional upheaval is necessary if you are ever going to be able to manage it at all. There can be no more significant personal resolution at the beginning of the New Year than this: I will face the problem I have been putting off because of too much fear, of too many tears, of too much resentment, even if it means crying all the way through, in order that I may deal with it without fear, tears, or resentment.

BLESSINGS AT YEAR'S END

I remember with gratitude the fruits of the labors of others, which I have shared as a part of the normal experience of daily living.

I remember the beautiful things that I have seen, heard, and felt—some as a result of definite seeking on my part and many that came unheralded into my path, warming my heart and rejoicing my spirit.

I remember the moments of distress that proved to be groundless and those that taught me profoundly about the evilness of evil and the goodness of good.

I remember the new people I have met, from whom I have caught glimpses of the meaning of my own life and the true character of human dignity.

I remember the dreams that haunted me during the year, keeping me ever mindful of goals and hopes which I did not realize but from which I drew inspiration to sustain my life and keep steady my purposes.

I remember the awareness of the spirit of God that sought me out in my aloneness and gave to me a sense of assurance that undercut my despair and confirmed my life with new courage and abiding hope.

LONG LIVE LIFE!

There is something which seems utterly final about the end of a year. It means that we are one year older; this is a fact definite and inexorable. We are twelve months closer to the end of our physical time span—one year closer to death. It means that in some important ways we are taken farther from, or brought closer to, the goal of our living, whatever that goal may be. It means that some crucial questions which were unanswered twelve months ago have been finally and decidedly answered, and whatever doubts there may have been about the result are completely removed; now we know. It means that we are in fuller or lesser possession of ourselves and our powers than ever before.

During the passing of the twelve months, experiences have come into our lives which revealed certain things about ourselves which we had not suspected. Some new demand was made upon us which caused us to behave in a manner that was stranger to our established pattern of life, and we felt shocked, surprised, enraged, or delighted that such was possible for us. We met someone with whom we built the kind of relationship which opened up to us new worlds of wonder and magic, which were completely closed to us a year ago. It means that we are wiser by far than we were at year's beginning.

The circling series of events upon whose bosom we have been wafted cut away our pretensions, stripping us bare of much beneath which we have hidden even from ourselves; when we saw ourselves revealed, there was born a wisdom about life and its meaning that makes us say with all our hearts, this day, that life is good, not evil. It means that we have been able to watch, as if bewitched, while

the illumined finger of God pointed out a path through the surrounding darkness where no path lay; exposed to our surprised gaze
a door where we were sure there was only a blank wall; revealed the
strong arms and assuring voices of friends when we were sure that
in our plight we were alone, utterly and starkly alone.

All of these meanings and many more counsel us that because
life is dynamic and we are deeply alive, the end of the year can mean
only the end of the year, not the end of life, not the end of us, not
even the end of time. We turn our faces toward the year being born
with a riding hope that will carry us into the days ahead with courage and with confidence. The old year dies; the new year is being
born—Long live Life!

THE TRIUMPHANT ENTRY

Searching indeed must have been the thoughts moving through the mind of the Master as he jogged along on the back of the donkey on that fateful day which marks in the Christian calendar the Triumphant Entry. The experience must have been as strange and out of character for him as it was for the faithful animal on whose back he rode.

For more than two years, Jesus had been engaged in a public ministry. Once when there were those who wanted to make him a king, he had refused. "My kingdom is not of this world." He had walked the countryside with his band of disciples, preaching, teaching, healing, and spreading a quality of radiance that could come only from one whose overwhelming enthusiasm was for God and His Kingdom. He had kept many lonely trysts in the late watches of the night, trueing his spirit and his whole life by the will of his Father. So close had he worked with God that the line of demarcation between his will and God's Will would fade and reappear, fade and reappear. Step by resolute step, he had come to the great city. Deep within his spirit there may have been a sense of foreboding, or the heightened quality of exhilaration that comes from knowing that there is no road back.

He had learned much. So sensitive had grown his spirit and the living quality of his being that he seemed more and more to stand inside of life, looking out upon it as a man who gazes from a window in a room out into the yard and beyond to the distant hills. He could feel the sparrowness of the sparrow, the leprosy of the leper, the blindness of the blind, the crippleness of the cripple, and the frenzy of the mad. He had become joy, sorrow, hope, anguish, to the joyful, the sorrowful, the hopeful, the anguished. Could he feel his way into the mind and the mood of those who cast the palms and the flowers in his path? Was he in the cry of those who exclaimed their wild and unrestrained Hosannas? Did he mingle with the emotions that lay beneath the exultations ready to explode in the outburst of the mob screaming, "Crucify him! Crucify him!" I wonder what was at work in the mind of Jesus of Nazareth as he jogged along on the back of the faithful donkey.

Perhaps his mind was far away to the scenes of his childhood, feeling the sawdust between his toes, in his father's shop. He may have been remembering the high holy days in the synagogue, with his whole body quickened by the echo of the ram's horn as it sounded. Or perhaps he was thinking of his mother, how deeply he loved her and how he wished that there had not been laid upon him the Great Necessity which sent him out on the open road to proclaim the Truth, leaving her side forever. It may be that he lived all over again that high moment on the Sabbath when he was handed the scroll and he unrolled it to the great passage from the prophet Isaiah, "The spirit of the Lord is upon me, for he has anointed me to preach the gospel to the poor, to open the eyes of the blind, to unstop the ears of the deaf, to announce the acceptable year of the Lord." I wonder what was moving through the mind of the Master as he jogged along on the back of the faithful donkey.

" M Y   G O D !   M Y   G O D ! . . ."

He was dying!
Jesus had come to the cross by a direct path
Despite the agony of all the pain

There was the sense of pure relief
That he and the dogging shadow were face to face.
Nothing could reach him now.
He was beyond the violence of all his foes,
He thought.
He gripped the pain.
He established its place and bade it stay.
Death was at hand, he knew:
A zone of peace holds fast the place
Where pain and death are met.
Pinnacled on its lonely height, he waited.
Then came the crash of words:
   "Come down! Come down!
   If you believe your words,
   Call the angels to do their work."
   "If you are God's son, make good your claim!
   Come down! Come down! Come down!"

His spirit quaked. His mind tilted.
The pain escaped; his whole world shifted.
   "My God! My God! Hast Thou forsaken me?"
The words leaped forth.

He wondered had he missed the way.
Could it be true that he was sure of God
But God not sure of him?
The day at the Jordan his mind recalled;
Into the desert wilderness he sought the clue.
The mount with Moses and Elijah came to mind.
He remembered the Cup
And the long night beneath the olive trees.
   "This is the Cup; not Death!
   To yield the right to prove the Truth
   As if it could not stand alone.
   This is the Cup; not Death!
   Father, into Thy Hands, I give my life."

THE GLAD SURPRISE

There is ever something compelling and exhilarating about the glad surprise. The emphasis is upon *glad*. There are surprises that are shocking, startling, frightening and bewildering. But the glad surprise is something different from all of these. It carries with it the element of elation, of life, of something over and beyond the surprise itself. The experience itself comes at many levels: the simple joy that comes when one discovers that the balance in the bank is larger than the personal record indicated—and there is no error in accounting; the realization that one does not have his doorkey—the hour is late and everyone is asleep—but someone very thoughtfully left the latch off, "just in case"; the dreaded meeting in a conference to work out some problems of misunderstanding, and things are adjusted without the emotional lacerations anticipated; the report from the doctor's examination that all is well, when one was sure that the physical picture was very serious indeed. All of these surprises are glad!

There is a deeper meaning in the concept of the glad surprise. This meaning has to do with the very ground and foundation of hope about the nature of life itself. The manifestation of this quality in the world about us can best be witnessed in the coming of spring. It is ever a new thing, a glad surprise, the stirring of life at the end of winter. One day there seems to be no sign of life and then almost overnight, swelling buds, delicate blooms, blades of grass, bugs, insects—an entire world of newness everywhere. It is the glad surprise at the end of winter. Often the same experience comes at the end of a long tunnel of tragedy and tribulation. It is as if a man stumbling in the darkness, having lost his way, finds that the spot at which he falls is the foot of a stairway that leads from darkness into light. Such is the glad surprise. This is what Easter means in the experience of the race. This is the resurrection! It is the announcement that life cannot ultimately be conquered by death, that there is no road that is at last swallowed up in an ultimate darkness, that there is strength added when the labors increase, that multiplied, peace matches multiplied trials, that life is bottomed by the glad surprise. Take courage, therefore:

MOMENTS OF CELEBRATION

When we have exhausted our store of endurance,
When our strength has failed ere the day is half done,
When we reach the end of our hoarded resources,
Our Father's full giving is only begun.

THE CENTERING
MOMENT

Prayer and the Search for Community

It was the year of Halley's comet. I was a little boy living in a saw-mill town in Florida. I had not seen the comet in the sky because my mother made me go to bed with the setting of the sun. Some of my friends who were more privileged had tried to convey to me their impression of the awe-inspiring spectacle. And I heard my step-father say one day when he came home for lunch that a man had been down at the mill office selling what he called "comet pills." The theory was that if these pills were taken according to directions, when the tail of the comet struck the earth the individual would be immune. As I remember it, the owner of the sawmill made several purchases, not only for himself and family, but for his key workmen—the idea being that after the debacle he would be able to start business over again.

One night I was awakened by my mother, who asked if I would like to see the comet. I got up, dressed quickly, and went out with her into the backyard. There I saw in the heavens the awesome tail of the comet and stood transfixed. With deep anxiety I asked, without taking my eyes off it, "What will happen to us when that thing falls out of the sky?" There was a long silence during which I felt the gentle pressure of her fingers on my shoulders; then I looked into her face and saw what I had seen on another occasion, when without knocking I had rushed into her room and found her in prayer. At last she said, "Nothing will happen to us, Howard. God will take care of us." In that moment something was touched and kindled in me, a quiet reassurance that has never quite deserted me. As I look back on it, what I sensed then was the fact that what stirred in me was one with what created and controlled the comet. It was this inarticulate awareness that silenced my fear and stilled my panic.

Here at once is the primary ground and basis of man's experience of prayer. I am calling it, for the purpose of this discussion, the "givenness of God" as expressed in the hunger of the heart. This is native to personality, and when it becomes part of a man's conscious focus it is prayer at its best and highest. It is the movement of the heart of a man toward God; a movement that in a sense is within God—God in the heart sharing its life with God the Creator of all Life. The hunger itself is God, calling to God. It is fundamental to my thought that God is the Creator of Life, the Creator of the living substance, the Creator of existence, and as such expresses Himself through life. This is the meaning, essentially, of the notion that life is alive and that this is a living universe. Man himself cannot be an exception to this fact.

It has always seemed curious to me that man should investigate the external world, recognize its order, and make certain generalizations about its behavior which he calls laws, that he should study his own organism and discover there a kind of orderliness of inner behavior, which he seeks to correct when it acts out of character by a wide variety of ministrations, from drugs and surgery to hypnosis and faith—and yet that he should be inclined, at the same time, to regard himself as an entity apart from all the rest of creation, including his body. Man is body, but more than body; mind, but more than mind; feelings, but more than feelings. Man is total; moreover, he is spirit. Therefore it is not surprising that in man's spirit should be found the crucial nexus that connects him with the Creator of Life, the Spirit of the living God. The apostle is utterly realistic when he says that in Him we live and move and have our being. The most natural thing in the world for man, then, would be to keep open the lines of communication between him and the Source of his life, out of which he comes and into which (it is my faith) he goes.

Prayer is a form of communication between God and man and man and God. It is of the essence of communication between persons that they shall talk with each other from the same basic agenda. Wherever this is not done, communication tends to break down. If, however, an atmosphere of trust can be maintained, then one learns how to wait and be still. It is instructive to examine the prayer life of the Master from this point of view. I am always impressed by the fact that it is recorded that the only thing that the disciples asked Jesus to teach them how to do was to pray. The references are many to His own constant dependence on prayer:

. . . when Jesus had been baptized and was praying, heaven opened and the holy Spirit descended in bodily form like a dove upon him (LUKE 3:21).

In the early morning, long before daylight, he got up and went away out to a lonely spot (MARK 1:35).

. . . after saying good-bye to them, he went up the hill to pray (MARK 6:46).

. . . and he took the five loaves and the two fish, and looking up to heaven he blessed them (MARK 6:41; MATT. 14:19. Cf. MARK 8:6, 14:22; MATT. 26:26; LUKE 24:30).

. . . large crowds gathered to hear him . . . while he kept in lonely places and prayed (LUKE 5:15, 16).

This filled them with fury, and they discussed what they could do to Jesus. It was in these days that he went off to the hillside to pray. He spent the whole night in prayer to God (LUKE 6:11, 12).

Now it happened that while he was praying by himself, his disciples were beside him. So he inquired of them, "Who do the crowds say that I am?" (LUKE 9:18).

. . . he took Peter, John, and James, and went up the hillside to pray. While he was praying, the appearance of his face altered and his dress turned dazzling white. . . . Now Peter and his companions had been overpowered with sleep, but on waking up they saw his glory (LUKE 9:28, 29, 32).

The seventy came back with joy. . . . He said to them, "Yes, I watched Satan fall from heaven like a flash of lightning. . . . I praise thee, Father, Lord of heaven and earth" (LUKE 10:17, 18, 21).

"Simon, Simon, Satan has claimed the right to sift you all like wheat, but I have prayed that your own faith may not fail" (LUKE 22:31, 32).

Then he went outside and made his way to the Hill of Olives, as he was accustomed. The disciples followed him, and when he reached the spot he said to them, "Pray that you may not slip into temptation." He withdrew about a stone's throw and knelt in prayer, saying, "Father, if it pleases thee, take this cup away from me. But thy will, not mine, be done" (LUKE 22:39–42).

Jesus gave a loud cry, "My God, my God, why forsake me?" (PS. 22:1; MARK 15:34).

Then with a loud cry Jesus said, "Father, I trust my spirit to thy hands" (PS. 31:5; LUKE 23:46).

To Jesus, God breathed through all that is: the sparrow overcome by sudden death in its flight; the lily blossoming on the rocky hillside; the grass of the field and the clouds, light and burdenless or weighted down with unshed waters; the madman in chains or wandering among the barren rocks in the wastelands; the little baby in his mother's arms; the strutting insolence of the Roman Legion, the brazen queries of the tax collector; the children at play or old men quibbling in the marketplace; the august Sanhedrin fighting for its life amidst the arrogances of empire; the whisper of those who had forgotten Jerusalem, the great voiced utterance of the prophets who remembered—to Jesus, God breathed through all that is.

To Jesus, God was Creator of life and the living substance, the Living Stream upon which all things moved, the Mind containing time, space, and all their multitudinous offspring. And beyond all these, He was Friend and Father. The time most precious for the Master was at close of day. This was the time for the long breath, when all the fragments left by the commonplace, all the little hurts and big aches, came to rest; when the mind could be freed of the immediate demand, and voices that had been stilled by the long day's work could once more be heard; when there could be the deep sharing of innermost secrets and the laying bare of heart and mind—yes, the time most precious for him was at close of day.

But there were other times: "A great while before day," says the Book—the night was long and wearisome because the day had been full of jabbing annoyances; the high resolve of some winged moment had spent itself, no longer sure, no longer free, and then vanished as if it had never been; the need, the utter urgency was for some fresh assurance, the healing touch of a heavenly wing—"a great while before day" he found his way to the quiet place in the hills. And prayed.

· 2 ·

The Master was always concerned about his Father's agenda. In reflecting on the discipline of prayer, I asked myself how I may find a clue to God's purposes in the world? How may I sense Him at work? Already I am aware of Him in the hunger of my heart; this is a crucial clue. In the depths of my own spirit, then, I may be aware of His Presence, share His Mind, and establish true communication because my will comes to rest in His Will. We shall return to this later in the discussion.

The work of God in the world is another important clue to His agenda. If I can understand this, a rapport is established between God and me which becomes the prelude to communion or communication in prayer. This is what the Psalmist is talking about when he says,

The heavens declare the glory of God;
    and the firmament sheweth his handywork.
Day unto day uttereth speech,
    and night unto night sheweth knowledge.
There is no speech nor language,
    where their voice is not heard.
Their line is gone out through all the earth,
    and their words to the end of the world.
In them hath he set a tabernacle for the sun,
    Which is as a bridegroom coming out of his chamber,
    and rejoiceth as a strong man to run a race.
His going forth is from the end of the heaven,
    and his circuit unto the ends of it:
    and there is nothing hid from the heat thereof.

The law of the Lord is perfect, converting the soul:
    the testimony of the Lord is sure, making wise the simple.
The statutes of the Lord are right, rejoicing the heart:
    the commandment of the Lord is pure, enlightening the eyes.
The fear of the Lord is clean, enduring for ever:
    the judgments of the Lord are true and righteous altogether.
More to be desired are they than gold, yea, than much fine gold:
    sweeter also than honey and the honeycomb.
Moreover by them is thy servant warned:
    and in keeping of them there is great reward.
Who can understand his errors? Cleanse thou me
    from secret faults.
Keep back thy servant also from presumptuous sins;
    let them not have dominion over me:
    then shall I be upright,
    and I shall be innocent from the great transgression.
Let the words of my mouth, and the meditation of my heart,
    be acceptable in thy sight,
O Lord, my strength, and my redeemer.

PSALM 19

Or when he bursts forth:

O Lord our Lord,
    how excellent is thy name in all the earth!
    who hast set thy glory above the heavens.
Out of the mouth of babes and sucklings has thou ordained strength because of thine enemies,
    that thou mightest still the enemy and the avenger.
When I consider thy heavens, the work of thy fingers,
    the moon and the stars, which thou hast ordained;
What is man, that thou art mindful of him?
    and the son of man, that thou visitest him?
For thou hast made him a little lower than the angels,
    and hast crowned him with glory and honour.

Thou madest him to have dominion over the works of thy
  hands;
  thou hast put all things under his feet: All sheep and
  oxen,
  yea, and the beasts of the field;
The fowl of the air, and the fish of the sea,
  and whatsoever passeth through the paths of the seas.
O Lord, our Lord, how excellent is thy name in all the
  earth!

PSALM 8

Any close examination of the world of nature reveals that everything is painstakingly structured. In its functioning, nature operates on the basis of a rather definite agenda. All animals and plants live intentional lives. We cannot dismiss this fact by saying that it is blind instinct or merely a pattern of conformity on the basis of which the continuity of the particular species is guaranteed. Here the activity of an innate order is at work. When I am able to read the specifications, then I can understand the behavior. The same thing is at work in me as elsewhere in the whole process. This is why so much knowledge about our own bodies is secured from the study of other forms of life. Such study is mandatory for all who would acquire a working knowledge of the human organism. If I regard this understanding as a part of God's—the Creator's—working paper, then I relate to it not only with my mind but also with my feelings. I react to what I observe: this is the Hand of God fashioning His creation. Such a mood of reverence has a transfer value for me also. It moves me directly into the experience of what Schweitzer calls "reverence for life." But there is much in familiarity with technology (which is the pragmatic application of a knowledge of the behavior of particles) that stifles any mood of reverence. So rapid and astounding have been our developments in this area that there is little time for the element of reverence to emerge. I doubt very seriously if a scientist who knew reverence as a part of his own response to what his investigation of nature revealed could ever bring himself to the fashioning of atomic or hydrogen bombs.

Now, the mood of reverence opens up the spirit to a receptivity of the greatness of God at work in the world of nature. It heightens one's sensitivity to meaningful overtones of beauty that enliven the

spirit and enrich the awareness of values. Here, then, is one important clue to the divine agenda or working paper. Harmony becomes
a language the understanding of which opens up a whole world of
communication between God and me.

> The universe is not dead. Therefore, there is an Intelligence there,
> and it is all-pervading. At least one purpose, possibly the major pur-
> pose, of that Intelligence is the achievement of universal harmony.
>
> Striving in the right direction for Peace (Harmony), therefore, as
> well as the achievement of it, is the result of accord with that Intel-
> ligence.
>
> It is desirable to effect that accord.
>
> The human race, then, is not alone in the universe. Though I
> am cut off from human beings, I am not alone.
>
> For untold ages man has felt an awareness of that Intelligence.
> Belief in it is the one point where all religions agree. It has been called
> by many names. Many call it God.*

There is an element of profound truth in the outlook of panthe-
ism, which sees the work of God in the world of nature with such
clarity as to identify God with His world; the temptation is hard to
resist. But this is not enough. God must never be a prisoner in His
creation. When I look carefully at my own body, I see at once that
my body functions are so closely meshed and integrated that, under
ordinary circumstances, I am not aware of any part of my body as
such unless the inner harmony breaks down at the point of function. I do not become little-finger-aware unless my little finger no
longer functions as a little finger should. When the harmony is broken, I say that the part is ill or the body is ill. The body is quite
literally a dwelling place of the Most High God, Creator of the Universe. The mood of reverence applies here with telling effect upon
man's whole world of values, meaning, and morality.

Further, I seek a clue to God's working paper, His agenda in
the world of men, in the whole story of man's collective or social life
on the planet. At first look, human relations as experienced in human history, or in the immediate social environment in which we
live, seem quite chaotic. The casual view discovers no valid intent;
if there be an intent, it seems more evil than good, more diabolical

*Richard E. Byrd, *Alone* (New York: Putnam, 1938), p. 183.

than benevolent. In the language of faith, the kingdoms of this world often conflict with the Kingdom of God. It cannot be denied that a part of the fact of human society is the will to destroy, to lay waste, and to spend. There is often so much that casts down and so little that uplifts and inspires. The bloody carnage of fratricide is a part of the sorry human tale. And yet always, against this, something struggles. Man does not ever quite make the madness total. Always there is some voice that rises up against what is destructive, calling attention to an alternative, another way. It is a matter of more than passing significance that the racial memory as embodied in the myths of creation, as well as in the dream of prophet and seer, points ever to the intent to community as the purpose of life. This is no mere incident of social evolution, or growth toward civilization from times more primitive. It goes to the very heart of all human striving. It is basic to the aspirations of the entire human race. The dramatic character of this phenomenon can be seen during periods of the greatest violence among men—in war. In the midst of the vast death-dealing moments of war between nations there are always voices speaking out for peace. They are not tolerated; they are taken out of circulation so that their spirit may not become contagious; but they always appear and reappear.

Occasionally there comes into view on the horizon of the age a solitary figure who, in his life, anticipates the harmony of which he speaks. No one dreamed that Mahatma Gandhi would be able to introduce into the very center of a great modern empire such as Britain a principle contrary to empire, and abide. For Gandhi to have come out of the womb of a religion outside the Christian faith and address himself to an empire whose roots were nurtured by that faith is the most eloquent testimony of the timeless, universal character of what was working in him. It is as though there were at work in this little man an Intent by which he was caught up, and of which in some way he became the living embodiment. The moving finger of God in human history points ever in the same direction. There must be community. Always, in the collective conscience and in the private will, this intent appears and reappears like some fleeting ghost. It is a fact that mankind fails again and again, but the sense of not being mistaken in the fundamental intention never deserts the final purpose, or the judgment that is passed upon all social behavior.

When the hunger in a man's heart merges with what seems to

be the fundamental intent of life, communion with God the Creator of Life is not only possible but urgent. The hunger of the heart, which is a part of the givenness of God, becomes one with the givenness of God as expressed in the world of nature and in human history. It must be pointed out that this hunger may function merely at the level of human striving and enlightened social concern. In this sense it may be regarded simply as a characteristic of personality; only this and nothing more. In other words, it may not become personal in terms of the devotional response of the individual to Life. Or, it may be a clue to the Father's house, to the Holy of Holies, wherein the Creator of Life and the King of the Universe has His dwelling place. Prayer is the means by which this clue is pursued. The hunger cannot be separated from God. For many this is what makes any communication between God and man possible. This is the swinging door that no man can shut. This is not to say that the great God of Life is reduced to or squeezed into the hunger of the heart of man, but that the hunger is an expression of the givenness of God. I repeat: it is the trysting place where the God and the soul of man meet, where they stand on a common ground and the wall or partition between them has no status. It is what Eckhart calls the "apex of the soul—the uncreated element in the soul of man." This is the citadel of encounter.

The true purpose of all spiritual disciplines is to clear away whatever may block our awareness of that which is God in us. The aim is to get rid of whatever may so distract the mind and encumber the life that we function without this awareness, or as if it were not possible. It must be constantly remembered that this hunger may be driven into disguise, may take a wide variety of twisted forms; but it never disappears—it cannot. Prayer is the experience of the individual as he seeks to make the hunger dominant and controlling in his life. It has to move more and more to the central place until it becomes a conscious and deliberate activity of the spirit. When the hunger becomes the core of the individual's consciousness, what was a sporadic act of turning toward God becomes the very climate of the soul.

· 3 ·

It will be in order to suggest certain simple aids to this end. One of these is the practice of silence, or quiet. As a child I was accustomed to spend many hours alone in my rowboat, fishing along the river, when there was no sound save the lapping of the waves against the boat. There were times when it seemed as if the earth and the river and the sky and I were one beat of the same pulse. It was a time of watching and waiting for what I did not know—yet I always knew. There would come a moment when beyond the single pulse beat there was a sense of Presence which seemed always to speak to me.

Silence is of many kinds. There is a silence which is the prelude to prayer—the moment of hush and ingathering. There is a silence that tends to quiet the soundless words that fall from the tongue and to calm the noises of the mind and spirit. Every person who is concerned about the discipline of prayer must find the ministry of silence in accordance with his particular needs. Certain mechanical devices are helpful. We must seek a physical place of withdrawal, a place of retreat, if this is possible. It may be achieved merely by closing the door as a signal that one wishes to be alone; it may be by remaining in bed for a spell after everyone else is up and about; it may be by taking a walk or by extending a walk beyond the initial requirement or demand; it may be by withdrawing one's participation in conversation, even though one has to remain in the midst of company.

Once the physical silencing has been achieved, then the real work must begin. The calming of the mind as an effort to exclude distraction is a complex necessity. The soundless voices take the form of thoughts that distract. One of the most helpful things to do is to read or recall some stilling passage or thing—words that place before the mind a picture or a feeling tone that quiets or subdues and settles. The Psalms are very helpful here. "The Lord is my shepherd, I shall not want." Or, "Lord, Thou hast been our dwelling place in all generations." Or, "Lord, Thou hast searched me and known me." There are many. One may find helpful the literature of devotion aside from the Bible; sometimes a great poem of remembered radiance or a picture which speaks peace to the spirit at a time of great upheaval. Often there is a person whose life gives forth a quality of tranquility as one who has come through troubled seas into a place of calm and confidence.

He understood what it is that we are trying to work out.
He was very old, and from the secret swing of planets
To the secret decencies in human hearts, he understood.

I used to watch him watering his lawn, scattering the food for the
  woodpecker,
Sweeping the crossing before his house. It was not that there was light
About him, visible to the eye, as in the old paintings.
Rather, an influence came from him in little breaths.
When we were with him we became other.
He saw us all as if we were that which we dreamed ourselves.
He saw the town already clothed on for its Tomorrow,
He saw the world, beating like a heart, beating like a heart.
"How may I, too, know?" I wanted to cry to him. Instead
I only said: "And how is it with you?" But he answered
Both questions by the look in his eyes. For he had come to quietness.
He had come to the place where sun and moon meet
And where the spaces of the heavens open their doors.
He was understanding and love and the silence.
He was the voice of these, as he fed the woodpecker.*

For many Christians the contemplation of Jesus Christ is the
most helpful aid. I know a man who always, at this point in his
preparations, selects some incident in which Jesus is expressing his
love for someone. He moves into identification, sometimes with the
Master himself, sometimes with the object of the Master's love.

It may be that some problem is so central in thought and concern that it pushes everything else aside. If this happens to be the
case, it should not cause undue distress as regards the business at
hand. The problem itself may clear away everything else and in a
sense perform an important task. This is one of the real services
that an overriding problem may render the life of the spirit. It clears
the decks for action. If such be the situation, then the individual
can attack the problem itself as something that deadens the hunger;
thus that which threatens is included in the process itself. If the
problem is considered in the light of what it does to the hunger for
God, this alone will put it into a different context and a new perspective. It will no longer be regarded merely as something that an-
noys, frustrates, or discourages, but rather as something that stands
squarely in the way, blocking the pathway to God. Under such circumstances fresh insight is apt to come, and even if there is no im-

*Zona Gale, "The Sky-Goer," from *The Le Gallienne Book of English and American Po-
etry*, Richard Le Gallienne, ed. (New York: Garden City Books, 1935), p. 293. Used by permission of the author's estate.

mediate solution one is now in a position to challenge the integrity of the problem by raising his sights—looking at it from the other side, from the point of view of what it obscures.

Once the interference that drowns out the hunger has been stilled or removed, real communion between man and God can begin. Slowly the hunger begins to stir until it moves inside the individual's self-consciousness, and the sense of the very Presence of God becomes manifest. The words that are uttered, if there be words, may be halting and poor; they may have to do with some deep and searching need of which the individual now becomes acutely aware; it may be a sin that had become so much a part of the landscape of the soul that the soul itself has the feeling of corruption—but this may not last long. On the other hand, it may be a rather swift outpouring of a concern, because here is the moment of complete understanding and the freedom it inspires.

Several years ago I was talking with a very old lady about prayer, and particularly her own experience in prayer. She told me a story from her own most recent past. In her little Congregational church in a small New England community there was an extended crisis over the minister. The congregation felt he should leave because his usefulness was over. He prayed about the matter and as a result was convinced that, all evidence to the contrary notwithstanding, he should remain at his post. My friend said that she decided to take the matter directly to God in her prayer time. I quote her:

> I gave myself plenty of time. I went into a thorough review of the highlights of the sixty years I have been a member of the church right up to the present situation. I talked it through very carefully. It was so good to talk freely and to know that the feelings and the thoughts behind the words were being understood. When I finished I said, "Now Father, these are the facts as best I can state them. Take them and do the best you can. I have no suggestions to make."

The experience of communion may elicit an expression of concern for someone whose need is great or for whom one has compelling love. Such a person may be ill, or in trouble, or in deep quandary before the exacting demands of fateful decision. To bring him and his need clearly to mind, or into complete focus, and expose him tenderly to the scrutiny and love of God through our own thought is to pray for him. At such a moment questions as to the efficacy of intercessory prayer become merely academic. I share my concern with God and leave the rest to Him. Does such a sharing do any good? Does it make a difference? The conviction of the praying person is that it does some good, that it does make a difference. Can you prove it? he may be asked. In what does proof of such a thing consist? The question of the effectiveness of intercessory prayer does not belong in the experience of the man who prays for his friend—it is his care that is poured out when he is most conscious of being cared for himself. When the hunger for God becomes articulate in a man so that it is one with his initial experience of God, it is the most natural thing in the world to share whatever his concerns may be. A man prays for loved ones because he has to, not merely because his prayer may accomplish something beyond this.

There is no attempt here to deal with the problems and issues that center in a discussion of what is called intercessory prayer. With reference to these I permit myself one comment only. The man who shares his concern for others with God in prayer does two things at the same time. He exposes the need of the other person to his total life and resources, making it possible for new insights of helpfulness and creativity to emerge in him. In other words he sees more clearly how to relate himself to the other person's need. In the second place, he may quicken the spirit of his friend to a sudden upsurging of the hunger for God, with the result that he is in the way of help from the vast creative energies of God. How this is done we may never explain. That it happens again and again in the religious experience of the race is a part of the data of the prayer experience itself.

Communion may be an overflowing of utter praise, adoration, and celebration. The sense of awe becomes trumpet-tongued, and the sheer joy of the beauty of holiness overwhelms the mind and enlivens all the emotions with a kindling of spiritual fervor. It is at such a moment that one feels he was created to praise God and to enjoy Him forever.

The communion may be an overflowing of thanksgiving. Here I do not mean an order of thanks for services rendered or for goods received. Here is no perfunctory grace before meals, when a person chooses to mumble gratitude either out of habit, or superstition, or because of spiritual breeding of a high order. No, I do not mean this sort of thing, but rather the overflowing of the heart as an act of grace toward God. The overflow is not merely because of what has taken place in life or in the world or because of all the manifestations of benevolence that have covered a life. Something far more profound is at work. It is akin to adoration; it is the sheer joy in thanksgiving that God is God and the soul is privileged and blessed with the overwhelming consciousness of this. It is the kind of thanksgiving that sings itself to the Lord because He is God. This praiseful thanksgiving overshadows any bill of particulars, even though many particular things crowd into mind. We can get some notion of what is meant here when, under some circumstances, we encounter a person who, for what seems to be a swirling temporary moment, enjoys *us*—not what we say or what we are doing or what we represent, but who reaches into the core of our being and touches us purely. How such moments must rejoice the heart of God! I agree most heartily with Rufus Jones when he says that prayer at its best is when the soul enjoys God and prays out of sheer love of Him.

There is one remaining crucial element that must be taken into account in the experience of communion. I refer here specifically to the sense of sin, of unworthiness, that often takes on a dramatic character in the experience with God. Here I am not thinking primarily of human nature and man's general frailty, but more precisely of those awarenesses of having denied the hunger and, in the denial, having done violence to the integrity of the soul and to the sense of goodness and righteousness which became manifest along our journey. This goes deeper than the guilt one feels for going counter to a convention. That may be included, but I refer now specifically to the residue that remains as a man's own deep, personal, and private sense of sin and guilt. Sin has to be absorbed and the guilt washed from the spirit. How this is done we do not know. There are Christians who experience the redeeming love of Christ, which sets them free of guilt because they believe that in some miraculous way He takes their guilt upon Him and absorbs in His Body and Spirit the virus of their sins. For those who believe, the offering of Christ is made to God on their behalf, and in Christ's name they pass from darkness into light.

For many others this whole experience involves something more than can be managed with the mind. There is a strange necessity in the human spirit that a man deal with his sin before God. This necessity is honored in prayer when the deed is laid bare and the guilt acknowledged. I do not know how it happens or quite how to describe it, but I do know that again and again man has come away from prayer freed of his guilt, and with his sin forgiven; he then has a sense of being totally understood, completely dealt with, thoroughly experienced, and utterly healed. This is not to suggest that after the experience a man is always through with his sin. No, but now a solvent is at work on it which dissolves it, and the virus begins to be checked in its breeding place.

The experience of prayer, as I have been describing it, can be nurtured and cultivated. It can create a climate in which a man's life moves and functions. Indeed, it may become a way of living for the individual. It is ever possible that the time may come when a man carries such an atmosphere around with him and gives its quality to all that he does and communicates its spirit to all who cross his path. This was the most remarkable impact of the life of the Master upon those whom he encountered. It was this that stilled the ragings of the madman, that called little children to Him, that made sinners know that their sins were forgiven. His whole countenance glowed with the glory of the Father. And the secret? "A great while before day, he withdrew to a solitary place and prayed, *as was his custom.*"

Meditations and Prayers From the Pulpit

THE SACRAMENT OF LIFE

We celebrate the sacrament of life, the simple delights of being alive with varying measures of health, strength, and vitality. We are blessed with so many things that we did not create ourselves, but are ours because of the labor, the work, the sacrifice, and the dreaming of many people whose names we shall never know—all of the little things by which our days are surrounded to make us secure, to make us happy, and to give to us a quiet sense of joy in being alive.

We make a sacrament of thanksgiving for all of these things, even as we remember those who are not blessed as we are blessed— the little children who are not comfortably housed, who do not have warm clothes to wear, who did not have breakfast this morning because there was no food for them; all of the frightened and lonely and desperate little children, all over the world—we remember them, in our comfort, in our plenty. In the quietness we seek to know how we may learn to be more sensitive, to be more charitable, to be more gracious, to be more sharing, if indeed we are to be true to ourselves. We make a sacrament of our determination to be better tomorrow than we are today, to be more thoughtful of our own needs and the needs of others, to be more gracious in the way we live, to the end that through us there shall come no violence to anyone; through no word of ours shall there be a heart broken, or a spirit injured. We make a sacrament of our determination in this regard, that we may be blessed by Thy spirit, O God, not because we are worthy or unworthy, but because we cannot live without Thy grace and benediction.

THE WATERING OF OUR ROOTS

Surrounded by all of the memories and the dreams and the hopes and the desires of so great a host of witnesses, we still ourselves in the presence of God, gathering together all of the things that are needful for our peace. The mood of thanksgiving overwhelms us when we remember how good and great is our fortune, even as we are mindful of the ways that are hard and difficult for so many whose names are known to us and whose pictures are vividly in our minds. It is so great a privilege to experience the watering of one's roots at a time of such dryness in the world.

Thus, our Father, we expose ourselves to Thy spirit, daring not at all to make even the simplest request of Thee. We let ourselves down in Thy grace and Thy holiness, waiting for the movement of Thy spirit.

THE LITTLE GRACES OF LIFE

Our Father, we turn aside from the things that ordinarily occupy our waking hours and we wait in Thy presence. We are reminded of the graces of life that are so commonplace, so much a part of our daily living that the grace of them is lost sight of. Each day for many days we have been able to arise from our beds and be active, to do our work, to live our lives with the full function of our bodies. Each day we have been greeted by a few people who understand us and who salute us. We have been smiled upon, we have been blessed by the countenances of many of Thy children. The little graces of life.

We have been visited also, our Father, by concerns to which

we have responded, sometimes with enthusiasm and conviction; and other times we have been so overwhelmed with our own personal needs and disorders and complexities that we have not had any time to give to the needs and disorders and complexities of other people, and we feel just a little guilty about it as we linger in the quietness, sorting out the details of our lives. We do not want to have hard hearts, we do not want to close the windows of our spirits to the cries and to the agonies of those whose needs cry out to Thee. There seems to be no ear to hear, no hand to succor. We do not wish to be this way, but our own lives are hard and our frustrations are very great. Thus, our Father, we try to loosen ourselves up, so that we may become aware of what it is that Thou art seeking to do in us and in our world, so that after this hour we may not only be refreshed and renewed but we may be on the scent of that which is Thy will for us. To know Thy will, O God, and to sink these little minds and little purposes of ours into Thy will—this is the heart of our hunger, O God of our spirits, as we wait in Thy presence.

FOR THE STUDENTS OF THE WORLD

We pray for the students of the world:

Those in refugee camps who are straitened by the vast uncertainties of all their waking moments.

Those in Egypt, Israel, South Africa, Europe, and all the centers of the earth where they live and learn.

Those in our own land who are lonely, homeless, aimless, confused, dedicated.

We pray for the students of the world!

We hold ourselves and them steadily, quietly, with great concentration before Thy altar. Invade their lives, their living contexts, their surroundings, not only with Thy wisdom and understanding but also with Thy judgment and its vitality, to the end that something will become manifest in them that will make Thy kingdom, Thy rule, effective in the way that they take. We do not ask. We do not plead. We do not beg. We offer them and ourselves and we wait. In Thy presence we wait; Thou wilt not reject our spirits.

OUR HEARTS ARE WOOED

Again and again we find ourselves deeply distressed because there is so much that is dependent upon us as individuals carrying specific responsibilities within a world which is small and compact and demanding. So overwhelming is this kind of pressure upon us that we are tempted to rely, despite all of our inadequacies, upon our own strength. Again and again we say to ourselves, if I do not depend upon myself, if I do not depend upon that which I am able to do for myself and those for whom I am responsible, then there is no other source upon which I may be dependent. And even as we say it and as we feel it, our minds are flooded with multitudinous instances in which strength did come to us that was not of our making, a lift to our burden did come, even though it could not be measured by anything that we ourselves were doing. All around us there are these surprises of kindly interference manifesting the grace of life and the tenderness and the mercy of God.

Thus our hearts are wooed into thanksgiving and praise for so much that has come to us, transcending our merit and our demerit, so much thoughtfulness, so much reassurance, so many little ways by which our spirits have been renewed and revived. Even against our disposition, we offer our thanksgiving to Thee. Accept it, our Father, as our sacrament and as our offering to Thee, totally, wholeheartedly, that after this hour has passed each may know for himself that he is Thy child and Thou art his Father.

Our times are in Thy hand.

WE ARE VISITED

It is our great and blessed fortune that our lives are never left to themselves alone. We are visited in ways that we can understand and in ways that are beyond our understanding by highlights, great moments of inspiration, quiet reassurances of grace, simple manifestations of gratuitous expressions of the goodness of life. These quiet things enrich the common life and give to the ordinary experiences of our daily grind a significance and a strength that steady and inspire. We are also surrounded by the witness of those others whose strivings have made possible so much upon which we draw from the common reservoir of our heritage, those who have carried the light against the darkness, those who have persevered when to persevere seemed idiotic and suicidal, those who have forgotten themselves in the full and creative response to something that calls them beyond the furthest reaches of their dreams and their hopes.

We are surrounded also by the witness of the life of the spirit in peculiar ways that speak directly to our hearts and to our needs: those men and women who walk the pages of the holy book; those men and women with whom in our moments of depression and despair, and in our moments of joy and delight, we identify.

We are grateful to Thee, our Father, for all of the springs of joy and renewal and recreation that are our common heritage and our common lot. We offer in thanksgiving to Thee the fruits of our little lives that they may in turn be to others a source of strength and inspiration, that apart from us they may not find fulfillment and apart from them we may not know ourselves.

We thank Thee, our Father, for so holy a privilege and we offer our thanksgiving, our dedication, and our response, not only to Thee, but to the life which is ours.

CREATURES OF PAIN AND HURT

We are buffeted about by so rich a variety of circumstances that it is often very difficult for us to find our own ways. We are creatures of pain and hurt, of joy and ecstasy, of despair and hope. All around us we see great stretches of unrelieved human misery: hunger of body, with all the wasting away of the flesh that comes in its wake; upheaval of mind, with all of the inward torture with which the skill of man finds no way to deal. We are surrounded by so much that casts doubt and so often so little that uplifts and inspires. And when we think about our own selves, each within the tight circle of his little life, the same picture presents itself. We have found no satisfying answer for the pain of our lives.

At such a time as this, our Father, enveloped by the great quietness instilled by Thy presence, we want to offer the part of us that is clear, unsullied, fresh, clean, untainted, and to hold back under the shadow of our own feelings the things that are tainted and painful and tragic.

Teach us, our Father, how we may be so worthy of our living experience, that we may even now offer to Thee our pain, our suffering, our miseries—all the stains of our lives, even as we offer to Thee our best. What a relief it is, O God, to have somewhere to pour it all out. Our Father, our Father, accept us totally.

IN SEARCH OF EACH OTHER

We are aware of the circle that shuts us in—cutting us off from each other. Despite our many-sided exposure to each other we are alone in our solitariness even in the midst of the congregation. Much of our aloneness is in the nature of things; much of it is due to the uncertainties of our own feelings about ourselves and about others who make up the world of our familiars. At times, our Father, we are conscious of what we do to each other. The careless word, the unseeing look into another's face, the mood out of which all kindness is drained; these often undermine the confidence and the strength of someone who walks beside us in our journey. Preoccupied with the urgencies of our own lives we are insensitive to the ways in which we turn others away from our door empty and afraid. We cannot separate ourselves from our own hurts, our own wounds and injuries—out of the depths of our private agonies we are tempted to feel that no one understands or that those who do understand, do not care.

Thus we are in search of each other as well as of Thee in this act of worship which is our sharing. May Thy Presence invade our being until at last there begins to stir within us that which breaks the circle, spilling over into the lives of each other and we are no longer alone.

Forgive us our trespasses
As we forgive those who trespass against us.
Deliver us from evil, for Thine is the Kingdom and the Glory.

SOME CENTERING MOMENT

We wait in the quietness for some centering moment that will re-define, reshape, and refocus our lives. It does seem to be a luxury to be able to give thought and time to the ups and downs of one's private journey while the world around is so sick and weary and desperate. But, our Father, we cannot get through to the great anxieties that surround us until, somehow, a path is found through the little anxieties that beset us. Dost Thou understand what it is like to be caught between the agony of one's own private needs and to be tempest-tossed by needs that overwhelm and stagger the mind and paralyze the heart? Dost Thou understand this, our Father?

For the long loneliness, the deep and searching joy and satisfaction, the boundless vision—all these things that give to Thee so strong a place in a world so weak—we thank Thee, Father. For whatever little grace Thou wilt give to Thy children even as they wait in confidence and stillness in Thy presence, we praise Thee. O love of God, love of God, where would we be without Thee? Where?

THE HURT OF ISOLATION

So much of our common life is spent in seeking ways by which we may break the isolation and solitariness and loneliness of the individual life. There is within us the hunger for companionship and understanding, for the experience of free and easy access to the life of another, so that in the things which we must face, the enemies with which we must do battle, we shall not be alone. Sometimes this isolation is brought about because life has eliminated from our world, one by one, those who have won the right to companion us on our journey. Sometimes the isolation is due to evil things which we have done deliberately or against our conscious wills, rendering those around us afraid and injured, and we are alone. Sometimes the isolation is due to a demand which our hearts make upon ourselves—the right to be free from involvements, the right to experience detachment, the right to take the long, hard look in solitariness and in isolation. But whatever may be the cause, it is so very good to sense the common character of our quest and the mutual support by which we are sustained.

We thank Thee, our Father, that this is so. Thy rod and Thy staff they comfort us and we thank Thee, O God; we thank Thee, our Father.

THE PRESENCE OF THE FACT

Our spirits and our minds stand at attention in the presence of the fact, which is our little life. Our days are crowded by events, sometimes cruel, sometimes heartless, sometimes meaningless, sometimes full of joy and richness. We finger them one by one in Thy presence, our Father—the grief that we have known that lingers long after the moment of its first great wild tearing at the fibers of the heart; the anguish we have felt because the thing for which we have worked so long and so hard, that into which we have poured so much of the living stuff of our days, has turned sour in our spirits or become whitened ashes in our hands and we are bereft; the temptations that have been our daily companions from our youth and which, through all the leaden-footed months and years of our living, we have not found a way to escape; the great resolutions of our spirits that stirred in us at other times, sending us on a joyful journey, questing, full of confidence that life would hold in its hands that which we wrought with all of our passionate endeavor. We sit now in the quietness before Thee, having not found it.

O God, God our Father, hold us in the sweep of Thy hands under the shadow of Thy wing, until at last all of our anguish dies and our fears are removed, and the joy of Thy spirit possesses our lives. Thus we may know for ourselves this day and tomorrow and tomorrow, not only that Thou canst be trusted, our Father, but that life itself can be counted on. With this assurance we can stand anything that life can do to us; without this assurance our souls are desolate, it is night, and we are afraid.

FLOATING HOPES

Each of us is mindful of the tight circle in which his life is lived; all of the ways by which life closes in, stultifies, frightens, disturbs; all of those private regions of the heart where desires have their beginnings, the quiet anxieties of the spirit that express themselves in many ways that defeat the outward life. We remember the floating hopes and dreams and desires that surround us but do not quite take hold upon us.

As we still ourselves in Thy presence, O God, our Father, we trust that there may be visited upon us that which can widen the narrowness of our little lives, that which can make room within us for love where there now is hate, for understanding where there is misunderstanding, for courage where there is fear. We want this so much for ourselves. We are tired, our Father, of the narrowness and the weariness and the littleness of our lives. This we know, but again and again, our Father, we do not know how to go any other way. We try. Thou knowest it. Now we wait, we wait with confidence, that what we have been unable to do, using all the powers of our minds and imaginations, Thou mayest show us how to do as we wait in Thy presence. O God of our spirits, we await Thy pleasure.

WALLS OF DISAPPOINTMENT

When trapped by walls of disappointment and tempted to panic by disordered thinking, calmness is the only solution for men, for the acts of Providence are so hidden it is hard to understand how delicate are the influences emanating from our own mind. There are great changes that come about in the darkest hours where there is no hope and the encircling gloom is terrifying to the heart. It is difficult to understand the power at that moment. Calmness in the midst of chaos, serenity in the midst of feverish activity, are the secret that all commanders must know, the secret revealed in crisis, that the soul that is calm with controlled emotion is performing an act of faith. To do this we must remember our way back into the very center of our being, to that eternal fountain of refreshment within. Otherwise we block, frustrate, and delay, giving over to a frantic spirit and a mind glutted with panic. It is a hard lesson; perhaps it should be an easy one.

Consider: you believe that you are a child of God. You have a vision, however vague, of your own sense of godhood. Your bewildered, tired, impatient self can only glimpse this in moments far between as you conceive time. But what is a week, a month, yea, even a year? In the deep, inner quietness of your spirit, time stands still— before and after are lost in now, there is no movement, no action, even the outer edges of awareness blend into the surrounding calm.

It is this calmness that now you must carry with you into the maelstrom of your hectic days. Let it be a remembered grace and a nourishing companion. And this is enough!

THOU DOST NOT BECOME WEARY

It is our faith and our confidence, our Father, that Thou dost not become weary, because always before Thee we present the same sorry spectacle. It is our trust that Thou dost not get tired of us but that always Thou dost remain constant, even as we do not; that Thou dost remain true even when we take refuge in falsehood and error; that Thou dost remain kind and gracious when our hearts are hard and callous; that Thy scrutiny and Thy judgment hold despite all of our whimpering, self-pity, and shame. It is so good to have this kind of assurance and to know, as we move into the days and the hours that are still left to us, that we are not alone but that we are comforted and straightened by Thy brooding presence.

We would ask forgiveness for our sins, but of so much that is sinful in us we have no awareness. We would seek to offer to Thee the salutation of our spirits and our minds were we able to tear ourselves away from preoccupation with our own concerns, our own anxieties, our own little lives. We would give to Thee the "nerve center" of our consent if for one swirling moment we could trust Thee to do with us what our lives can stand.

O God, our Father, take the chaos and confusion and disorder of our minds and spirits and hold them so completely in Thy grasp that the impure thing will become pure, the crooked thing will become straight, and the crass and hard thing will be gentled by Thy spirit. Oh, that we may have the strength to see and the vision to comprehend what in us is needful for Thy peace.

PRAYER FOR
A FRIENDLY WORLD

Our Father, fresh from the world, with the smell of life upon us, we make an act of prayer in the silence of this place. Our minds are troubled because the anxieties of our hearts are deep and searching. We are stifled by the odor of death which envelops our earth, where in so many places brother fights against brother. The panic of fear, the torture of insecurity, the ache of hunger, all have fed and rekindled ancient hatreds and long-forgotten memories of old struggles, when the world was young and Thy children were but dimly aware of Thy Presence in the midst. For all this, we seek forgiveness. There is no one of us without guilt and, before Thee, we confess our sins: we are proud and arrogant; we are selfish and greedy; we have harbored in our hearts and minds much that makes for bitterness, hatred and revenge.

While we wait in Thy Presence, search our spirits and grant to our minds the guidance and the wisdom that will teach us the way to take, without which there can be no peace and no confidence anywhere. Teach us how to put at the disposal of Thy Purposes of Peace the fruits of our industry, the products of our minds, the vast wealth of our land and the resources of our spirit. Grant unto us the courage to follow the illumination of this hour to the end that we shall not lead death to any man's door; but rather may we strengthen the hands of all in high places, and in common tasks seek to build a friendly world, of friendly men, beneath a friendly sky. This is the simple desire of our hearts which we share with Thee in thanksgiving and confidence.

SOURCES OF
SELECTIONS

(For additional bibliographical information, see pp. 301–302.)

CM   *The Centering Moment*
DH   *Deep Is the Hunger*
DR   *Deep River* (Friends United Press ed.)
DS   *Disciplines of the Spirit*
IJ   *The Inward Journey*
JD   *Jesus and the Disinherited*
MC   *The Mood of Christmas*
MH   *Meditations of the Heart*
ML   *Mysticism and the Experience of Love*
NS   *The Negro Spiritual Speaks of Life and Death*

SOURCES OF SELECTIONS

SOURCES OF SELECTIONS

SELECT BIBLIOGRAPHY OF HOWARD THURMAN'S WRITINGS

Apostles of Sensitiveness. Boston: American Unitarian Association, 1956.

The Centering Moment. New York: Harper & Row, 1969. Paperback ed., Richmond, Ind.: Friends United Press, 1980.

The Creative Encounter. New York: Harper & Row, 1954. Paperback ed., Richmond, Ind.: Friends United Press, 1972.

Deep Is the Hunger. New York: Harper & Row, 1951. Paperback ed., Richmond, Ind.: Friends United Press, 1978.

Deep River: An Interpretation of Negro Spirituals. Mills College, Ca.: Eucalyptus Press, 1945.

Deep River and *The Negro Spiritual Speaks of Life and Death* (single volume). Richmond, Ind.: Friends United Press, 1975.

Deep River: Reflections on the Religious Insight of Certain of the Negro Spirituals. New York: Harper & Row, 1955. (Revised ed. of the 1945 publication, with illustrations by Elizabeth Orton Jones.)

Disciplines of the Spirit. New York: Harper & Row, 1963. Paperback ed., Richmond, Ind.: Friends United Press, 1973.

The First Footprints—The Dawn of the Idea of the Church for the Fellowship of All Peoples: Letters Between Alfred Fisk and Howard Thurman, 1943–44 (editor). San Francisco: Lawton and Alfred Kennedy, 1975.

Footprints of a Dream: The Story of the Church for the Fellowship of All Peoples. New York: Harper & Row, 1959.

The Greatest of These. Mills College, Ca.: Eucalyptus Press, 1944.

The Growing Edge. New York: Harper & Row, 1956. Paperback ed., Richmond, Ind.: Friends United Press, 1974.

SELECT BIBLIOGRAPHY

The Inward Journey. New York: Harper & Row, 1961. Paperback ed., Richmond, Ind.: Friends United Press, 1971.

Jesus and the Disinherited. Nashville: Abingdon Press, 1949. Apex ed. paperback, Abingdon Press, 1969. Reprint ed., Richmond, Ind.: Friends United Press, 1981.

The Luminous Darkness: A Personal Interpretation of the Anatomy of Segregation and the Ground of Hope. New York: Harper & Row, 1965.

Meditations for Apostles of Sensitiveness. Mills College, Ca.: Eucalyptus Press, 1947.

Meditations of the Heart. New York: Harper & Row, 1953. Paperback ed., Richmond, Ind.: Friends United Press, 1976.

The Mood of Christmas. New York: Harper & Row, 1973.

Mysticism and the Experience of Love. Wallingford, Pa.: Pendle Hill Pamphlet 115, 1961.

The Negro Spiritual Speaks of Life and Death. New York: Harper & Row, 1947.

The Search for Common Ground: An Inquiry into the Basis of Man's Experience of Community. New York: Harper & Row, 1971.

Temptations of Jesus: Five Sermons. San Francisco: Lawton Kennedy, 1962.

A Track to the Water's Edge: The Olive Schreiner Reader, by Olive Schreiner (editor). New York: Harper & Row, 1973.

With Head and Heart: An Autobiography. New York: Harcourt Brace Jovanovich, 1979. Paperback ed., Harcourt Brace Jovanovich, 1981.

Readers interested in a more complete bibliography are referred to *God and Human Freedom: A Festschrift in Honor of Howard Thurman* (Richmond, Ind.: Friends United Press, 1983), pp. 196–207.